A Historical Morphology o

A Historical Morphology of English

Don Ringe

EDINBURGH
University Press

Edinburgh University Press is one of the leading university presses in the UK. We publish academic books and journals in our selected subject areas across the humanities and social sciences, combining cutting-edge scholarship with high editorial and production values to produce academic works of lasting importance. For more information visit our website: edinburghuniversitypress.com

Edinburgh University Press Ltd
The Tun – Holyrood Road, 12(2f) Jackson's Entry, Edinburgh EH8 8PJ

Typeset in Janson MT by
Servis Filmsetting Ltd, Stockport, Cheshire,
and printed and bound in Great Britain.

A CIP record for this book is available from the British Library

ISBN 978-1-4744-5976-1 (hardback)
ISBN 978-1-4744-5978-5 (webready PDF)
ISBN 978-1-4744-5977-8 (paperback)
ISBN 978-1-4744-5979-2 (epub)

Contents

Preface

Like the other volumes in this series, this is intended to be a textbook for students who already have a solid elementary grounding in linguistics. Of course, I hope that it will prove to be more broadly accessible, but it still seems advisable to make some remarks about the book and its subject with students specially in mind.

As many of you already know, morphology is perhaps the least tractable area of linguistic structure. Unlike syntax, which has to be a maximally general set of rules for generating sentence structures, and phonology, in which exceptionless rules are not rare, morphology seems to be characterized by lists of exceptions to general rules. Though there is often more orderly structure in morphological systems than initially meets the eye, it is true that idiosyncratic details matter and that they can differ dramatically from language to language—and it follows that you must engage with the details if you want to understand the system.

Morphological change has also been rather poorly served by linguistic science. The overwhelming regularity of sound change—a statistically robust *fact*, not a hypothesis—has provided a solid framework for historical phonology since its discovery in the 1870s, and while historical syntax is still in its infancy, several useful hypotheses have already been proposed (see, e.g., Kroch 1989 and Walkden 2014). Yet for the past century and a half, historical linguists have relied on "proportional analogy" between surface forms to explain morphological changes, even though such a framework is patently inadequate, both overgenerating and undergenerating the set of actually observed changes (see, e.g., Ringe and Eska 2013: 152–3). We have begun to do better, especially by thinking in terms of rules rather than proportions, by exploiting the notion of defaults and the ranking of morphosyntactic features, and by trying to ask what a given system of morphology might look like to a three-year-old native learner who has acquired only the most frequent lexemes of her language. I will try to use those approaches whenever feasible. But much work remains to be done, and it seems fair to say that the generation of linguists now being trained has a unique opportunity to discover much more about the principles of morphological change.

Of course, in order to do competent research on any language from any perspective *you must acquire a solid control of the data*. If a language is still spoken, you can work with native speakers, but historical linguists do not have that option. Our data are texts, so at a minimum we must each acquire a comfortable knowledge of the relevant texts. That means, in the first instance, learning to read every stage of the language under study *fluently*, without making chronic errors. If you are considering a scholarly career in the history of English, you must learn Old English as soon as possible—and you should start with that stage of the language, because it is maximally different from Modern English. When you have learned to read Old English well, you will find that it is surprisingly easy to read early Middle English; later Middle English will be less of a problem, since the closer it is to us in time, the more like Modern English it becomes. (There will still be occasional setbacks—the vast and unfamiliar vocabulary of the Gawain poet comes to mind—but in general a concentration on the earlier stages of English will yield results quickest.) Above all, once you have mastered Old and Middle English, you should read as much text as you can pack into each working day, because any language-learning task succeeds quickest by relentless repetition; if you can make medieval English your leisure reading, so much the better. Whenever possible, read with a Modern English translation and a grammar, the former to catch errors, the latter to explain constructions that you do not at first understand; for Old English, Henry Sweet's edition of the *Cura Pastoralis* (which includes a translation), together with Fulk's introductory textbook, should enable you to make rapid progress.

This textbook assumes that you have *not* completed that task. Nevertheless, I have tried to encourage you to engage with short excerpts from relevant texts, especially in the early chapters of Section B, with translations when the text is very different from its modern equivalent. I urge you to read those excerpts closely and analyze them in any way that seems appropriate, comparing your analyses with those of your fellow-students and asking your instructor questions about anything that puzzles you. This is an important part of your education in linguistics. It is possible to work your way into an unfamiliar language from any point using what you know about related languages and the structure of human language in general; hands-on experience teaches best, and if you do become a professional linguist, you will be repeating this sort of intellectual adventure for the rest of your life. Remember that you are not expected to get everything right every time; taking risks, making mistakes, and having them corrected is actually the quickest way to learn—and it can be fun. I have been having that sort of fun for more than fifty years, and I wish you no less.

Acknowledgments

I am grateful to Ronald Kim, Margaret Laing, Roger Lass, Donka Minkova, Patrick Stiles, Michael Weiss, and several anonymous readers for helpful feedback on the book proposal and early drafts of this book. I owe a special debt of gratitude to Heinz Giegerich, who asked me to submit the proposal and has been an unfailing source of support and helpful criticism, and to Bettelou Los, who gave me excellent advice about what to include and how to structure its presentation, and who then read the entire draft and suggested numerous improvements. No doubt there are still errors and other shortcomings, but those are mine.

Section A

Concepts

1 Morphology

This section is intended as a review of material with which students are expected to be familiar. Good short introductions to morphology with a focus on English are Don 2014 and Carstairs-McCarthy 2018; more extensive introductions are Spencer 1991 and Booij 2007.

In this chapter I present some concepts and categories of morphology in an informal framework that does not adhere to any single theory of morphology, though I will make use of theoretical concepts when they are convenient. Since this is a general discussion, not a discussion of English in particular, illustrations will occasionally be drawn from other languages. It must be borne in mind that morphology is a SYSTEM, or perhaps a pair of systems (see below), not an incidental collection of details that interact in unpredictable ways. A history of a language's morphology is therefore a history of systems; specific details are of interest insofar as they shed light on the system.

In Chapter 2 I will outline what is currently known about the sources of linguistic changes.

1.1 The relation(s) of morphology to other components of the grammar

In a natural human language the contrast between LEXICAL items, or LEXEMES, and FUNCTIONAL items is the most fundamental distinction among the language's contentful (or "meaningful") material. Roughly speaking, lexical items are those that can refer to entities and events of the real or imagined world; functional items signal the relations between the lexemes in an utterance, as well as providing information about the nature of the speech event (e.g. whether the utterance is a statement or a command, or whether the speaker, the addressee, or some other entity is being referred to). Because our experience of real-world entities and events is effectively unbounded, the LEXICON—the list of lexemes—is open-ended. By contrast, a language's functional machinery constitutes a closed system within which the functional oppositions between items are categorical, not gradient.

The organization of morphology reflects that dichotomy. The (non-phonological) structure of a language's lexemes is described by its DERIVATIONAL morphology; the structure of its functional (or "grammatical") machinery is described by its MORPHOSYNTAX. The asymmetry between those two statements is important. Derivational morphology is often contrasted with INFLECTIONAL morphology, the latter being defined as that subsystem of morphology which interacts with the syntax. But precisely because of that interaction, inflection and syntax are a single integrated system, and it is not always easy to draw a sharp line between them; some discussion is necessary before we proceed.

In principle, inflectional morphology is that part of morphosyntax which is internal to "words". Unfortunately it is notoriously difficult to give a universal definition of the term *word*. At a minimum, we need to distinguish between phonological words and morphological words. The former are the smallest units of a language that can be pronounced in isolation; the latter are the smallest units which are adequately marked by the functional machinery *in the context in which they occur*. The boundaries of the two types of words very often coincide, but not always.

The mismatch between types of words can be exemplified by the Modern English (ModE) CLITIC *'s*, which is an independent morphological item but not a phonological word. Not only does *'s* not constitute a "word" in all senses of the term, but the items to which it is appended often also exhibit such a mismatch. For instance, in the phrase

  the king of France's ancestors

the clitic *'s* is attached to the entire phrase *the king of France*, not merely to the word *France*; the structure is

  [*the king of France*] *'s ancestors*.

By itself, *France's* is a phonological word, and in some contexts it could be a well-formed morphological word, but not in this context; here the well-formed morphological word is actually the phrase *the king of France's*, because otherwise *the king of* is not adequately accounted for by the morphosyntax.

Several practical consequences follow from these facts. Most obviously, inflectional morphology cannot be discussed without reference to syntax; almost equally obviously, we must deal with morphological words, whether or not they are also phonological words, and the relation between the two types of words must be stated explicitly whenever their boundaries do not coincide. For both reasons, a discussion of clitics—

functional items whose behavior is clearly syntactic but which are not phonological words—must be included.

1.2 The relation(s) between morphemes and functions

The relation between functional items and their functions is not always straightforward either. In a maximally transparent morphosyntactic system, each identifiable functional item would be matched to a single function, and the items would be concatenated with minimal interaction between their forms. Such an "agglutinative" system is well exemplified by Turkish, in which (for example) the number, case, and possessor of nouns are marked by separate suffixes (see, e.g., Underhill 1976 for details). At least the following types of deviation from such a system are actually attested in natural human languages.

1. A language can employ completely different markers for the same function with different lexemes. For instance, though most ModE nouns mark the plural with the ending spelled *-(e)s*, the plural of *ox* is *oxen*, that of *child* is *children*, and *sheep* and *deer* have plurals with no overt expression at all (a "zero ending").
2. A language can exhibit "fused" inflectional markers, which express two or more morphosyntactic categories simultaneously. For instance, in the Latin genitive singular ending *-is* and genitive plural *-um* no separate exponents of "genitive", "singular", or "plural" can be identified; each of the endings marks case and number together.
3. A language can express a single morphosyntactic category in two or more places in a single form. For instance, in the Ancient Greek future passive form ποιηθήσονται /poiɛ:tʰέ:sontai/ 'they will be made' the category *passive* is marked both by the suffix /-tʰɛ:-/ and by the ending /-ntai/; the latter also marks the 3pl. subject and nonpast tense,[1] and the future tense marker /-so-/ intervenes between the two passive markers.
4. A language can express a morphosyntactic category by modifying or replacing part of a form rather than by adding a separate "piece"; an obvious example is ModE pl. *teeth* /tiːθ/, formed from the singular *tooth* /tuːθ/ by replacing the vocalic part of the stem.

---

1. In an alternative analysis /-nt-/ marks the 3pl. subject, while /-ai/ marks passive and nonpast simultaneously; the point of the example is the same. Note that we cannot say that /-ntai/ is merely the 3pl. marker that is SELECTED by passive forms, because in the present passive 3pl. it is the only marker of the passive (cf. pres. 3pl. passive ποιοῦνται /poiô:ntai/ vs. active ποιοῦσι /poiô:si/).

Nor are the complications restricted to inflectional morphology; a ModE derivational example will be adduced at the end of Chapter 11.

In sum, the definition of morphemes as contentful units represents a norm from which deviations are possible. While a one-to-one matching of morphemes with functions or meanings is the ideal situation (because it is maximally easy to learn and parse), one-to-many, many-to-one, and even many-to-many matchings are not all that rare. What defines a morpheme is not its content, but its behavior in a system of morphology.

1.3 Alternations

There is a final point about morphology in general that needs to be addressed. Identifiable morphemes often exhibit somewhat different phonological shapes in different contexts, but the ALTERNATIONS between the sounds of those shapes are not all of a single kind. Consider first the default plural ending of ModE nouns. After sibilant fricatives and affricates (/s, z, ʃ, ʒ, tʃ, dʒ/) it is /-əz/ or /-ɪz/, depending on one's dialect (e.g. *horses*, *churches*); after other voiceless consonants it is /-s/ (e.g. *cats*, *cliffs*); otherwise it is /-z/ (e.g. *dogs*, *days*). The alternants are very similar phonologically, and the context that determines which alternant appears is likewise statable in purely phonological terms, so that a purely phonological or morphophonemic[2] set of rules governing the alternation can be posited. That is confirmed by the fact that the present 3sg. ending *-(e)s*, the clitic *-'s*,[3] and the reduced forms of *is* and *has*[4] all exhibit the same set of alternations; since there is nothing common to them all in terms of morphosyntax, their identical behavior must be (morpho)phonological. At the other end of the spectrum is the suppletive relationship between *go* and its past tense *went*; it has to be described in lexical terms, though the forms are related to one another by the morphosyntax. In between there are cases of various kinds. The class of nouns exemplified by *wife*, plural *wives* is lexically defined (the relevant nouns have to be listed) but undergoes a rule which is phonological in content ("voice a stem-final anterior fricative") triggered by the morphosyntax ("in the plural"). Since the same process recurs in the derivation of verbs from nouns and

---

2. I am assuming that the underlying shape of the plural morpheme is /-z/; if it is not, then some reference to morphology will be necessary to account for the alternations (Bettelou Los, p.c.).

3. In the singular; after the default plural ending the clitic is reduced to zero by a morphological rule.

4. It is not clear that reduced /əz/ representing *is* or *has* is a product of this phonological rule, but it is significant that the nonsyllabic alternants /-z/ and /-s/ cannot appear after sibilants.

adjectives—e.g. *believe* from *belief,* or *save* from *safe*—it is reasonable to call it a (morpho)phonological rule, but it is clearly a "fragmented" rule, operating in contexts which have nothing in common, triggered by morphology rather than phonology, and applicable only to fixed lists of lexemes. Other rules altering the shapes of morphemes are not obviously phonological at all; ModE examples include the rules replacing the vowels of strong verbs in the past tense (*sing, sang; drive, drove; take, took,* etc.) and the rule replacing the codas of a short list of verbs with /-ɔt/ or /-ɔːt/, depending on dialect, in the past tense (*bring, brought; teach, taught,* etc.). The different plural markers of English *horses, sheep, oxen,* and *geese* do not even resemble one another phonologically. At least a large proportion of these alternations must be accounted for by morphology rather than phonology; each case must be judged on its own merits, and there will inevitably be examples in which it is not clear which solution is correct.

1.4 Derivational morphology: an overview

Since it deals with the structure of lexemes, derivational morphology is intimately connected with a language's lexicon. The latter cannot simply be a list of idiosyncratic items, because in any language there are derived (i.e. multimorphemic) lexemes whose meanings cannot be deduced entirely from their component parts. A standard example is ModE *gentleman*. The first component of that compound no longer means 'pertaining to the gentry' when it occurs in isolation, so it is clear that the simple word and the compound have "drifted" apart semantically. But even if *gentle-* did still mean 'gentry', the compound word has acquired a wider applicability than it originally exhibited; any male person who behaves politely can be described as a gentleman. Yet the structure of the word has not been obscured; any native speaker of English can see that it is a compound of *gentle* and *man*, and that fact ought to be reflected in any approximation of a native-speaker grammar. It follows that the lexicon, if it is a single thing, has a good deal of internal structure; the classic discussion is Jackendoff 1975.

A possible response to this situation is to link the form and meaning of lexemes less tightly together; that is the hypothesis pursued by Distributed Morphology (DM).[5] A DM analysis of a language includes lists of roots, affixes, and functional morphemes, with rules regulating their interaction, and a separate "Encyclopedia" that deals with all aspects of meaning. The advantage of this approach is that the Encylopedia also

---

5. Convenient short introductions to DM are Embick and Noyer 2007 and Siddiqi 2009: 7–26.

handles the meanings of idioms constructed by the syntax, ranging from (for example) *pay (someone) no mind*, which is a fixed phrase but is easily interpretable, to *eat crow*, which now requires an explanation, as well as the awkward fact that a simple lexeme like *wolf* is actually defined by real-world experience: if you have seen a wolf, you know what one is; otherwise not really.[6]

It is striking that the machinery of derivational morphology exhibits little variation from language to language. All languages possess a core of basic lexemes that are unanalyzable. Lexemes are derived from other lexemes by two basic processes, compounding and affixation. Most Indo-European (IE) languages, including English, employ both processes extensively; but there are languages that employ compounding almost to the exclusion of derivation, such as Chinese languages,[7] and others in which derivation is almost exclusively used, such as Semitic languages.[8]

An idiosyncratic (but not unique) complication of ModE derivational morphology is the presence of numerous sets of derivationally related French and Latin loanwords. Some of the derivational rules relating them are modestly productive; in some cases, an affix, such as *-able*, *-ize*, or *re-*, has been segmented off and has become highly productive. The origins of these systems represent the most important innovations in English derivational morphology and will therefore be discussed in detail. In addition, the Latinate vocabulary of ModE blurs the distinction between compounding and affixation (Plag 2018: 72–3, 152–6), a point which

---

6. Cf. Don 2014: 2–3. The classic illustration is perhaps the end of Chapter 2 of Grimmelshausen's *Simplicissimus*. A peasant boy guarding sheep is advised to play his bagpipe to scare off the wolf, *dann he iß a solcher feyerboinigter Schelm un Dieb, der Menscha und Vieha frißt* ('because he is such a four-legged scoundrel and thief that eats people and livestock'). He replies: *Knano, sag mir aa, wey der Wolf seyhet? Eich huun noch kan Wolf gesien.* ('Daddy, please tell me, who might the "wolf" be? I've not yet seen a wolf.') The answer is uninformative—*Ah dau grober Eselkopp, dau bleiwest dein Lewelang a Narr, geith meich wunner, was aus dir wera wird, bißt schun su a grusser Dölpel, un weist noch neit, was der Wolf für a feyerfeussiger Schelm iß.* ('Oh you clumsy blockhead, you'll be a fool all your life, it makes me wonder what will become of you, you're already such a big lout and still don't know what sort of four-footed scoundrel the wolf is.')—so that in the following chapter he mistakes a troop of mounted plunderers for wolves. I quote from the Reclam pocket edition of 1961.
7. The Mandarin pronoun pluralizer *-men* is best analyzed as an affix; it is unclear to me whether *-zi*, the second component of many disyllabic nouns, should be analyzed as an affix, or whether *-(e)r*, which is clearly a noun suffix, can be assigned any function at all.
8. Apparent exceptions are names, which are better parsed as sentences, e.g. Akkadian *Nabu-kudurri-uṣur* 'Nabu, protect the boundary!' ("Nebuchadnezzar") or Hebrew *'Ēliy-yāhū* 'My god (is) Yahweh' ("Elijah"). I am grateful to Akiva Bacovcin for helpful discussion of this point.

will also require discussion in Chapter 11.

1.5 Inflectional morphology: an overview

Inflectional morphology expresses morphosyntactic categories by means of affixes attached to lexemes (and, less often, by other modifications of lexemes—see the general discussion above). In terms of the derivation of a sentence the inflectional markers have the following sources.

1. Some categories are part of the identity of the lexical item.

    A type of category that is widespread in the IE family (though not in many others) is LEXICAL CLASS membership; an obvious example is the "conjugations" of Latin. Except for a tiny handful of irregular verbs, every Latin verb must exhibit one of five vowels at the end of its present stem: namely, *-ā-*, *-ē-*, *-ī-*, *-i-*, or a variable short vowel whose underlying shape is not obvious (possibly /-e-/). Though these stem vowels are not always completely functionless—for instance, a large number of derived statives have present stems in *-ē-* —in most cases the choice of present stem vowel must have struck native learners as arbitrary, and Latin verbs can be sorted into arbitrary lexical classes on that basis.

    A more widespread type of lexically inherent category is CONCORD CLASS membership. In many languages nouns are sorted into concord classes, and the concord class to which a noun belongs is part of its lexical identity. In some language families these classes are called "genders", and it is true that small concord class systems often exhibit a (typically weak) correlation with biological gender; perhaps the most familiar systems are masculine vs. feminine (e.g. in Semitic languages, Baltic languages, and most Romance languages) and masculine vs. feminine vs. neuter (e.g. in the most conservative Germanic languages and many other subgroups of IE). But a system animate vs. inanimate is also widespread (e.g. in Hittite, continental Scandinavian, and Algonkian languages), and some larger concord class systems, such as those of the Bantu languages, also exhibit no correlation with biological gender at all.[9] The function of concord classes is to mark relations between a noun and other elements of its clause (see below); for that reason, concord class markers copied onto adjectives, pronouns, verbs, etc. are usually overt, while marking on the noun itself may or may not be overt. (In Bantu languages it generally is; in German it mostly is not.)
2. Some categories are assigned semantically in a syntactic context.

---

9. An excellent discussion of concord class systems is Corbett 1991.

In those languages that mark NUMBER on noun phrases, the number of a noun phrase usually expresses an aspect of the real-world referent. In many languages some CASES are assigned in the same way; for instance, in Sanskrit a noun denoting the means by which something is done is assigned instrumental case. Both number and case are typically also part of the concord system (see below).

Depending on one's theory of syntax, similarly assigned categories of the verb might include TENSE, indicating temporal relations between the event referred to by the verb and the time of utterance; ASPECT, indicating the internal structure of the event;[10] and MOOD, indicating the speaker's intention or attitude toward the utterance. In many versions of generative syntax these categories are instead expressed by functional heads higher up the tree than the verb, and the verb is raised through them sequentially, acquiring morphosyntactic features as it goes. However, the assignment of these features to the functional heads is essentially the same as if they were assigned to the verb itself.

Perhaps the only category similarly assigned to adjectives is DEGREE: in many IE languages (though in surprisingly few others) adjectives regularly have comparatives, and in some languages they have superlatives as well.

3. Some categories are assigned on the basis of a lexeme's syntactic function.

The most obvious features assigned in this way are the "structural" cases. In IE languages (and many others) these typically include nominative case, assigned to subjects and to complements of verbs such as *be*, *become*, and *seem*; accusative case, assigned to direct objects; and dative case, assigned to indirect objects. Some languages and families have different case systems that mark the same relationships, e.g. the ergative and absolutive cases of Eskimo-Aleut and some other language families. Various cases can also be assigned under government by a preposition or postposition. Finally, there is usually also an adnominal case that marks noun phrases inside another noun phrase; it is typically called the genitive case.

VOICE is probably best regarded as a similarly assigned category for verbs, since the distinction between active and passive sentences is, at least primarily, a matter of syntax. As with the verb categories listed under (2) above, there is more than one way of handling passives formally; for an interesting discussion see, e.g., Baker 1988: 305–61 with references.

4. Finally, many categories which have been assigned in one or another of

---

10. The classic discussion of aspect systems is Comrie 1976.

the ways outlined above are copied onto other lexemes in an utterance.

The most obvious categories copied onto a verb form are the PERSON and number of the subject, in some languages also its concord class (see above), and in some languages the same information regarding the verb's direct object (and, in a few languages, its indirect object).

Many languages have nominal concord systems in which the number and concord class of a noun are marked on predicate adjectives, pronouns, and the like which are related to the noun by the syntax or which are coreferent with it within the discourse. The mechanism of concord marking is not the same in every instance. For example, the case of a noun phrase must be assigned to all components of the noun phrase by the syntax, since it is the entire noun phrase which is the argument of its verb or the object of a preposition (or bears some other relationship to the rest of the clause), so the parts of the noun phrase will exhibit case concord if marked separately; but the concord class of a noun is also copied onto any determiners and adjectives in the noun phrase, and so is its number. Presumably, case is also copied from a noun phrase embedded in a clause to any other noun phrases in apposition with it.

The pervasiveness of such a system of concord marking justifies treating those lexemes which are neither verbs nor adverbs together in discussions of inflectional morphology; a convenient cover term for them is NOMINALS.

From the foregoing discussion it is clear that an inflectional system can be very complex, but that most of the complexities mentioned are functional, in the sense that each inflectional marker expresses one or more morphosyntactic categories of the language which "do their work" in communication. The outstanding exception is lexical classes, which express identical morphosyntactic categories in arbitrarily different ways. Lexical classes can persist even in a language like ModE that has lost most of its inflection. For instance, the plurals *hands* and *feet* are used in all and only the same syntactic circumstances, yet *hands* belongs to the (huge) default class of noun plurals, while *feet* belongs to a small closed class and must be listed. In the same way, *spoke* and *talked* are grammatically identical (as well as more or less synonymous), yet the former belongs to a small class of verbs which replaces the root vowel /iː/ with /oʊ/ in the past and also adds *-en* in the past participle,[11] while the latter belongs to the (very large) default class of past tenses.

---

11. Namely, *freeze, speak, steal,* and *weave* in the author's speech.

1.6 Some useful concepts

The morphological structure of derived words can be irreconcilably different from their prosodic structure in the phonology. The classic case is ModE *unhappier*. The morphological structure of the word is clearly [un+happy$_{ADJ}$]+er$_{CPTV}$, with the comparative inflectional suffix added to a fully formed prefixed adjective, and its meaning 'more unhappy' is fully consistent with that analysis. However, the word's prosodic structure is ùn[háppier], the prefix constituting a foot with secondary stress while the remainder of the word, including the suffix, constitutes another foot with primary stress. It follows that the hierarchical morphological structure of words is not part of the input to the phonology; the phonological component of the grammar takes a string of segments and (perhaps) boundaries as input and constructs its own prosodic tree on that substrate. On the other hand, the prosodic structure of complex words can have consequences for morphological change; some ModE examples will be adduced in Chapter 12.

In languages which have fused inflectional markers, such as the case-and-number endings of Latin, SYNCRETISM is often a prominent feature. Syncretism can be defined as the expression of two or more contrasting morphosyntactic features, or bundles of features, by the same inflectional marker. Some syncretisms are clearly accidental; for instance, the fact that both the genitive singular and the nominative plural of Latin non-neuter second-declension nouns end in *-ī* must be the result of chance, since the two morphosyntactic bundles have nothing in common. On the other hand, if a syncretism is widespread in a language and "makes sense" in featural terms, native learners are very likely to posit a rule expressing it. For instance, in Latin the dative plural and ablative plural of any nominal are always identical—there are no exceptions at all—and in Old English (OE) the nominative plural and accusative plural are identical except for the 1st- and 2nd-person pronouns. The question is how best to analyze these systematic syncretisms in the grammar.

An especially promising approach employs the notion of DEFAULTS, which is useful in many areas of the morphosyntax. It is reasonable to suggest that in the category *number* the singular number is the default, that in the category *case* the nominative case is the default, that in the category *person* the 3rd person is the default (since its range of reference is widest, i.e. any entity not including the speaker or the addressee), etc. It is also reasonable to posit that defaults are unmarked morphologically; thus a nom. pl., for instance, is a form marked for plurality but not for case, while a nom. sg. is marked for neither. We can then account for the syncretism between the nom. pl. and acc. pl. in OE by suggesting that in the inflectional component of the grammar the morphosyntactic feature "accusative" is deleted in the presence of the feature "plural" unless the person feature "1" or "2" is also present. The result should be a form marked only for plural, i.e. a nominative plural form. If we have ranked our features, ranking number higher than case, all we need to do is prohibit any 3rd-person form from being overtly marked both for plural and for accusative; since case is the lower feature, accusative will be suppressed, leading to the desired result. The technical term for such a suppression is IMPOVERISHMENT. This is one of the most useful innovations of recent work in morphological theory, explored in detail in Noyer 1997. Whether it provides a general account of syncretism is still unclear.

1.7 Some unanswered questions

Most theories of morphology work with segmentable morphemes, simply because an agglutinative system of overt inflectional markers is a maximally simple and transparent ideal. Such theories can deal with fused markers, multiple markers of a single category, morphemes with no content, etc., by means of more or less obvious local adjustments. Markers that are processes rather than "pieces" are more of a challenge. ModE *teeth* /ti:θ/, the plural of *tooth* /tu:θ/, is a case in point. If we ask what the plural marker is, the most straightforward answer is the change in the vowel. However, there is an alternative: if we are determined to insist that morphemes be pieces, we could argue that the principal plural affix is actually zero, and that the change in the vowel is an ancillary marker. Such an analysis can be correct to the extent that, *in every instance that we encounter*, a language that appears to have such "process" morphemes also exhibits parallel formations with zero affixes but without the process. There is no apparent reason why that should be true, yet it is actually true in a wide range of cases. In ModE, for instance, there are zero plurals such as *sheep*, *deer*, and *fish* without the vowel-change process.

A different type of challenge is provided by suppletion. A ModE paradigm such as *go, went, gone* seems to show that a lexeme such as *go* is, in principle, an abstract entity: most of its forms contain a recognizable "root" beginning with /g.../, but the combination *go* + 'past tense' yields the formally unrelated /wɛnt/. But it turns out that that is not the only type of suppletion attested in natural human languages; we also find sets of homonymous lexemes which are defective—i.e. their paradigms lack certain members—and are in partial competition with one another. Ancient Greek provides some notorious examples. For instance, there are several verbs meaning 'say', none of which has a complete paradigm:

present	future nonpassive	aorist nonpassive	perfect active
φάναι /pʰánai/	φήσειν /pʰɛ́ːseːn/	(φῆσαι /pʰɛ̂ːsai/)	—
λέγειν /légeːn/	λέξειν /lékseːn/	(λέξαι /léksai/)	—
—	ἐρεῖν /erêːn/	—	εἰρηκέναι /eirɛːkénai/
—	—	εἰπεῖν /eipêːn/	—

There are also aorist (and future) passive and perfect mediopassive stems formed from the second and third of the verbs listed. The only common aorist nonpassive is *eipêːn* 'to say', and the only active perfect is *eirɛːkénai* 'to have said', but in the other stems there is vigorous competition. Clearly, these stems do not constitute a single paradigm in the same way that the ModE forms of *go* do. The historical relationships between these two types of suppletion, as well as the question of whether one can be reduced to a special case of the other, are of interest.

In the preceding paragraph the grammatical construct "paradigm" proved to be convenient. No one doubts that it is a useful descriptive device (and I will, in fact, use it throughout this book), but whether it is theoretically necessary is a question still being debated. Since the contents of a paradigm can be read off the list of morphosyntactic features in a language, it is not obvious that paradigms have an independent status in an adult native-speaker grammar. Andrew Carstairs-McCarthy has adduced possible evidence that paradigms are linguistically real (see especially Carstairs 1987), but the evidence is complex and messy.

The history of some instances of suppletion might actually demonstrate the psychological reality of paradigms. We often find that when suppletive lexemes are replaced in the history of a language, they are replaced piece by piece, yet the lexeme remains suppletive. English provides a spectacular example. It seems clear enough that the Proto-Germanic (PGmc.) verb 'go' was *ganganą and that its finite past began with the sequence *ijj- (cf. Gothic *gaggan*, past *iddja*). In OE the inherited past apparently survives (regularized with a suffix) as *ēode* (see Cowgill 1960 for discussion), but the present stem is undergoing replacement: *gangan* still occurs, but *gān* is in competition with it and is more common in the southern and Midland dialects. The Middle English (ME) descendant of this paradigm, *gōn*, past *ēde* or *yēde*, persists into the seventeenth century (and later in outlying dialects), but *went* (originally the past of *wend*) begins to compete with it in Chaucer's generation and eventually ousts its older rival. The result is that although no part of the ModE paradigm is inherited from PGmc., the modern paradigm is still suppletive in exactly the same way. Of course, the suppletion was not so neat while the replacements were occurring, but the paradigm always "settled out" eventually into a case of clean suppletion. If that is not evidence for the reality of paradigms, we need to account for that development in some other plausible way, e.g. as a natural consequence of native language acquisition.

It is time to take a look at the potential sources of linguistic change.

Exercises

Since this book is a history of English morphology, it seems reasonable at this point to review the inflectional categories of ModE. You should be able to answer the following questions. If you need to consult a ModE grammar, feel free to do so; what is important is to have a clear picture of the ModE inflectional system before embarking on a discussion of its history.

1. What morphosyntactic categories are marked on nouns in ModE? Which ones are marked on the demonstratives *this* and *that*? How about the personal pronouns? The interrogative pronoun? Make a table of pronoun forms and identify their functions.
2. Various ModE noun plural formations have been adduced in this chapter. Are there any which have not been mentioned? What is the membership of each of the nondefault lexical classes? Answers to the last question, especially, might vary, depending on an individual's native dialect.
3. Consider the way that ModE comparatives and superlatives of adjectives are formed. There are two formations, one using suffixes, the other periphrastic (i.e. consisting of a phrase). Can you state a general rule determining which formation is used for which adjectives? Are there irregularities in the suffixal formation, and if so, what are they? Are there adjectives which could have comparatives and superlatives but do not?
4. How many distinct forms does a ModE verb of the default lexical class have, and what are their morphosyntactic functions? What about a verb like *sing*, which constructs some of its forms by ABLAUT (i.e. the replacement of the vowel in its root syllable)? Is there any ModE verb that has more forms than *sing*? If there is, list its forms and their functions.
5. The "modals" of ModE include at least *can, could, may, might, must, shall, should, will,* and *would*. Do you see a pattern in these forms? How does it relate to the pattern of inflection of ordinary verbs? What forms do ordinary verbs have that modals do not?

2 Linguistic change and the evidence of the past

2.1 The nature of the evidence

Because the most immediate goal of linguistics is to elucidate the structure of native speaker grammars, only the speech of native speakers is ordinarily admitted as evidence; not only non-native speech, but also written language is too far removed from native speech to be entirely trustworthy. For historical linguists this poses a major problem. We want to study changes in the structure of native speaker grammars, but we have no native speech to work with. Recordings of speech adequate for scientific purposes are available only from the past sixty years or so, and usable scientific descriptions of languages based on fieldwork began to appear in any quantity only about a century ago.[1] Almost all our evidence is written evidence, at least one remove from actual speech. We are constrained to make the best of bad data, and we must begin by trying to recover what the speech of any writer of the distant past must have been like.

If we are to make intelligent use of our data, so as to transcend the limits imposed by the severely imperfect linguistic records of the past, we must adhere to the Uniformitarian Principle (UP). Originally formulated for historical geology late in the eighteenth century, the UP has become the basis of all historical sciences; it was applied explicitly to historical linguistics by Hermann Paul in 1880 (see Paul 1960). As applied to linguistics, the UP can be stated as follows:

> Unless we can demonstrate a relevant alteration in the conditions of language use or language acquisition between some time in the past and the present, we must assume that the same types, range, and distribution of language structures existed and the same types of linguistic change processes operated at that past time as in the present. (Ringe and Eska 2013: 3)

---

1. An outstanding exception is Kleinschmidt 1851, often cited precisely because it was so far ahead of its time.

In principle, all historical linguists accept the UP, but surprisingly little attention has been paid to its practical use. This book will insist on applying the UP whenever possible in as much detail as possible, using the insights of all subfields of modern linguistics that have any bearing on the questions at hand.

2.2 The sources and course of linguistic change

Many aspects of language change were discovered, explored, and formalized generations ago; the classic example is the regularity of SOUND CHANGE (i.e. spontaneous changes in pronunciation), which was discovered in the 1870s and formalized in phonemic terms in Hoenigswald 1960. As any historical phonologist with broad experience of languages is aware, the regularity of sound change is statistically overwhelming. However, within the past fifty years or so we have also begun to acquire substantial information about how linguistic changes begin and how they propagate through a speech community. As a result, we are now able to identify a *process* of sound change that appears to be exceptionless within speech communities (narrowly defined), and that must be the ultimate source of the large-scale regularity that we find in the historical record; for discussion see Fruehwald 2016 and Labov, forthcoming.

The spread of linguistic changes through speech communities is by now also fairly well understood, thanks to the work of William Labov and his colleagues and students in sociolinguistics. It is clear that we must recognize speech communities in the narrowest sense—sociologically coherent communities speaking single dialects narrowly defined—and progressively broader speech communities, the broadest being the sum of all narrower communities speaking mutually intelligible dialects. It is also clear that innovations occur locally and spread at first within narrow speech communities; they may or may not spread outward into the broader speech community. A good introduction to these phenomena is Trudgill 2000; a compendium of what the sociolinguistic community has learned about language change is Labov 1994–2010.

Particularly important for the history of English is the question of how innovations spread across dialect boundaries, because right from the beginning of its history English has been a group of (more or less) mutually intelligible dialects. Modern work has shown that almost any linguistic characteristic can spread across dialect boundaries, but also that innovations can be modified in various ways in the course of that spread (cf., e.g., Labov, Yaeger and Steiner 1972: 48–51). Trudgill 1986 is a good introduction to the mechanisms and results of dialect contact. Illustrations of the effects of dialect contact will appear occasionally in this book.

There is less unanimity regarding how linguistic changes originate, partly because there are several potential sources, but also because historical linguists have paid fairly little attention to modern work on language acquisition and language contact. The following points, while necessarily limited, seem securely established.

Changes in a language's lexicon are by far the least constrained, for several reasons. The lexicon is open-ended, so that new words can always be added. Most lexical items are not defined by strict opposition to one another; synonyms and words whose meanings overlap are not rare. Productive word-formation rules are part of the grammar of adult native speakers, and they are routinely used to coin new words; in recent generations, words with no antecedents at all have been coined for commercial purposes, in politics (cf. *Nazi*), in connection with the completely new world of electronic devices (cf. *wysiwyg*), etc. The borrowing of words from completely different languages is largely unconstrained; perhaps the only universal constraint is that the word must be pronounceable in the borrowing language.[2] Finally, new rules of word formation can be extracted from sets of borrowed words and become productive; the history of English provides some especially clear examples.

By contrast, changes in structure seem to be tightly constrained. That should not be surprising. A native speaker's grammar is almost entirely categorical, not statistical; except around the margins (e.g. when sentences become very complex, or in the presence of gaps in inflectional paradigms), an utterance either is grammatical or it is not. It follows automatically that every innovation in grammar must *at first* be an error; it can become a viable innovation only when it is used consistently enough by a group of speakers that it can be regarded as an option rather than just a mistake. Even then, speakers who are not participating in the innovation may disapprove of it—i.e. may continue to insist that it is an error; but by that point the innovation has at least a fighting chance of acceptance by the speech community. If we want to find the source(s) of grammatical innovations we must therefore ask: who makes grammatical errors consistently enough to have them copied by other native speakers, and who copies grammatical errors enough to make them potentially viable innovations?

It is easy to give a negative answer to the questions just asked. Adult native speakers of a language do not make errors which they are chroni-

---

2. In some languages there are additional constraints; for instance, if the inflection of verbs is idiosyncratic enough that it is difficult to inflect a borrowed verb straightforwardly, special strategies may be used to borrow verbs. See Ringe and Eska 2013: 60–1 for some examples.

cally unable to correct, and they do not copy traits of other speakers' speech which they regard as errors. However, there are two groups of speakers who do make consistent errors, and who are at least sometimes unable to recognize that an error is in fact an error (so that they have no disincentive to copy it): native learners still in the process of native language acquisition (NLA) and non-native adult speakers of a language. It follows that those two groups must be responsible for most changes in categorical grammar.

Children acquire the phonology and morphosyntax of their native language(s) not by imitation but by constructing and using rules; that has been known for more than sixty years (Berko 1958). In the course of that process, native learners construct incorrect rules, overapply correct rules, and in other ways generate forms and structures that are at variance with adult native-speaker norms—i.e. they are errors; any alert parent of a small child can cite at least a few anecdotal examples, and the CHILDES corpus is full of them. Moreover, the errors produced by children largely overlap with changes attested in the historical record; most obviously in the case of English, the formation of incorrect but regular past tenses like *knowed, holded*, etc. in NLA is no different from the formation of *helped* and *beseeched*, the former replacing inherited *halp* (now obsolete), the latter currently replacing inherited *besought*. It is true that catching such an error "in the act" of becoming an innovation is very much like looking for a needle in a haystack, but the inference that a large majority of recorded changes began as native-learner errors is overwhelmingly likely to be correct and is certainly the best hypothesis available.[3]

But how can children's errors, which are obviously errors from an adult point of view, be accepted by a whole speech community? Anecdotal evidence suggests that they are first copied by other native learners who are not aware that they are errors; that is possible because children talk much more to their peers than to adults, if given the chance, with the result that many learn their native language(s) more from their peers than from their parents (as not a few startled parents have discovered). Once the "errors" have become entrenched habits of speech within a peer group of children, they have some chance of surviving into adolescent speech and becoming markers of group solidarity (Ringe and Eska 2013: 38–9). Study of the latter process by sociolinguists has begun to yield interesting results (Labov 2001 passim, Ringe and Eska 2013: 51, 55–6).

That the errors of non-native adult learners might eventually become innovations in the native-speaker community is a much more interesting proposition. Adult native speakers do not normally copy the errors of

3. Nor is it new; this hypothesis too was first formulated by Hermann Paul.

non-native speakers; if the latter are to have any chance of becoming language changes, they must be learned by native learners who are not aware that they are errors because they do not have enough native models for comparison. In this case the fact that children learn their native language(s) preferentially from their peers militates against adult errors being learned—unless the adults in the community are all, or almost all, struggling to learn the dominant language non-natively, and their children must learn from their parents' non-native speech because they have almost no contact with children from outside the community who are learning the dominant language natively. This is very important for the history of English because we know that large numbers of speakers of Norse settled in northern and eastern England in the ninth and tenth centuries, and it is clear that whole communities shifted from Norse to English in subsequent generations—precisely the sort of scenario that might give rise to Norse errors becoming English changes if local conditions were favorable (cf. Thomason and Kaufman 1988: 275–304, Townend 2002). We will need to discuss the evidence in detail in Chapter 6.

Do adults, then, *never* introduce structural changes into their native language? From what has been said above it seems that that should be true, yet it is not quite true. Native bilinguals obviously have an opportunity to transfer structure from one of their native languages into the other, and it is reasonable to expect them to do so. What is surprising is how seldom it works. A case in which transfer of structure has been successful is Yiddish, originally a dialect of southern German, into which various Hebrew structures have been imported, most obviously Hebrew noun plural markers (Jacobs 2005: 135, 165). A parallel case in which transfer has largely failed is the attempt to import Latin and Greek noun plural markers, such as those of *data* and *genii* (plurals of *datum* and *genius*) into English; only *cacti* seems to be holding its own outside of the academic world (Ringe and Eska 2013: 37 and 8.4 below). The difference in outcomes is attributable, at least partly, to the fact that for many generations about half the Yiddish-speaking community (the male half) had a passive native command of Hebrew, whereas even a comfortable passive command of Latin and Greek was never characteristic of more than a tiny fraction of the English-speaking population. But other factors are probably also important. The best-studied example of the importation of foreign structure into a native language is the transfer (with reinterpretation) of pieces of English morphosyntax into the French of Prince Edward Island (PEI), explored in some detail in King 2000. It is clear that the transfer must have been accomplished by native speakers of PEI French because for the past two and a half centuries the status of French in PEI has been so low that there has been no incentive for native speakers of English to learn it. That situation also appears to be one factor that has made the transfer possible: for generations, every native speaker of PEI French has been obliged to speak English as well, though not necessarily natively, and English is unassailably the prestige language in PEI. In other words, the two languages have been in intimate contact with substantial bilingualism for generations, and throughout that period the pressure of English on French has been intense and unrelenting. Nevertheless the transfer of structure has been quite limited. As King demonstrates, PEI French has borrowed a number of English "function words", especially prepositions, and some have brought associated English syntactic structures with them. Such LEXICALLY MEDIATED borrowing of structure is just about all that has happened; notably, morphology has not been touched. Arguably, none of this is relevant to the history of English, simply because community-wide bilingualism has never been the norm in English-speaking communities.

Increased acceptance of the large-scale generalization that *change is due to failure to learn in detail* has transformed the discussion of language change. Older treatments regarded the process of change as a "black box" and attempted to access what might be going on inside by statistical studies; a respectable example of such an approach is Krygier 1994. Such studies are still valuable, not only as collections of data but as general indications of what needs to be accounted for, but recent work is a new departure based on radically shifted premises.

2.3 Contact and change

The last section dealt with a range of contact-induced changes, but the most obvious large-scale question has not yet been posed: to what extent is contact responsible for language change?

The educated public expects to find contact at the root of almost all linguistic changes, both because it is difficult for a nonlinguist to imagine where else changes might come from and because of a deep-seated conviction that a language, or at least one's own language, *should not* change without some obvious reason. The historical record shows that such expectations are misplaced. Even isolated languages do, in fact, change. Icelandic, most of whose speakers had little contact with speakers of other languages between the period of settlement and the industrial era, has undergone dramatic changes in pronunciation, notable changes in syntax, and even some changes in inflection over the past half-millennium or so. Greenlandic, an equally isolated Eskimoan language, has undergone a major simplification of its sound system since the mid-nineteenth century, as a comparison of Kleinschmidt 1851 and Fortescue 1984 demonstrates. All languages change all the time; the hypothesis that a particular change in a particular language is the result of contact must be supported by evidence.

This is important for the study of English because it is obvious that English has been in close contact with several other languages and has undergone a great deal of change. That numerous words have been borrowed into English from other languages is, of course, obvious; that some innovations can have been triggered by dialect contact is often at least plausible, given that mutually intelligible dialects in contact can trade material, including structure, fairly freely. That grammatical structure might have been transferred from other languages into English is a much less straightforward proposition, and if we take linguistics seriously as a science, we ought to demand proof for each specific hypothesis. This will be relevant in Chapter 6.

Exercise

A type of language change that straddles the interface between phonology and morphology is LEVELLING, which can be defined as the elimination of an alternation in a paradigm by spreading one alternant into the environment occupied by the other. The alternants can be either phonologically or morphologically defined. Here is a simple ME example. In the prehistory of OE, a series of regular sound changes had affected the paradigm of 'day', so that the nominative singular was *dæġ* but the nominative plural was *dagas*. (The nominative is the case which marks the subjects of verbs; it was the nominative forms that survived in later English.) By the early ME period further sound changes had produced the forms sg. *dei* (also spelled *dai*, etc.), pl. *dawes*, and if no levelling had occurred, the plural of ModE *day* would be **daws*. But already in early ME the singular stem was being levelled into the plural, producing a form *deies*, which is the ancestor of ModE *days*.

OE had four nouns which had an unusual inflectional peculiarity: they inserted -r- before the usual plural endings. Here are the Anglian nom. sg. and nom. pl. forms of those nouns and the ModE forms that would exist if only regular sound changes had affected them. (ModE is mostly descended from an Anglian dialect of OE.)

	Anglian OE		*expected ModE*	
	nom. sg.	*nom. pl.*	*sg.*	*pl.*
'child'	ċild	ċild ~ ċildru	child	*childer /tʃɪldəɹ/
'lamb'	lamb	lambru	*lomb /loʊm/	*lamber /læ·mbəɹ/
'calf'	calf	calfru	calf	*calver
'egg'	æ̇ġ	æ̇ġru	*ey /eɪ/	*eyer

I have given the phonemic shapes that the forms would have in my pronunciation of standard English in cases where the spelling might lead to
uncertainty; it should be easy to transpose them into your pronunciation.

As you can see, half the ModE singular forms and all the plurals are
different from those that would be expected by regular sound change.
Figure out what changes have occurred and determine which of those
changes were levellings. For a complete answer you need one further
piece of information: the Old Norse (ON) word for 'egg' was nom. sg.
egg, nom. pl. *egg*.

Section B
Inflectional morphology

3 Old English inflectional morphology

Hogg and Fulk 2011 is the most recent full presentation of OE inflectional morphology; older treatments that are still worth consulting are Campbell 1962 and Brunner 1965. The best introductory grammar is Fulk 2014.

This chapter is a sketch of the inflectional system of OE which focusses on the structure of the system; it will be the starting point for the discussion of subsequent chapters. Students should be aware that the inflectional system of OE was complex and intricate, with lexical exceptions to many general rules; I have included only the barest minimum of detail necessary to understand subsequent developments. In addition, OE inflection was complicated still further by the operation of phonological rules reflecting prehistoric sound changes. One example will have to suffice, since this is (fortunately!) not also a presentation of OE phonology. Several completely different grammatical endings had the shape *-u in prehistoric OE; that ending survived after light stressed syllables but was lost after heavy stressed syllables (and what happened in other circumstances was complicated and in part disputed). Thus in the nominative singular of the default class of feminine nouns *giefu* 'gift' retains the ending but *stōw* 'place' has lost it; in the nom.-acc. pl. of neuter nouns *sċipu* 'ships' retains the ending but *word* 'words' has lost it; in the nom.-acc. sg. of u-stem nouns we find *sunu* 'son' but *hand* 'hand'; and adjectives exhibit a similar distribution of *-u* in its different functions. Only in the present indicative 1sg. of verbs (in the Anglian dialects) was *-u* restored after heavy syllables, so that we find not only *beoru* '(I) carry', for example, but also *bindu* '(I) tie'. In what follows I will generally avoid discussing such phonological complications unless they were important for the later history of English.

3.1 The Old English verb system

3.1.1 Inflectional categories and stems

The OE verb system was based on a morphological opposition between a present tense and a past tense. Among finite forms both tenses distinguished an indicative and a subjunctive; there was also a present imperative. Singular and plural finite forms were always distinguished; in addition, the indicative distinguished person in the singular, though in the past indicative there was a systematic syncretism between 1sg. and 3sg. All imperative forms were 2nd-person, and there was a systematic syncretism between the imperative plural and the present indicative plural. The nonfinite forms were the present infinitive, with both an uninflected and an inflected form, the present participle, and the past participle. The past participle was the only passive form in the system (if the verb was transitive), all other forms being active; finite passive forms were constructed with the past participle and auxiliary verbs meaning 'be' and 'become'.

Here is the complete paradigm of OE *beran* 'carry, bear', illustrating the description just given.

	present	*past active*	*past passive*
infinitive	beran	—	
inflected inf.	berenne	—	
participle	berende	—	boren
indicative			
sg. 1	bere / beoru[1]	bær	
2	bir(e)st	bære	
3	bir(e)þ	bær	
pl.	beraþ	bæron	
subjunctive			
sg.	bere	bære	
pl.	beren	bæren	
imperative			
sg.	ber	—	
pl.	beraþ	—	

From the perspective of even a modern Romance language this is a small paradigm. However, though the number of different forms is modest, they are constructed from no fewer than four different stems. The pre-

---

1. The first of these forms occurred in the WS and Kentish dialects, the second in the Anglian dialects; see below for discussion.

sent stem is *ber-*, to which endings marking inflectional categories are added; before the indicative 2sg. and 3sg. endings *ber-* becomes *bir-* by a process called "i-umlaut", which will be discussed below. In the past, the default stem is clearly *bǣr-*, with a long vowel, but the endingless indicative 1sg. and 3sg. form is instead *bær*, with a short vowel, and the past participle *boren* has yet another vowel in the root syllable of the verb. In fact the paradigm of an OE verb can usually be constructed from its present infinitive, past indicative 3sg., past indicative pl., and past participle, which are therefore called its "principal parts". I will use the system of principal parts throughout this book, because it is a shorthand device which remains useful even in ModE (in which the principal parts of this verb are *bear, bore, borne*—there is now only one stem for the finite past).

Comparison of OE verb paradigms with those of other Germanic languages reveals an interesting pattern. The complex system of stems appears in all the languages and was clearly inherited from their common ancestor; for the history of English we simply have to take it for granted. The number of different forms, however, was considerably smaller in OE than in Old High German (OHG), which is relatively closely related to OE; moreover, the number was smaller in OHG than in Gothic, which is more distantly related. Evidently, a number of distinctions were lost in the development of English.

Among the attested Germanic languages only Gothic has forms for 1st-person dual and 2nd-person dual subjects; the other Germanic languages have lost the dual verb forms, but most retain the dual pronouns for several centuries. In English they survived into the thirteenth century. In every one of those languages the *dual* pronouns were used with the corresponding *plural* verb forms. This is one example of a broader crosslinguistic pattern: if a language makes a straightforward distinction between singular, plural, and dual, but provides dual forms only for some categories (e.g. only verbs, or only nominals, or only some persons), dual concord defaults to plural when no specifically dual form is available (cf. Noyer 1997: lxxv, 42).

One of the syncretisms in the table of forms above is characteristic of West Germanic languages, and it seems strange: the past indicative 2sg. of strong verbs (only) was formed from the default past stem, not the past indicative singular stem, and in OE it looks exactly like a subjunctive. That is clearly an innovation, not present in Gothic or ON, which demands an explanation. The oldest and least problematic hypothesis is that the subjunctive form took over indicative function as well (see Ringe and Taylor 2014: 67–9, Ringe 2018 with references), but there are alternative hypotheses (see Fulk 2018: 277–8 with references).

The major syncretisms in the table above follow a general pattern: in the plural of all categories, and also in the singular of the subjunctive, there was only a single form for all persons. In every instance the form was originally the 3rd-person form, as we can tell by comparison with the other Germanic languages. That reveals two fundamental points of the structure of verb paradigms: the 3rd person is the default person, because it is used with the widest range of subjects, so that if the distinction between persons is given up, we expect the 3rd-person form to be generalized; and in Germanic languages (though not in all languages) number appears to take precedence over person, so that the distinction between singular and plural survives even when the distinction between persons does not.

Finally, there is a syncretism in the table above which occurred only in some OE dialects. Whereas the inherited pres. ind. 1sg. ending -*u* survived in the Anglian dialects spoken north of the Thames, it was replaced by subjunctive -*e* in the West Saxon (WS) and Kentish dialects south of the Thames. A plausible formal reason for this dialect difference in development was advanced in Cowgill 1965;[2] but it is also interesting that this is an unambiguous case of a subjunctive form taking over indicative function. Apparently, that is not as odd as might be supposed.

Unfortunately (or delightfully, for those who really like inflectional morphology and/or phonology), the simple underlying system exemplified above was greatly complicated in its concrete expression, both by lexical and morphological idiosyncrasies and by phonological rules. The most fundamental complication was a large-scale lexical division of verbs into "strong" verbs, "weak" verbs, "preterite-present" verbs, and irregular ("anomalous") verbs on the basis of how their present and finite past tenses were constructed and inflected. I will deal with those lexical (super-)classes briefly in turn.

3.1.2 The inflection of Old English strong verbs

In any Germanic language, strong verbs are those verbs which form their past tenses by replacing the vowel in the root syllable; typical ModE examples, given as principal parts (see above), are *sing, sang, sung* and

---

2. Cowgill's explanation hinges on the fact that in some common verbs the endings contracted with the stem; because of the phonological details of the contraction, the pres. 1sg. indicative and subjunctive became identical by regular sound change in seventeen verbs south of the Thames, but in only three verbs in the Anglian dialects to the north. Whether those seventeen verbs could have been a sufficient basis from which to generalize the identity of the two forms to all verbs (except 'be') remains a matter of judgment.

drive, drove, driven. Whereas in ModE all strong verbs belong to small lexical classes and can reasonably be called irregular, in OE that was clearly not the case. Germanic strong verbs are conventionally sorted into seven major classes, identifiable by the system of vowel alternation, or "ablaut", observable in their root syllables. Some of those traditional classes were still reasonably coherent in OE, but others no longer were. A table of the classes and subclasses of OE strong verbs can be found in Ringe and Taylor 2014: 347–8. The strong verb classes that still contained subclasses with more than twenty members each were I, II, III, and arguably VII (if we disregard the wide variety of vowels in the present stems of class VII); many classes had been fragmented, some of them into many fragments, and uniquely inflected strong verbs were not rare already in OE. The ModE situation is different in only two respects: the number of subclasses is now smaller, and the large subclasses have been eroded, so that the largest now contains no more than a dozen members (see Chapter 8) instead of about fifty.

A full description of the ablaut system of strong verbs is beyond the scope of this book, but it may be instructive to list the principal parts of a few representative verbs here. Belonging to large subclasses are, for example:

> *drīfan, drāf, drifon, drifen* 'drive'
> *rīdan, rād, ridon, riden* 'ride'
> *frēosan, frēas, fruron, froren* 'freeze'
> *bindan, band, bundon, bunden* 'tie, bind'
> *singan, sang, sungon, sungen* 'sing'
> *feallan, fēoll, fēollon, feallen* 'fall'
> *grōwan, grēow, grēowon, grōwen* 'grow'

At the other end of the spectrum of regularity, very common verbs that were uniquely inflected or belong to very small subclasses include:

> *cuman, cōm, cōmon, cumen* 'come'
> *giefan, geaf, ġēafon, ġiefen* 'give'
> *sēon, seah, sāwon, sewen* 'see'
> *biddan, bæd, bǣdon, beden* 'ask for'

Most of the commonest verbs are still strong verbs today, no matter how irregular they were, simply because they are learned very early in NLA.

The endings of strong verbs are exemplified by the paradigm of *beran* above, but there is a further complication and a dialect difference that should be noted. In the Anglian dialects north of the Thames the pres. ind. 2sg. and 3sg. endings were usually syllabic *-es* and *-eþ*, and in most verbs the root syllables of those forms did not undergo the phonological rule called "i-umlaut", which was triggered by an *i in the endings that was subsequently lost. In the Kentish and WS dialects south of the Thames the corresponding endings for most verbs were nonsyllabic -*st* and -*þ*, which interacted with stem-final consonants in various ways, and in addition the vowel of the root was usually affected by i-umlaut. Thus north of the Thames the pres. ind. 3sg. of *hātan* 'call' was *hāteþ*, but to the south it was *hēt*; to the north we find *stondan* 'stand' and *stondeþ*, but to the south *standan* and *stent*; to the north *haldan* 'hold' and *haldeþ*, but to the south *healdan* and Kentish *helt*, WS *hielt*, later *hylt*, etc. These phonological complications in the southern dialects were vulnerable to paradigmatic levelling, as we will see.

Finally, it seems worth pointing out that the inflection of OE strong verbs challenges the claim that if a morphosyntactic category appears to be signalled only by a change in the root of a word, with no affix, there must also be instances of the same category in which there is only a zero affix with no change in the root (see 1.7 above). The past stems of strong verbs are marked only by ablaut, not also by an affix; for instance, the formal difference between pres. subj. sg. *singe*, pl. *singen* and past subj. sg. *sunge*, pl. *sungen* lies in the root vowel and nothing else. There are a couple of OE strong past stems which do not exhibit ablaut, but they occur only some half-dozen times in verse (Seebold 1970: 128, 213); in most dialects of OE the generalization is clearly violated. Apparently, we are not able to insist that morphemes must be "pieces", and that apparent examples of "process" morphemes (such as vowel changes) are really cases of zero affixation with the process as an ancillary marker, without doing violence to the OE facts.

3.1.3 The inflection of Old English weak verbs

The other large superclass of OE verbs is called weak verbs; as in other Germanic languages, they formed their past tenses and past participles in OE with a suffix containing a coronal obstruent (usually -*d*-, but occasionally -*t*-). Since all finite past forms were constructed to the same stem, it is not necessary to list the past ind. 3pl. as a principal part, and weak verbs therefore have only three. The endings of the past indicative differed from those of strong verbs, as can be seen by comparison of the forms of *beran* 'carry, bear' and *hīeran* 'hear':

		strong 'carried'	weak I 'heard'
past ind.			
sg.	1	bær	hīerde
	2	bǣre	hīerdest
	3	bær	hīerde
pl.		bǣron	hīerdon

There were two large lexical classes of weak verbs and a handful of irregular verbs, as follows.

Class I weak verbs, a very large lexical class, inflected their present stems like strong verbs. The suffix of the past and past participle was -ed- or -d-, depending on the shape of the root; after a voiceless obstruent -d- was assimilated to -t-. Common regular weak verbs of class I included, for example:

> *hīeran, hīerde, hīered* 'hear'
> *fēran, fērde, fēred* 'travel, go'
> *lǣdan, lǣdde, lǣd(ed)* 'lead'
> *fremman, fremede, fremed* 'accomplish, make, do'
> *herian, herede, hered* 'praise'

The sound change called i-umlaut affected all forms of regular class I weak verbs, because in all forms there was originally an *i or *j[3] immediately following the root syllable, so that there was no vowel alternation between the stems.

The operation of various phonological rules divided this class of verbs into subclasses. The most awkward consequences were caused by the general OE phonological rule that geminate consonants could not exist next to another consonant. Thus the past stem of *sendan* 'to send', which we might expect to have been *sendd- (i.e. *send-* plus suffix -d-) was reduced to *send-*, identical with the present stem. The result was an extensive homonymy of forms; for instance, *sende* might be the pres. ind. 1sg. or the pres. subj. sg., or it might be the past ind. 1sg. or 3sg. or the past subj. sg. That might have been a problem for native learners in the early stages of NLA; sometime in the eleventh century some clever toddler came up with a solution, as we will see in Chapter 4. Just as awkward was the fact that the past suffix was -t- or -d- even after light root syllables if they ended in -t- or -d-; thus the finite past tense and past participle of *settan* 'to seat, to set' are not *setede and *seted, as might be expected, but *sette* and *sett*. That gave rise to exactly the same homonymies, but in this case the problem (if there was one) was never solved; even in ModE the relevant forms of *set* are *set* and *set*.

A fairly small but significant minority of class I weak verbs were irregular. The nature of the irregularity can be seen from the principal parts of representative verbs:

---

3. This survives after a light syllable ending in *r*—for instance, in *herian* 'praise'—but was otherwise lost, with gemination of the preceding consonant if the root vowel was short.

sellan, sealde, seald 'give, sell'
weċċan, weahte, weaht 'wake up' (transitive)
tǣċan, tǣhte, tǣht, Anglian *tǣċan, tāhte, tāht* 'teach'
sēċan, sōhte, sōht 'seek, look for'
þenċan, þōhte, þōht 'think'
þynċan, þūhte, þūht 'seem'
wyrċan, worhte, worht 'work, make'
byċġan, bohte, boht 'buy'

The present stems of these verbs were completely normal: i-umlaut appeared in all forms, gemination was in evidence if the root syllable was light, root-final velars were palatalized, etc. In the finite past and the past participle, however, i-umlaut had not occurred,[4] and there were various other phonological irregularities. Most verbs with presents in *-ell-* inflected like *sellan*, most with presents in *-eċċ-* inflected like *weċċan*, and *rǣċan* 'reach' was like *tǣċan*; the others were unique.

The other large class of weak verbs, weak class II, was enormous, though it included fewer common verbs. The past suffix was *-od-*, and the inflection of the finite past was exactly like that of weak class I. The present stem inflected differently, however. Compare the present of 'hear' with that of weak class II 'answer':

infinitive	hīeran	andswarian
inflected inf.	hīerenne	andswarienne
participle	hīerende	andswariende
indicative		
sg. 1	hīere	andswarie
2	hīerst	andswarast
3	hīerþ	andswaraþ
pl.	hīeraþ	andswariaþ
subjunctive		
sg., pl.	hīere, -en	andswarie, -en
imperative sg.	hīer	andswara

As the chart shows, for the most part, class II had the same endings as class I (and the strong verbs) preceded by an *-i-*, which was syllabic. However, in the pres. ind. 2sg. and 3sg. and in the imperative sg. the stem ended in *-a-*.

Half a dozen common weak verbs are best described as irregular. It is not necessary to deal with them in detail, but the principal parts of the commonest ones give some idea of their irregularities:

4. In *tǣhte, tǣht* the umlauted vowel of the present stem had been levelled into the past; the Anglian forms preserved the original situation.

bringan, brōhte, brōht 'bring'
secġan (3sg. *sæġþ*), *sæġde, sæġd* 'say'
habban (3sg. *hæfþ*), *hæfde, hæfd* 'have'
libban (3sg. *leofaþ*), *lifde, lifd* 'live'

3.1.4 The inflection of Old English preterite-present verbs

These verbs are so called because the inflection of their presents is more or less like that of a strong past (preterite) stem. Already in PGmc. they were an archaic relic, and the explanation of how they arose and developed is not useful for understanding their OE inflection; interested students should consult Ringe 2017: 177–9 with references. A comparison of *witan* 'to know' with the strong verb *bītan* 'to bite' will show the peculiarities of preterite-present inflection:

	present	past	present	past
infinitive	witan	—	bītan	—
inflected inf.	witenne	—	bītenne	—
participle	witende	witen	bītende	biten
indicative				
sg. 1	wāt	wisse	bīte	bāt
2	wāst	wissest	bītst	bite
3	wāt	wisse	bīt(t)	bāt
pl.	witon	wisson	bītaþ	biton
subjunctive				
sg.	wite	wisse	bīte	bite
pl.	witen	wissen	bīten	biten
imperative				
sg.	—	—	bīt	—
pl.	witaþ	—	bītaþ	—

It can be seen that, with the exception of the archaic ind. 2sg. *wāst*, the pres. ind. and subj. of the preterite-present were inflected exactly like the past ind. and subj. of the strong verb. Of course, OE past stems did not have imperatives, infinitives, or active participles, so preterite-presents had to construct those forms in some other way. The infinitives and present participle were formed by adding the usual suffixes to the default stem, in this case *wit-*, which corresponds to the strong past default stem; that is not surprising. Most preterite-presents had no imperatives at all, using the subjunctive instead; *witaþ* 'know ye' is an exception, and it too was formed to the default stem with the usual ending. Like all finite past stems of preterite-present verbs, *wisse* was a weak past, and over time it was remodelled by native learners as *wiste*, conforming somewhat better to the formation of irregular weak past stems (cf. *brōhte, worhte, bohte*, etc.). Most preterite-presents had no attested past participle, but *witen* and the few others that do occur were strong in form—which is surprising.

Because their inflection was so unusual, the principal parts of a preterite-present verb are rather different from those of other verbs: the present infinitive, the *present* indicative 3sg., the past indicative 3sg., and the past participle (if any). A list of the common ones shows that most preterite-presents had roughly the same types of ablaut alternations as strong verbs, though there were some differences:

> *witan, wāt, wisse ~ wiste, witen* 'know'
> *cunnan, cann, cūþe, cunnen* 'know (how)'
> *þurfan, þearf, þorfte* 'need'
> **durran, dearr, dorste* 'dare'
> **sċulan, sċeal, sċolde* 'owe; ought to, shall'
> *ġemunan, ġeman, ġemunde, ġemunen* 'remember'
> **mōtan, mōt, mōste* 'be allowed, be able; must'
> *āgan, āh, āhte* 'have'
> *magan, mæġ, meahte* 'be able'

(See immediately below on the asterisked infinitives.) Also worth mentioning here is the single form *uton* 'let's', which seems to have been parallel to many preterite-presents both formally and functionally (Warner 1993: 95). In addition to archaic pres. ind. 2sg. forms (*wāst, canst, þearft, dearst, sċealt, ġemanst, mōst, āht ~ āhst, meaht*), several of these verbs variably exhibited i-umlaut in the pres. subj. (*þyrfe ~ þurfe, dyrre ~ durre, sċyle ~ sċule, ġemyne ~ ġemune*); that is another archaism that had been eliminated from the past subjunctive of OE strong verbs.

Though this was a small, closed class of verbs—indeed, a relic class—it is important because it was a major source of ModE modals. There is a serious debate among syntacticians about the extent to which some of these verbs were modals already in OE (see Warner 1993: 92–109, 135–55, Ringe and Taylor 2014: 424–8, both with references). For the most part, that is a syntactic question, but it has a morphological corollary. ModE modals have no nonfinite forms—no infinitives or participles—and in the context of ModE syntax that is a natural consequence of the fact that they are generated somewhere in the Tense (formerly INFL) complex of functional nodes, not as heads of full VP's that can (for example) govern objects of their own. Historically, however, it is the other way round: at some point, various preterite-presents (and *willan* 'to want', on which see below) lost their nonfinite forms because they had become too rare to be acquired by some significant proportion of native learners, and at that point they could be reanalyzed as genuine modals. It is therefore more than a little interesting that nonfinite forms of some of these verbs are rare or unattested in our OE documents. The absence of past participles might or might not be significant—they are rare in all Germanic languages—but the absence of infinitives is less easily explained. It seems possible that at least some preterite-presents had begun their gradual development into modals already in the OE period. On the other hand, that development was clearly not monotonic, since 'dare' did acquire an infinitive in ME, and many of these verbs acquired participles during the same period (Warner 1993: 144–8). For the purposes of the present book we can do no more than note the morphological facts.

3.1.5 The inflection of Old English anomalous verbs

This is, of course, a grab-bag of irregular verbs; they are important because they were very common and have remained so throughout the history of English.

Two of these verbs had strong presents, weak finite pasts, and strong past participles; they are treated here because the finite past of one was uniquely constructed, while that of the other was suppletive:

dōn, dyde, dōn 'do'
gān, ēode, gān 'go'

A third had no past participle:

willan, wolde 'want'

This verb exhibited a unique irregularity in the inflection of the pres. ind.:

sg. 1	wille
2	wilt
3	wile
pl.	willaþ

Though *wilt* has the same ending as preterite-present *sċealt*, 3sg. *wile* is an unparalleled archaism, cognate with OHG and Gothic *wili*.

The most irregular verb was also the commonest by far: namely, multiply suppletive 'be', for which a complete paradigm must be given.

	default present	*perfective present*	*past*
infinitive	(wesan)	bēon	—
inflected inf.	(wesenne)	bēonne	—
participle	(wesende)	(bēonde)	(ġebēon)

indicative

sg. 1	eom (*Angl.* eam)	bēo	wæs
2	eart (*Angl.* earþ)	bist	wǣre
3	is	biþ	wæs
pl.	sint ~ sindon	bēoþ	wǣron
	(*Angl.* arun)		

subjunctive

sg.	sīe	bēo	wǣre
pl.	sīen	bēon	wǣren

imperative

sg.	(wes)	bēo	—
pl.	(wesaþ)	bēoþ	—

The forms in parentheses do not occur in early WS texts. Present forms of *wesan* do occur in late WS; they also occur in early Mercian documents and in verse, which suggests that they were originally only Anglian. The participles *bēonde* and *ġebēon* do not appear before the eleventh century. There was an actual contrast between the default present and the perfective present only in the indicative and the subjunctive. In those categories the perfective present was used to indicate (1) future time and (2) statements which are always true; thus 'be' was the only verb in which the future was systematically distinguished from the present.

3.1.6 Lexical classes, productivity, and defaults in the Old English verb system

In 3.1.2 I noted that a few subclasses of OE strong verbs were substantial, many more were small, and there were numerous uniquely inflected verbs. Though I did not discuss the subclasses of weak verbs, their situation was similar. Regular class I weak verbs with heavy roots were very numerous, and there were even more class II weak verbs of the default type; there were also a few smaller subclasses of weak verbs, but a significant number of irregular verbs as well. Preterite-present and anomalous verbs were all uniquely inflected (except that the rare *unnan* 'grant' rhymed with *cunnan* 'know how' in all its forms). Except for the fact that there were still some large subclasses of strong verbs in OE and more than one large subclass of weak verbs, *the situation was actually comparable to the ModE situation*; in other words, much of the fragmentation of lexical classes of English verbs had already occurred in the prehistoric period. For the purposes of comparison with ModE, consider the following table:

OE verb subclasses by size	no. of classes	no. of verbs
uniquely inflected verbs	47	47
pairs of identically inflected verbs	13	26
membership 3–6	12	50
membership 7–9	5	39
membership 13–19	7	106
membership 20–51	5	227
membership larger	3	very numerous

Though this is a rough approximation (and could have been constructed differently), the overall distribution is clear. A comparable ModE table can be found in 8.1.1.

The OE verb system was also like the ModE system in another way that is not immediately apparent: weak class II had a special status, comparable to—though *not* identical with—the status of the default class of ModE verbs which is its direct descendant. The similarities and differences between the two lexical classes can be appreciated by making a series of comparisons.

Suppose we sort OE verbs into four categories: weak class II, weak class I (all types), strong verbs, and verbs of other classes. In a typical piece of West Saxon OE prose, the forms of class II weak verbs encountered will be outnumbered by the forms of *each* of the other categories encountered, so that they amount to less than one-fourth of the total (sometimes much less). In a typical piece of ModE prose, if auxiliary verbs are excluded,[5] the ratio of verbs inflected in the default pattern to other verbs is often roughly one to one—though in novels written in colloquial English default-pattern verbs can be modestly less common, simply because so many of the commonest and most basic verbs either are inflected according to minority patterns or are irregular, while in technical discourse the imbalance is reversed because virtually all Latinate verbs inflect according to the default pattern. Since the ModE default class is descended (as a class) from OE weak class II, we can say that the incidence of this class in texts has increased dramatically over the past millennium, though it is still not overwhelmingly dominant.

Lexical lists of verbs occurring in text corpora tell a somewhat different story, but with a parallel development from OE to ModE. For early WS[6] Cosijn 1888: II.174–5 lists more than 300 weak verbs of class II. That is slightly greater than the number of strong verbs in *all* OE texts taken together; it is also substantially greater than the number of class

---

5. Auxiliary verbs were uncommon in typical OE prose, so that it makes little difference whether they are tabulated separately.

6. Effectively, only three long texts: the *Cura Pastoralis*, the OE translation of Orosius, and the *Anglo-Saxon Chronicle* up to about 900.

I weak verbs discussed in Cosijn 1888: II.152–73 (more than 200, but considerably less than 300). It appears that class II weak verbs were already the largest class around the year 900, though on the average they were so much less common than verbs of other classes that they were much less prominent in running text. In ModE, of course, the default class has become overwhelmingly the most numerous class; even colloquial English has a couple thousand verbs, of which only about 160 (and their compounds) fail to inflect according to the default pattern.[7] Yet those 160 are still so much commoner than the rest, on the average, that they account for about half of all main-verb tokens heard or read.

Comparison of the productivity of OE and ModE lexical classes is also enlightening. In ModE only the default pattern is more than marginally productive; though innovative past stems such as *dove* and *snuck* are occasionally coined, any new verb entering the language by any route adopts default inflection automatically. Surprisingly, that was already almost true of weak class II in OE. Not only can verbs of that class be derived productively from nouns and adjectives, but most verbs borrowed into the language are inflected as class II weak verbs (Campbell 1962: 210, Durkin 2014: 113–14, 119). Here is a representative sample of OE class II weak verbs borrowed from Latin, the only significant source of OE loanwords:

> *culpian* 'humble oneself' ← Lat. *culpāre* 'blame'
> *dīlegian* 'delete' ← Lat. *dēlēre*
> *gecorōnian* 'crown' ← Lat. *corōnāre*
> *offrian* 'offer' ← Lat. *offerre*
> *pinsian* 'consider' ← Lat. *pēnsāre*
> *plantian* 'plant' ← Lat. *plantāre*
> *predician* 'preach' ← Lat. *praedicāre*
> *sealtian* 'dance' ← Lat. *saltāre*
> *trifolian* 'grind' ← Lat. *tribulāre*
> *turnian* 'turn' ← Lat. *tornāre* 'turn on a lathe'

This is by no means a complete list. A couple of these verbs might have been borrowed when the ancestors of the English were still living on the continent (cf. Ringe and Taylor 2014: 137–8); that suggests that weak class II might already have been the default lexical class of verbs fairly early in the separate prehistory of the language, or even in Proto-West Germanic. A few might actually be OE derivatives of borrowed Latin nouns (Durkin 2014: 121–3).

However, that is not quite the whole story. There are also a handful of Latin verbs that appear in weak class I in OE, e.g. (Ringe and Taylor 2014: 137–8, Durkin 2014: 121–3):

---

7. Modals have been omitted from this calculation.

āspendan 'spend' ← Lat. *expendere* 'weigh out, disburse'
dihtan 'direct' ← Lat. *dictāre* 'dictate, prescribe'
pynġan 'prick' ← Lat. *pungere*
tyrnan 'turn' ← Lat. *tornāre* 'turn on a lathe'

Though *dihtan* might have been borrowed on the continent (Ringe and Taylor 2014: 137–8), the shape of *āspendan*, at least, shows that it was borrowed not earlier than the seventh century, since the root of the OE verb is obviously intended to match that of the Latin verb and would not have done so until after i-umlaut had run its course (ibid. pp. 133–4). Thus it seems clear that weak class I retained at least some productivity well down into the prehistory of OE and possibly even in the attested period. By contrast, the only borrowed OE strong verb, *scrīfan* 'prescribe' (← Lat. *scrībere* 'write'), was almost certainly borrowed on the continent and does not demonstrate even marginal productivity of strong verbs in OE.

In addition to the loanword evidence, there is evidence from morphological change that weak verbs were the default superclass and that within the weak verbs class II was the ultimate default. In the WS dialect the class VII strong verbs *rǣdan* 'advise; read' and *ondrǣdan* 'dread' became class I weak verbs (pasts *rǣdde*, *ondrǣdde*) within the OE period; in the prose of all dialects class VII strong *slǣpan*, Angl. *slēpan* 'sleep' likewise became a class I weak verb (past *slǣpte*, Angl. *slēpte*; see Brunner 1965: 307). Within the weak verbs there was apparently a transfer of verbs from class I to class II in the WS dialect, beginning already in early WS: most verbs with light root syllables ending in a sonorant or a fricative replaced the forms exhibiting a geminate consonant with forms exhibiting a single consonant plus *-i-*. The change proceeded on a lexical basis. Thus while *fremman* 'further, accomplish, do' retained its inherited forms *fremme*, *fremmaþ*, etc. until quite late in the OE period, **gremman* 'anger' is unattested, having been replaced by *gremian* (*gremie*, *gremiaþ*, etc.) by around 900. Admittedly, it is not quite clear what this change amounted to at first. It might not be impossible that the spelling "*gremian*" represented not trisyllabic *gre.mi.an*, an unambiguously class II form, but disyllabic *grem.i̯an*, like the class I weak type *her.i̯an* 'praise' with /rj/ in place of the gemination that affected other consonants. That is perhaps suggested by the fact that we still find only pres. ind. 3sg. *gremeð* and past ind. pl. *gremedon* in the early WS documents. But by the late WS of Ælfric's prose we find *gremaþ* and *gremodon* respectively, the former (at least) an unambiguously class II form. I doubt that we can reconstruct how this change started, but I do not doubt that in the long run it effected a transfer of a number of class I weak verbs into class II, which is thus revealed as the ultimate default class of OE verbs.

The long-term development of weak class II reveals a characteristic pattern in the history of inflectional morphology. The default lexical class need not be the majority class within its major class of lexemes; it can even be one of the less important lexical classes. However, if it remains the default class, it will steadily acquire new members, and if that situation continues for long enough, it will eventually become the majority class, first in terms of a lexical list, then even in terms of tokens in running discourse.

3.1.7 Periphrastic verbs in Old English

We have already considered the extent to which some preterite-presents might have begun to become modals in OE (see 3.1.4). Periphrastic constructions—i.e. collocations of auxiliary verbs and participles—also occur in OE, though they are less common than in ModE. The following clearly occur (see Mitchell 1985: 271–360 for the facts in great detail, Warner 1993: 92–109, and Ringe and Taylor 2014: 428–38 with references for analysis and discussion):

> *bēon/wesan* plus the present participle, parallel to ModE *were fighting*;
> *habban* plus the past participle, parallel to ModE *had sent*;
> *bēon/wesan* plus the past participle of motion verbs and change-of-state verbs, parallel to archaic ModE *is come*;
> *bēon/wesan* plus the past participle of transitive verbs, parallel to ModE *was wounded*;
> *weorþan* 'become' plus the past participle of transitive verbs, roughly parallel to ModE *got killed*.

I have said "parallel" in the above discussion for a specific reason: the function ("meaning") of the OE constructions sometimes appears to be identical with that of their ModE equivalents, sometimes is clearly different, and in many instances is difficult to determine; the discussion of Ringe and Taylor 2014: 428–38 gives a good idea of the uncertainties involved, while Mitchell 1985: 271–360 provides numerous examples. The following summary merely scratches the surface.

The tenses constructed with *habban* and the past participle are usually straightforward: they are anterior tenses corresponding to the perfect and pluperfect tenses of ModE and might as well be called by the same names. A typical example is found in the entry of the *Anglo-Saxon Chronicle* (ms. A) for 905:[8]

---

8. I do not usually cite specific editions of OE texts, since the readings have typically not been in question for a century or more. Passages quoted can be found by

Þā ætsǣton ðā Centiscan þǣr beæftan ofer his bebod, and seofon ǣrendracan hē
him hæfde tō āsend.
'Then the Kentishmen remained behind there against his orders, and he <u>had</u>
<u>sent</u> them seven messengers.'

It is true that the present perfect is not always used where it would be in
standard ModE; the classic example is *þīn ġelēafa þē ġehǣlde* (Matthew
9: 22) vs. *þīn ġelēafa hæfð þē ġehǣled* 'your faith has healed you' (Ælfric,
Catholic Homilies 1.10.258; see Ringe and Taylor 2014: 453 with references). But since the same variation is widespread in colloquial ModE it
seems inadvisable to attach much importance to it in OE. As in many
other European languages, a small group of verbs, mainly verbs of motion,
use *bēon/wesan* plus the past participle to form these tenses, e.g. in *Orosius*
5.47.19:

Hīe wǣron cumen Leoniðan tō fultume
'They <u>had come</u> to Leonidas's aid'.

As Mitchell emphasizes, already in early OE documents most of the participles in these tenses are uninflected, which shows clearly that they are
not adjectival but are part of genuine verbal periphrases; Warner 1993: 97
comes to the same conclusion.

The passive periphrases are a bit less straightforward (Ringe and Taylor
2014: 429–33 with references). For one thing, it is not always easy to
distinguish a genuine passive from 'be' or 'become' with an adjectival
participle; for another, *bēon/wesan* and *weorþan* seem to be isofunctional
when the passive describes an action, though *bēon/wesan* is generally used
when the passive describes a state. However, in this case too the situation
is similar enough to that of ModE that we can plausibly ascribe the periphrastic passive to OE (so also Warner 1993: 96 with references).

The tenses constructed with *bēon/wesan* plus the present participle are a
different matter. They are much less common in OE than in ModE, and
it seems reasonably clear that they do not have the same function. Often
the phrase means 'continue Xing', e.g. in the famous story of Cynewulf
and Cyneheard in the *Chronicle*:

and hīe ealle on þone cyning wǣron feohtende oþ þæt hīe hine ofslægenne hæfdon
'and they all <u>continued fighting</u> with the king until they had killed him'.[9]

searching the *Dictionary of Old English Web Corpus* (Healey, Wilkin, and Xiang
2009). For analysis and commentary the best modern editions are, of course,
essential; outstanding recent editions by Janet Bately, Susan Irvine, and Roy Liuzza
are listed in the bibliography.
9. Or perhaps 'got him killed', i.e. 'managed to kill him', since for once the participle is
inflected.

However, there are other examples that cannot reasonably be interpreted in that way (Mitchell 1985: 272–7, Warner 1993: 95–6). What there does not seem to be is continuity between the OE construction and the superficially similar construction at any later stage of English (Warner 1993: 95–6, who emphasizes a discontinuity in early ME and the full appearance of the modern pattern only in early ModE).

3.2 The inflection of nouns in Old English

Every OE noun was assigned to one of three concord classes, or genders, traditionally called masculine, feminine, and neuter; the concord system will be discussed at length in Chapter 4. OE nouns distinguished four cases: nominative, accusative, genitive, and dative. A fifth case, the instrumental, was already merging with the dative in early OE and is unimportant for the further development of the language (see Freeman 2018).

Traditional descriptions of OE noun inflection treat the system in terms of PGmc. lexical classes, but for OE the synchronic situation was already different. There was a single default inflection for each of the genders, plus a number of minority patterns. Leaving aside phonological complications that affected the stems of relatively few nouns, the default patterns are the following.

	masculine	neuter		feminine	
	'king'	'word'	'kingdom'	'place'	'answer'
sg. nom.	cyning	word	rīċe	stōw	andswaru
acc.	cyning	word	rīċe	stōwe	andsware
gen.	cyninges	wordes	rīċes	stōwe	andsware
dat.	cyninge	worde	rīċe	stōwe	andsware
pl. n.-a.	cyningas	word	rīċu	stōwa	andswara
gen.	cyninga	worda	rīċa	stōwa	andswara
dat.	cyningum	wordum	rīċum	stōwum	andswarum

All masculine nouns of the default class were essentially inflected alike; those that ended in -e (e.g. ende 'ende') simply dropped that vowel before overt endings. The same can be said of default neuters, with one qualification. If the noun ended in -e, or was a monosyllable with a short vowel ending in a single consonant, the nom.-acc. pl. ended in -u; if the noun was a "heavy" monosyllable, its nom.-acc. pl. was endless (see the beginning of this chapter). Polysyllables exhibited complex variation between the two patterns. A similar alternation affected the nom. sg. of default feminines, with an ending -u after light monosyllables (and their compounds, like *andswaru*) and an endingless form for all other nouns.

Several large-scale generalizations can be made about these paradigms. The following seem especially worth noting:

1. The nom. pl. and acc. pl. were always identical; that was true of all OE nominals except the 1st- and 2nd-person pronouns.
2. The dat. pl. of all these nouns ended in *-um*. In fact the dat. pl. of all nominals except the 1st- and 2nd-person pronouns ended in *-um* if the relevant syllable was unstressed, otherwise in *-m*.
3. The gen. pl. always ended in *-a*; that also held for all nominals except the 1st- and 2nd-person pronouns, though some had an additional consonant before the *-a*.
4. The dat. sg. always ended in *-e*. That was true only of default-class nouns.
5. The masc. and neut. forms were identical in the gen. and dat. of both numbers; that was true of all OE nominals.

It seems fair to say that many case-and-number combinations were not very well marked on default nouns; when unstressed vowels merged as /ə/ in late OE, they would be very poorly marked.

A substantial minority paradigm were the "n-stems", which included all masculine nouns with nom. sg. ending in *-a*, all feminines with nom. sg. in *-e*, and two neuters, *ēage* 'eye' and *ēare* 'ear'. Their inflection was completely different from the default type, except for the dat. pl. and (modulo one detail) the gen. pl.:

	masculine	*feminine*	*neuter*
	'name'	'heart'	'eye'
sg. nom.	nama	heorte	ēage
acc.	naman	heortan	ēage
g.-d.	naman	heortan	ēagan
pl. n.-a.	naman	heortan	ēagan
gen.	namena	heortena	ēagena
dat.	namum	heortum	ēagum

Once again, the functional oppositions were not very well marked. Comparison of the neuter paradigm with the others reveals a further principle of OE nominal inflection: for neuters, the nom. sg. and acc. sg. were always identical.

There were two relic inflectional patterns that were followed by significant numbers of OE nouns; they are traditionally called "u-stems" and "root nouns". There were no neuters in either class. I exemplify each pattern with one masculine noun and one feminine.

	u-stems		root nouns	
	masculine	feminine	masculine	feminine
	'son'	'hand'	'human'	'book'
sg. n.-a.	sunu	hand	mann	bōc
gen.	suna	handa	mannes	bōce ~ bēċ
dat.	suna	handa	menn	bēċ
pl. n.-a.	suna	handa	menn	bēċ
gen.	suna	handa	manna	bōca
dat.	sunum	handum	mannum	bōcum

Fewer than half a dozen nouns, all fairly common, were u-stems. Root nouns were significantly commoner. Their distinctive characteristic was i-umlaut, but no ending (because the *-i had been lost), in the nom.-acc. pl. *and the dat. sg.*[10] The only masculines were *mann (menn), fōt (fēt)* 'foot', and *tōþ (tēþ)* 'tooth', but there were more than a dozen feminines, including, for example, *gōs (gēs)* 'goose', *mūs (mȳs)* 'mouse', and *gāt (gǣt)* 'goat'. One feminine noun, *niht* 'night', had a vowel that was unaffected by i-umlaut; it was effectively uninflected except in the gen. pl. and dat. pl.

Numerous nouns and small classes of nouns exhibited isolated irregularities. Two are worth mentioning here. The kinship terms *mōdor* 'mother', *brōþor* 'brother', *dohtor* 'daughter', and *sweostor* 'sister' often had endingless forms except in the gen. pl. and dat. pl., like *niht*; those with o-vowels in the root exhibited i-umlaut in the dat. sg., but not in the nom.-acc. pl. *Fæder* 'father' was similar, except that it was shifting into the default paradigm (nom.-acc. pl. *fæderas*, optional gen. sg. *fæderes*). There were also a few neuter nouns that inserted an -r- before the plural endings; thus the nom.-acc. pl. forms of *lamb* 'lamb', *ċealf* 'calf', and *ǣġ* 'egg' were *lambru, ċealfru, ǣġru*, while *ċild* 'child' varied between *ċild* (according to the default pattern) and *ċildru*.

3.3 The inflection of other nominals in Old English

The remaining classes of OE nominals usually had forms for all three genders, since they participated in the nominal concord system. The only exceptions are the 1st- and 2nd-person and interrogative pronouns and the numerals above 'three'. I begin with adjectives.

The inflection of OE adjectives was organized completely differently

---

10. Also the gen. sg. for some feminine nouns. It is important to remember that i-umlaut was not a plural marker for these nouns; note that it did not appear in the gen. or dat. pl.

from the inflection of nouns: there were only two inflectional paradigms, and most adjectives inflected according to *both*. In general, the "weak" inflection was used for adjectives in noun phrases modified by a determiner, a possessive adjective, or a genitive, while the "strong" inflection was used in all other syntactic environments. Thus the strong vs. weak distinction was usually predictable from the syntax.

The weak paradigm was identical with the paradigm of n-stem nouns. For instance, the weak nom. sg. of *gōd* 'good' was masc. *gōda*, fem. and neut. *gōde*, etc., exactly as in the n-stem table given above.

The strong paradigm mostly had the endings of the default determiner (on which see below) whenever they were different from the corresponding endings of nouns. The strong paradigm of *gōd* 'good' was the following:

		masc.	*neut.*	*fem.*
sg.	*nom.*	gōd	gōd	gōd
	acc.	gōdne	gōd	gōde
	gen.	gōd e s		gōdre
	dat.	gōd u m		gōdre
pl.	*n.-a.*	gōde	gōd	gōda
	gen.	gōd r a		
	d.-i.	gōd u m		

Since a large majority of adjectives had heavy root syllables, this is the variant of the strong paradigm that is most frequently encountered. Those with light root syllables, as well as those ending in *-e*, had an ending *-u* in the fem. nom. sg. and the neut. n.-a. pl., so that for *sum* 'some' those forms were *sumu*, while for *grēne* 'green' they were *grēnu*. In later OE the fem. nom. sg. ending was lost, so that the nom. sg. became endingless for all concord classes, while the masc. n.-a. pl. *-e* was extended to all concord classes (Hogg and Fulk 2011: 152–3 with references).

Some adjectives were inflected only according to one paradigm or the other, usually because they never occurred in a syntactic position in which the other inflection would be required; thus the possessive adjectives *mīn* 'my, mine', etc., were always inflected strong, and so was *sum* 'some', while *ilca* 'same' was always inflected weak. But *ōþer* 'other; second' was always inflected strong even when a determiner or possessive adjective preceded; conversely, the other ordinal numerals were always inflected weak, so that we find only *forma* 'first', *þridda* 'third', etc. Moreover, comparative adjectives (on which see further below) were always inflected weak, though superlatives were inflected both strong and weak.

It might be supposed that a system of functionless distinctions like this one would be targeted for destruction. However, even a glance at a grammar of modern German will show that that is not necessarily true; though some inconsistencies have been ironed out over time, as expected, German still maintains the formal distinction between strong and weak adjectives. Evidently, native learners have no inherent difficulty learning an apparently crazy system such as this one. Since the system was, in fact, lost in English, we will have to consider why that might have happened.

Like other Germanic languages, OE had a comparison paradigm for adjectives, with comparative and superlative degrees. The comparative suffix was *-r-*; since comparatives were inflected weak, the masc. nom. sg. ended in *-ra*, and it is in that form that OE comparatives are usually cited. The usual superlative suffix was *-ost*, though its vowel was variously spelled (see Hogg and Fulk 2011: 176–8 for details). Typical comparison paradigms are *earm, earmra, earmost* 'poor', *hāliġ, hāliġra, hālgost* 'holy', etc., essentially as in ModE.

A handful of comparatives and superlatives exhibited i-umlaut of the root. The following are usual:

eald, ieldra, ieldest 'old'
ġeong ~ iung, ġingra, ġingest 'young'[11]
strang, strengra, strengest 'strong'[12]
lang, lengra, lengest 'long'
sċort, sċyrtra, sċyrtest 'short'
hēah, hīerra, hīehst 'high'

In addition, four very common adjectives had suppletive comparison paradigms:

gōd, betera, betst and *sēlra ~ sella, sēlest* 'good'
yfel, wiersa, wierst ~ wierrest 'bad, evil'
miċel, māra, mǣst 'big, great'
lȳtel, lǣssa, lǣst 'little, small'

Most parts of these suppletive paradigms were inherited, but the ancestors of *lǣssa, lǣst* replaced *minnirā, *minnist in the northern West Germanic (WGmc.) dialects ancestral to OE and Old Frisian (cf. OHG *minniro, minnisto* and Gothic *minniza, minnists*); this is a typical example of the replacement of part of a suppletive paradigm without eliminating the suppletion.

---

11. It seems clear that "*ġeong*" was actually the usual spelling for /jung/.
12. Though a positive *strenge* and comparative and superlative *strangra, strangost* also occurred (Campbell 1962: 274), all were much rarer than the forms given here; it seems clear than an i-umlauting comparison paradigm was normal for this adjective.

Though the formation of adverbs from adjectives is, strictly speaking, derivation rather than inflection, OE adverbs did have comparison paradigms, and it is convenient to treat them here. The default formation of adverbs from adjectives was in -*e*, with comparative in -*or* and superlative in -*ost*. Adverbs corresponding to adjectives with i-umlauting and suppletive comparison paradigms had similar paradigms; the most notable divergence is that the adverb corresponding to *gōd* was *wel*.

The default determiner is probably the commonest nominal in any OE text of substantial length. It functioned both as a definite article and as the distal deictic 'that'. In addition, it was used with and without the relative particle *þe* as a relative pronoun.[13] Here is its paradigm:

	masc.	*neut.*	*fem.*
sg. nom.	sē	þæt	sēo
acc.	þone	þæt	þā
gen.	þ æ s		þǣre
dat.	þǣm ~ þām		þǣre
pl. n.-a.		þ ā	
gen.		þ ā r a	
d.-i.		þǣm ~ þām	

It can be seen that the endings of this extremely common and pivotal nominal were the source of the strong adjective endings (for the most part), though the stressed vowels of this paradigm had been reduced to *e* or *u* in the unstressed endings of adjectives. The multiple irregularities were, of course, the results of many linguistic changes of various kinds, and some of them (such as the anomalous *s*- of the non-neuter nom. sg. forms) go all the way back to Proto-Indo-European, but from an OE point of view they were simply anomalies to be learned. The ability of native learners to acquire such a system accurately is evidenced by the fact that virtually all these irregularities reappear in the other early Germanic languages and were obviously inherited from their common ancestor.

The proximal deictic 'this' was an innovation of the North and West Germanic languages; it does not appear in Gothic, which used the default determiner for all deixis (!). However, the innovation was, at least partly, a parallel development, because the forms of the individual languages do not match in such a way as to permit the reconstruction of a common ancestor. I first give the OE paradigm, then note how it seems to have been constructed.

---

13. The relative particle could also be used by itself to introduce a relative clause. Its subsequent development will be relevant in the following chapter.

	masc.	*neut.*	*fem.*
sg. nom.	þēs	þis	þēos
acc.	þisne	þis	þās
gen.	þisses		þisse
dat.	þissum		þisse
pl. n.-a.		þ ā s	
gen.		þ i s s a	
d.-i.		þ i s s u m	

From a purely descriptive point of view, this paradigm can be constructed from the paradigm of the default determiner by the following rules.

1. Replace any initial *s-* with the default initial *þ-* (cf. *þēs, þēos*).
2. If the form is a monosyllable ending in a vowel, add *-s* (cf. *þēs, þēos, þās*).[14]
3. Otherwise use the stem *þiss-* plus the strong adjective endings.
4. Reduce *þiss-* to *þis(-)* when endingless or when followed by a consonant.
5. **-sr- > -ss-* (cf. *þisse, þissa*).

The last two rules were the results of regular sound changes; native learners eventually undid the last change in these forms to produce *þis(se)re, þis(se)ra* with more transparent endings. The first rule was a simple levelling (i.e. the elimination of an alternation in a paradigm). It is the second and third rules that reveal something of how this paradigm came into existence. The forms *þēs, þēos, þās* are fully inflected forms of 'that' with *-s* added *after* the inflection. That must have been the original structure of the paradigm; the additional *-s* (or possibly **-si*, with the short vowel later lost) must at first have been a clitic meaning approximately 'here'. Other such paradigms are known from other languages; for instance, the paradigm of Latin *hic* 'this' contains several forms with a clitic *-c(e)* 'here' added after the original endings. But for native learners used to finding the concord markers at the ends of nominals, a deictic inflected in the middle is anomalous, and it is not surprising that this OE paradigm also contains innovative forms, based on a stem *þiss-*, in which the endings have been moved to the end where they "belong". The source of *þiss-* is the major puzzle, to which no generally accepted solution has been proposed; fortunately, it is not important for the subsequent history of English.

14. So also masc. and neut. instrumental sg. *þȳs*, formed from *þȳ*, the corresponding form of the default deictic, in the same way.

The OE 3rd-person pronoun had essentially the same endings as the default determiner, attached to a stem that is recognizably /hi-/ (in spite of the operation of various phonological rules):

		masc.	neut.	fem.
sg.	nom.	hē	hit	hēo
	acc.	hine	hit	hīe
	gen.	h i s		hire
	dat.	h i m		hire
pl.	n.-a.		h ī e	
	gen.		h e o r a	
	d.-i.		h i m	

Remarkably, there was no 3rd-person reflexive pronoun in OE, nor in any of the other northern WGmc. languages; the inherited reflexive preserved in (acc.) Gothic, ON *sik*, OHG *sih*, etc. (and cognate with Latin *sē*) had simply been lost. Like the 1st- and 2nd-person pronouns, the ordinary 3rd-person pronoun was also used in reflexive function, giving rise to serious ambiguity in not a few sentences. The OE adjective *self* was used with pronouns to emphasize them; it was not a reflexive marker.

As in many IE languages, the interrogative pronoun had an impoverished paradigm: the masc. and fem. forms were identical, and there were no plural forms. Such a paradigm makes sense in terms of real-world reference, because one typically does not know the gender and number of persons that one is asking about; only the basic distinction between people and everything else is expressed. Here is the paradigm:

		masc.-fem.	neut.
sg.	nom.	hwā	hwæt
	acc.	hwone	hwæt
	gen.	h w æ s	
	dat.	hwǣm ~ hwām	
	inst.	h w ȳ	

I give the instrumental sg. form because it is the one such OE form that still survives in ModE (as the adverb *why*; development of fossilized caseforms into adverbs is a common type of change). Interrogatives other than this most basic pronoun were inflected like ordinary adjectives.

The inflection of 1st- and 2nd-person pronouns in IE languages is usually aberrant, retaining a number of extreme archaisms; for a discussion of the whole family Katz 1998 is the classic reference. Within the Germanic subfamily the earliest-attested languages preserved the PGmc. system more or less intact, and OE is no exception. Here are the paradigms:

		1st-person	*2nd-person*
sg.	*nom.*	iċ	þū
	acc.	mec (*Angl.*) / mē	þec (*Angl.*) / þē
	dat.	mē	þē
pl.	*nom.*	wē	ġē
	acc.	ūsic (*Angl.*) / ūs	ēowic (*Angl.*) / ēow
	dat.	ūs	ēow
du.	*nom.*	wit	ġit
	acc.	uncet (*Angl.*) / unc	incit (*Angl.*) / inc
	dat.	unc	inc

In the accusative of all numbers there was a systematic dialect difference: the Anglian dialects had forms ending in -*c* or -*t* (the latter by dissimilation from **-c*, see Stiles 1996) while the southern dialects had forms identical with the respective datives. The prehistory of these forms was not the same, however. In the singular, Anglian *mec* and *þec* were the inherited forms, and the southern dialects had syncretized accusative and dative under the form of the latter; such a syncretism would be odd for nouns and adjectives but is actually typical of non-neuter personal pronouns, in which the dative is very salient in daily use. In the nonsingular, the syncretism was inherited, and the longer Anglian forms are innovations on the model of the singular accusatives. This is an interesting example of a desyncretism—an uncommon type of change, though not as rare as is sometimes supposed.

I have given no genitive forms for a specific reason: the uninflected forms of the possessive adjectives were used as the genitives of the corresponding pronouns. The adjectives in question were 1sg. *mīn*, 2sg. *þīn*, 1pl. *ūser ~ ūre*, 2pl. *ēower*, 1du. *uncer*, 2du. *incer*. Since possession by a 1st- or 2nd-person referent was normally expressed by these adjectives, fully inflected, the genitives of the pronouns occurred only rarely, when governed lexically by a verb or a preposition; a typical example is early OE *help mīn* 'Help me!'

As in other conservative IE languages, the numerals had inflectional peculiarities of their own; interested students should consult the standard grammars.

Exercises

1. Compare the paradigms of the personal and interrogative pronouns given in the last section with the ModE ones you produced for exercise (1) in Chapter 1. Describe the changes that have occurred between OE and ModE.

2. OE is so different from ModE that it has to be learned as a foreign language, yet the similarities between the two are obvious (and helpful, naturally). Those similarities make close comparison of parallel texts illuminating. Here is a short passage (edited) from the WS translation of the *Gospel of John*, with a word-for-word gloss and an idiomatic ModE translation. Examine them closely and answer the questions that follow. One idiosyncrasy of the OE translation should be noted in advance: the translators regularly render the name 'Jesus' as *sē Hǣlend* 'the Savior', which leads to discourse infelicities of various kinds.

Đā sē Hǣlend fōr, þā ġeseah hē ānne man þe wæs blind ġeboren,
when the Savior travelled, then saw he one man that was blind born,

and his leorningcnihtas hine āxodon and cwǣdon, Lārēow, hwæt syngode
þēs
and his disciples him asked and said, Teacher, what sinned this

oððe his māgas þæt hē wǣre blind ġeboren? Sē Hǣlend answarode and
cwæð,
or his kinsmen that he be blind born? The Savior answered and said,

Ne syngode hē ne his māgas, ac þæt Godes weorc wǣre ġeswutelod on
him.
Not sinned he nor his kinsmen, but that God's work be manifested in
him.

Þā spǣtte hē on þā eorþan and worhte fenn of his spātle and smyrede mid
þām fenne
Then spat he on the earth and worked mud from his spittle and smeared
with the mud

ofer his ēagan and cwæð tō him, Gā and þweah þē on Syloes mere.
over his eyes and said to him, Go and wash you in Siloam's pool.

Hē fōr and þwōh hine and cōm ġesēonde. Witodliċe his nēahġebūras
cwǣdon,
He went and washed him and came seeing. Certainly his neigbors said,

Hū nis þis sē þe sæt and wǣdlode? Sume cwǣdon, Hē hit is; sume
cwǣdon,
How not is this that that sat and begged? Some said, He it is; some said,

Nese, ac is him ġelīċ. Hē cwæþ sōðliċe, Iċ hit eom.
No, but is him similar. He said truly, I it am.

As Jesus was walking he caught sight of a man that had been born blind, and his disciples questioned him, saying, "Teacher, what sin did this guy or his family commit for him to be born blind?" Jesus answered, saying, "Neither he nor his family sinned; rather (it is) so that God's work could be made evident in his case." Then he spat on the ground and made mud with his spittle and smeared the mud on his eyes and said to him, "Go and wash yourself in the pool of Siloam." He went and washed himself and returned able to see. Of course his neighbors said, "Hey, isn't this the guy that used to sit and beg?" Some said, "It's him;" others said, "No, he just looks like him." But he said, "It's me."

Some of the differences between the OE and ModE texts are syntactic; for instance, *þā ġeseah hē* shows inversion of the subject and verb, and at the end of the story the formerly blind man says literally 'I'm it' in OE, but *it's me* in ModE. We need to take those differences for granted in discussing the differences in inflectional morphology.

a. As you can see, both the accusative *hine* and the dative *him* occur in this passage. How are they distributed in syntactic terms? How does this distribution compare with that of the noun forms *fenn* and *fenne*?

b. In the sentence in which Jesus makes mud and smears the blind man's eyes, there is a potential ambiguity in the use of *his* in ModE (though in context there is no confusion: it is clear enough that Jesus is not putting the mud on his own eyes). But in OE there is an ambiguity in the use of *hine* (and *him*) that is resolved in ModE. What is it?

c. Consider the past tense verb forms 3sg. *fōr, ġeseah, syngode, andswarode, cwæð, spætte, worhte, smyrede, þwōh, cōm, sæt, wædlode,* and pl. *āxodon, cwædon.* Can you classify them into strong, class I weak, and class II weak verbs on the basis of the information in this chapter? If you were pressed to guess what the plural form of *sæt* is, what would you suggest, judging from forms of other verbs cited in the first two sections of this chapter?

d. Much of the inflectional machinery of OE has been lost in ModE; for instance, the past pl. ending -*on* has vanished without a trace, and the past subjunctive descended from *wære* has a very restricted distribution even in dialects in which it still occurs (namely, counterfactual: *If I were you, . . .*). But ModE has also acquired a range of innovative phrasal verb forms. Compare the OE verb forms in this passage with their ModE translations, paying particular attention to instances in which ModE conveys a more precisely defined meaning than OE.

3. Read a standard discussion of the OE subjunctive, e.g. Fulk 2014: 27–9. The subjunctive has almost disappeared in ModE, but we still need to say all the things that it expressed in OE. Discuss briefly the ModE constructions that fulfill the same functions as an OE subjunctive. If you have a solid knowledge of German, Latin, or any Romance language, you can substitute it for OE in this exercise.

4 Inflectional change in late Old English

The sketch of OE inflectional morphology given in Chapter 3 describes the system found in most OE documents written before about 1100, more than a generation after the Norman Conquest; at that date significant changes begin to appear. However, some of those changes are already apparent in glosses written in the Northumbrian dialect between about 950 and 1000 (Brunner 1965: 7–8, Hogg 2011: 5). Since those are the only substantial northern texts that survive from between the eighth century and c. 1300 (!; Fernández Cuesta and Rodríguez Ledesma 2007: 117–18), we have no way of knowing exactly when these "late" OE changes began in the north. In fact, the problem is broader and more serious than that: nearly all the surviving OE documents from between about 950 and 1100 are written in a semistandardized literary dialect called Late West Saxon (LWS), based on the southwestern OE dialect (see, e.g., Smith 1992: 582–3 with references); and though forms of other dialects and innovative forms occasionally appear in them, it seems clear that by 1000 or so LWS had become an artificially conservative literary standard, in which the development of spoken OE, even in the southwest, was no longer accurately reflected (Liuzza 2000: 144 with extensive references). For the last century or more of the OE period, then, we can identify linguistic innovations only from isolated failures to write the standard dialect.[1]

Nor does the problem disappear in the twelfth century, because OE documents continued to be copied and used through that century and into the thirteenth (see especially the papers in Swan and Treharne 2000). It is true that some of the scribes modernized their exemplars—the discussion of the Tremulous Hand in Collier 2000 is especially fascinating and instructive—but such modernizations are not reliable evidence for

---

1. Kitson has argued persuasively that late OE charters preserve lexical items peculiar to various dialects (Kitson 1995), but little information about inflection can be gleaned from them; the only results involving inflectional morphology that he has published so far involve the paradigms of individual nouns (ibid. pp. 51–5).

twelfth- and thirteenth-century English inflectional morphology, if only because they are at least one more step removed from actual contemporary speech. We must concentrate on documents which were composed, or are likely to have been composed, in the years after 1100.

This chapter will discuss the most important inflectional innovations which can be detected in later OE and twelfth-century documents. The most important was the collapse of the OE system of concord classes, or genders; the rise of a new subclass of weak verbs was also significant (though exceptionally hard to trace and analyze), there was a morphologically conditioned sound change that had an impact on English inflection, and a new pronoun, *she*, made its first appearance. The case system began to erode during this period too, but the survival of gen. sg. *-es* and its eventual transformation into a phrasal clitic, as well as the persistence of casemarking on pronouns, makes it convenient to postpone discussion of casemarking until the following chapter.

4.1 Loss of the gender system

4.1.1 Gender in Old English

It is reasonable to ask whether any of the three genders to which OE nouns were assigned was the default gender. The only possible evidence is the assignment of loanwords to gender classes. Since nearly all loanwords in OE were borrowed from Latin, which had a superficially identical gender system, the evidence largely amounts to shifts in gender, i.e. the assignment of a Latin noun to a concord class different from its Latin class. Early Latin loanwords—e.g. those that occur in *Beowulf*—are too few to reveal any clear pattern. However, the comprehensive count attempted in Wełna 1980 yielded the following numbers for OE as a whole:

masc. → fem. 8	masc. → neut. 5
fem. → masc. 61	fem. → neut. 10
neut. → masc. 43	neut. → fem. 33

Though the data are messy, suggesting that multiple factors conditioned these shifts (as argued at length, with varying plausibility, by Wełna), it is clear that there were almost twice as many shifts into the masculine class as into the others combined (104 vs. 56) and more than ten times as many shifts out of the other classes as out of the masculine (147 vs. 13).[2] Though certainty is unattainable, it is reasonable to suggest that by

---

2. This is not simply a matter of shifting nouns into the default masculine lexical class; as Wełna notes, various feminines and neuters became OE masc. weak nouns with nom. sg. in *-a*.

the eleventh century the masculine gender was the default gender for OE nouns. We might therefore expect that loss of gender as a morphological category would be accomplished by the shift of all nouns into the masculine class. As we will see, that is not exactly what happened; what did happen was more complex, and to understand it fully we need to look at OE gender in more detail.

As is usual in IE languages, the fit between the concord classes and natural gender was not perfect—most notably, the common words for 'child', *ċild* and *bearn*, were both neuter, as was the commonest word for 'woman', *wīf* (the less common compound *wīfmann* was masculine, while the still rarer *cwene* was feminine); in addition, diminutives like *mæġden* 'girl' were neuter (much like modern German *Mädchen*). When these words are the antecedents of 3rd-person pronouns, we might expect those pronouns to agree with them in concord class, and sometimes they do. However, there are also examples of masculine *hē* referring back to neuter *ċild* or *bearn*, and of feminine *hēo* referring back to neuter *wīf* or *mæġden* or to masculine *wīfmann* (Mitchell 1985: I.24, 35–7). From Ælfric's homilies can be cited, for example,

> *Đā ðā him ċild cōm, þā cōm hit mid Godes foresċēawunge and bletsunge . . .*
> 'When a child arrived for him,[3] it arrived with God's providence and blessing
> . . .'

but also

> *Þæt ċild is tuwa ācenned: hē is ācenned of þām Fæder on heofonum . . .*
> 'That child is twice begotten: he is begotten of the Father in heaven . . .'

In fact, it seems to be normal for *wīf* or *wīfmann* to be referred back to by a feminine pronoun, e.g. from Ælfric's homilies:

> *Gyf þonne hwylċ wīf tō ðām unspēdiġ wǣre þæt hēo þās ðing begytan ne myhte,*
> . . .
> 'If therefore any woman were so poor that she could not acquire these items,
> . . .'

Examples of neuter *hit* referring back to *wīf* 'woman' are rare, though at least one can be cited:

> *Sē ðonne hæfð wīf swelċe hē nān næbbe, sē ðe hit hæfð for līcumlicre frōfre . . .*
> 'He therefore has a wife as if he had none, who has her for bodily consolation
> . . .'
> (*Cura Pastoralis* 395.15–16)

---

3. The patriarch Abraham, aged and childless.

Examples of neuter pronouns referring back to unambiguously masculine or feminine nouns which denote inanimate objects are very rare (Mitchell 1985: I.24, 35–7). It seems fair to say that the OE concord system had begun to yield to natural gender insofar as persons are concerned, but not otherwise.

However, there is a further complication. As in other IE languages, a neuter pronoun can refer back to a preceding statement or real-world situation—and in OE that applies even to statements or situations which amount to the description, appearance, or identification of a person. A familiar early example occurs in line 11 of *Beowulf*, in which the poet, having given a brief description of the reign of the mythical Scyld, concludes:

> *Þæt wæs gōd cyning!*
> 'That was a good king!'

In principle, the neuter *þæt* could be said to refer to the poet's account, or to the activities of Scyld as an example of a good king but, in practice, it might as well refer to Scyld himself. A familiar later example occurs twelve times in the WS translation of the gospels, namely:

> *Iċ hit eom.*
> 'It is I.' / 'It's me.'

That is what Jesus says to the apostles when they think they are seeing a ghost, to the men who have come to arrest him, to the Samaritan woman who expresses belief in a messiah, etc. The literal translation is 'I am it', with the same use of the neuter pronoun as in the idiomatic ModE translation 'It's me', though the order of the equation has been reversed. These usages amount to a gender mismatch in the other direction, with neuter pronouns and demonstratives effectively used to refer to persons. In addition, the neuter is used to introduce explanations of the sort introduced in ModE by 'that is' (or, in writing, 'i.e.'). Mitchell 1985: I.130–1 gives a range of examples, including:

> *Wihtsǣtan, þæt is sēo ðēod þe Wiht þæt ēalond oneardað*
> 'Wihtsætan, that is the people that inhabits the island of Wight'

in which the antecedent is plural;

> *hē is heora bēgra gāst, þæt is heora bēgra lufu*
> 'he is the spirit of them both, that is to say the love of them both'[4]

in which the antecedent (*gāst*) is masculine singular, etc. Moreover, when there is no antecedent and a demonstrative is the subject of the copula,

---

4. I.e. the Holy Spirit is the spirit/love of God the Father and God the Son.

the neuter singular is used, irrespective of the gender and number of the complement (Mitchell 1985: I.136–7), e.g. in the gospels:

> *þis is mīn līchama*
> 'this [neut.] is my body [masc.]'

or in charters:

> *Ðis sint þā landgemǣru . . .*
> 'These are the boundaries . . .'

—literally 'this are', because the verb agrees with the complement rather than the subject if the latter is a non-agreeing neuter singular.

In sum, the concord system of OE included a number of systematic exceptions to the most generally statable rule. On the one hand, natural gender tended to override the strict class concord of nouns referring to human beings, inconsistently but nevertheless very often; on the other hand, the neuter singular had a much wider range of use than might be expected—though not in a way that had anything to do with natural gender. Whether these complications made learning of the system error-prone is difficult to say, but it is obvious that such a hypothesis is plausible enough to be entertained.

4.1.2 Gender in the Lindisfarne Gospel glosses[5]

In one group of pre-Conquest documents the OE concord system has broken down. In the Northumbrian glosses to the *Lindisfarne Gospels* and the *Durham Ritual*, written between about 950 and 1000,[6] masculine and feminine nouns referring to inanimate objects are frequently, though not consistently, accompanied or referred to by neuter determiners and pronouns (Brunner 1965: 194–5 with references, Millar 2016b). The data are not always easy to interpret. For one thing, it is not absolutely certain that the abbreviation *þ̄* always stands for neuter nom.-acc. sg. *þæt*; it is conceivable that its convenience and conciseness led the glossator to use it also for other forms of the default determiner, with or without any

---

5. A great deal of information about the use of different forms of the default determiner and its descendants in the documents discussed in this chapter (and several other documents as well) can be found in Millar 2000. Other useful collections of data are mostly much older; they will be cited as appropriate below.

6. For the most part not, however, in the Northumbrian parts of the glosses to the *Rushworth Gospels*, written around the same time in a more southerly subdialect (Lindelöf 1901: 98). Since the situation in the *Ritual* glosses is essentially the same as in the *Lindisfarne* glosses, examples will be drawn only from the latter.

conscious decision to treat *þæt* as the default form.[7] In addition, some uses of *þæt* not obviously within a noun phrase might have resulted from a modest expansion of those outlined above. But such a collocation as accusative singular *ðæt stān* at Mark 15: 46 (Lea 1894: 173) necessarily demonstrates a collapse of the concord class system, because (1) the noun is masculine, (2) the neuter determiner is spelled out unambiguously, and (3) in the Latin vulgate the noun *lapidem* is not accompanied by any deictic in this passage. Yet the "correct" *ðone stān* occurs twice a few verses later (Lea, op. cit.). Nor are these isolated facts; apparently random variation between the inherited concord system and a natural gender system is widespread in these glosses (see Carpenter 1910: 66–8 with references). What are we to make of this situation in our text?

The most basic conclusion forced by the Uniformitarian Principle is that acc. sg. *ðæt stān* and *ðone stān*, for instance, cannot be part of the same stable inflectional system, because systems of inflectional morphology are categorical and do not normally allow for widespread alternatives. It follows that we are in the presence either of a system in rapid change or of diglossia—the stable coexistence of two grammatical systems distributed according to some principle well understood by native speakers.[8] Jones 1988 sees the problem clearly, but the explanation that he offers is not convincing. He suggests that *þæt* (and its abbreviation) is used to indicate coreference with a noun already introduced into the discourse (pp. 45–8), to mark nouns representative of their class, or which have unique reference characteristics (pp. 49–59), etc. But those are all core functions of the default determiner; to say that *þæt* is used in such functions is no different from saying that the neuter form of the determiner is being generalized (so Ross 1936: 326–7).

In that case, how are we to explain the continued, but inconsistent, use of masculine and feminine forms of the determiner? The crucial fact is that they too are not always used correctly according to the "classical" OE system outlined above (Ross 1936: 323, Millar 2016b). Jones attempts to explain their misuse by complex functional hypotheses (pp. 70–81), but a much simpler hypothesis accounts more convincingly for the data: the glossator had a native command of the innovative colloquial register in which gender distinctions had collapsed, but not of the formal register in which they were still preserved; to the extent that he tried to reproduce

---

7. If such a decision was made, the glossator could have glossed forms of Latin deictics without regard to their inflection or context with a default *þæt* or *þ* (cf. Lea 1894: 175 with references).

8. The distinction between these two alternatives is, of course, not absolute; a system in change often passes through a diglossic stage.

the formal register, he made errors simply because it was not native to him. The way the glossator used feminine forms is especially revealing. In at least one passage, Matthew 9: 22, the glossator writes *of ðæm ł ðær tīð*, giving both the nonfem. and the fem. form of the dat. sg. of the determiner; as Millar asks rhetorically, "Does this distribution mean that Aldred had two competing systems in his head?" (Millar 2016b: 156). In fact, feminine forms are used (inconsistently) not only with nouns denoting females and with etymologically feminine nouns, but with OE masc. and neut. nouns *which translate Latin feminine nouns* (Ross 1936: 323); in other words, the glossator was apparently using the gender of Latin feminines, which is often well marked, to guess at the form appropriate for an OE gloss. He certainly would not have done that if the "classical" OE feminine gender were still a part of his native-speaker grammar.

It would be natural to suppose that the formal register which the glossator often tried to reproduce was the LWS literary dialect, but that is not obviously the case. In particular, nom. sg. fem. *ðīo ~ ðȳ* 'the, that' and inst. sg. masc. *ðīo* (Ross 1937: 115–17) seem to reflect not only native Northumbrian *īo* in place of WS *ēo*, but even a monophthongization of *īo* to *ȳ* in the local subdialect, probably under weak stress, leading to a phonological merger and reverse spellings; the corresponding forms of 'this' (ibid. pp. 117–18) point in the same direction. Apparently, we must entertain the possibility that the glossator might not have acquired native competence in the formal register of his own dialect. That is not necessarily surprising; a precisely similar situation is reported for Fox, an Algonkian language, in the twentieth century (Goddard 1988).

If the neuter of the default determiner was being used to refer to inanimates in the innovative colloquial register of the glossator's dialect, what was happening to the inflection of nouns, which in "classical" OE was differentiated by gender? In assessing the evidence it is important to realize that the glossator's unstressed vowels had undergone extensive mergers. Probably he had only a single unstressed vowel, phonemically /ə/; conceivably he still distinguished a front from a back unstressed vowel, in effect a front schwa and a back schwa[9] (Ross 1937: 53, summarizing an extensive analysis). Bearing that in mind, it is clear that the only gender-distinguishing endings in the default noun paradigms adduced in 3.2 above were the genitive singular and the nominative-accusative plural. Gen. sg. /-əs/, originally proper to default masculine and neuter nouns, has spread to most other nouns, though the older endings are

---

9. Such a system of unstressed vowels is well attested in Chuvash and in some dialects of Mari; the Old Church Slavonic vowels transliterated *ĭ* and *ŭ* were almost certainly similar.

also sometimes written (Ross 1937: 99). Nom.-acc. pl. /-əs/, originally proper only to default masculines, has also spread widely (ibid. p. 100). These changes could be another indication that the masculine gender was the default in at least late OE (see above). Though neuter concord forms had been generalized for inanimate nouns, masculine forms were being generalized in noun inflection.

However, a nom.-acc. pl. ending written *-a ~ -o* has also spread to some extent (Ross 1937: 101), and it is etymologically ambiguous (as Ross duly notes): since final *-n* in unstressed syllables had been lost in Northumbrian, it can reflect the n-stem ending *-an*, which was gender-neutral; on the other hand, it can also reflect *-u*, which, though originally proper only to some subclasses of default neuters (see 3.2), had spread variably to all of them (Ross 1937: 55–6). More than that cannot be said with confidence.

The glosses also exhibit levelling in the inflection of adjectives, including levelling of masculine/neuter forms into the feminine paradigm; the details are summarized in Ross 1937: 104–8.

4.1.3 Gender in the Peterborough Chronicle

In 1116 a fire destroyed most of the monastery of Peterborough, including the library. The monks borrowed at least one copy of the *Anglo-Saxon Chronicle* from another center and made a new copy in 1121, using other sources as well (see Irvine 2004: xxxii–ci for extensive discussion). For the most part, the copyist reproduced the LWS forms which he saw in front of him. However, he also inserted interpolations relating events of local interest, and the entries from 1122 through 1154 (when the *Peterborough Chronicle* ends) reflect local continuations of the chronicle, at least for the most part. It is clear that all the additions through 1131 are the work of the scribe who copied the older parts and made the interpolations; I will refer to those additions as *Peterborough1*. The remaining annals, called the "Second Continuation" (*Peterborough2*), were added by a different scribe in 1154 or shortly thereafter.[10] In all these additions we find evidence of a collapse of the OE gender system, but the details are rather different from what we see in *Lindisfarne*.

Like late tenth-century Northumbrian, the twelfth-century dialect of Peterborough had merged all unstressed vowels in /ə/, variously spelled (Irvine 2004: cxxvi, cxxxvi–ii). However, it had also merged the *eo*-diphthongs with the *e*-vowels (ibid. pp. cxvi, cxxiii, cxxxiii, cxxxvi), and that is important for our assessment of one piece of evidence: the use

10. See the discussion of Clark 1970 and Irvine 2004.

of nom. sg. *sēo* with masculine nouns and *sē* with feminines can simply reflect phonological merger; it is not necessarily evidence for the collapse of gender. Most importantly, there is no evidence for a local formal register; the "classical" OE system of gender marking in use is indistinguishable from that of the LWS literary language, and the scribes' imperfect command of it can simply be a defect of their education, as I will argue below.

In *Peterborough1* the neuter default determiner *þet ~ ðet* (as it is usually spelled in this document) is rarely used with masculine and feminine nouns, though there are a few examples; for instance, we find *ðet stede* 'the place (masc.)' (interpolation in the annal for 656), *þet dugeð* 'the vassals, the following (fem.)' (1114), and *eall þet lententīd* 'the whole of Lent (fem.)' (1127).[11] More often, we find masculine and feminine forms used incorrectly, e.g. *þet sēo mynstre bēo frēo* 'that the monastery (neut.) should be free' (interpolation 675), *of þēre minstre* '(the monks) of the monastery' (interpolation 777), *þone mynstre* 'the monastery' (interpolation 1070), *in þone cyrce* 'into the church (fem.)' (ibid., beside correct *in þǣre cyrce* 'in the church'), *on þone lententȳde* 'in Lent (fem.)' (1122), *þone godspell* 'the gospel (neut.)' (ibid.), *sē fīr* 'the fire (neut.)' (ibid. 2x), *wið þone eorðe* 'along the earth (fem.)' (ibid.), etc. A large majority of the incorrect forms are masculine. It is clear that the scribe had an imperfect command of the gender system of LWS, and that for him, at least, the masculine forms were the most salient set, perhaps the default (Clark 1957: 112–13, 115). We also find plurals in /-əs/ to (formerly) feminine and neuter nouns, e.g. *þās landes and þās wateres* 'these lands and these waters (both neut.)' (interpolation 656), *ealle þā munece hūses* 'all the monks' houses (neut.)' (interpolation 1070), *bōkes* 'books (fem.)', etc. Finally, there are a few gen. sg. forms in /-əs/ to (formerly) feminine nouns, e.g. *be his swustre rēd Kyneburges and Kyneswiðes* 'on the advice of his sisters Cyneburg and Cyneswith' (interpolation 656) and *ðurh his dohtres rēd* 'by his daughter's advice' (1126). In the dialect that the scribe actually spoke, the OE system of gender must no longer have been present; otherwise he would not have made so many and such diverse mistakes in attempting to write LWS (Clark 1957: 110).

In *Peterborough2* the situation is much simpler. The determiners are usually uninflected *þe* 'the' and *þis* 'this'; we also find *þat* with nouns of

---

11. Some care is needed in assessing apparent examples because in this document *þet* has also largely replaced the relative particle *þe*, which had never marked gender; for instance, the first example cited continues *ðet stede þet man cleopeð Folies* 'the place which one calls F.', and we also find *ðā hwīle þet* 'for as long as' (1123), *his dohter þet hē ǣror hafde given* 'his daughter, whom he has previously given' (1126), and *for þī þet* 'for þȳ þe, because' (1127).

all genders (*ðat mynstre, ðat abbotrīċe* (neut.), 1132; *ðat ōþer dæi* 'on the second day (masc.), 1135; *al þat īren* 'all that iron (neut.)', 1137; *tō ðat forewarde ðat* 'on condition (fem.) that'[12]). Since *þat* is also the conjunction and the inanimate singular relative pronoun (Dekeyser 1987: 99), it might have been the stressed form corresponding to *þe*, though it is not clear whether a categorical distinction between article and demonstrative already existed (as explored in detail in Millar 2000). The noun phrase *þe sunne* 'the sun', formerly feminine, is apparently coreferent with *him* in a following prepositional phrase, as though it were a masculine or neuter noun, in the entry for 1135. Nearly all nouns have plurals in /-əs/ (masc. n-stems *sterres* 'stars', *neves* 'nephews', 1135; neut. *landes*, 1135, *weorkes* 'works', *limes* 'limbs', 1137; fem. *trēothes* 'agreements', *sinnes* 'sins', 1137, etc.); the few exceptions are endingless forms inherited from OE (fem. *niht*, 1135; neut. *dǣr* 'animals', *wunder* 'outrages', 1137), one with i-umlaut (*men*, 1135). There happen to be no feminine nouns in the genitive in this short passage (six printed pages). This is the earliest ME text that closely resembles ModE in its complete absence of grammatical gender.

How is it possible for two scribes from the same community writing only thirty years apart to produce such different-looking systems of grammar? One might have been a generation older than the other (Millar 2012: 115–18, 2016a: 124–5), and the date of the Norman Conquest suggests how the consequences might have played out. From the fact that the sons of Edgar the Peaceful each declared his majority at the age of sixteen, it is reasonable to infer that that was the age of full manhood in late Anglo-Saxon England. We might further infer that a scribe being trained to write LWS should have completed his training at about that age. However, after 1066 there was no further reason to train monks to write LWS; thus the youngest scribes who had completed their training were probably born in the early 1050s, and nearly all will have died by the 1120s at the latest (cf. Millar 2016a: 124). That explains why a monk writing in and after 1121 might not have had a good command of the old written standard, and why a monk writing in 1154 should have been unable to write it at all, being constrained instead to write as he spoke. I suggest that that is what we see in the additions to the *Peterborough Chronicle*. Probably the dialect of *Peterborough2* was also what the earlier scribe spoke (more or less), though he had just enough education to make a fair attempt to write the obsolete literary language (so Clark 1970: lix–lxi, Allen 2008: 128–30).

---

12. Cf. *be þisre sylfan forewarde* 1091, *sēo forewarde* 1094.

4.1.4 Dialect differences in the loss of gender

The loss of gender that we see in the late additions to the *Peterborough Chronicle* did not affect all dialects of English at the same time. A few other short documents contemporary with the earlier additions survive; perhaps the best known is a homily entitled "Sermo in festis S. Marie virginis" in manuscript Vespasian D.XIV (R. Warner 1917: 134–9; cf. Laing 1993: 83). Unlike most of the homilies in that collection, this one was not updated from OE; it was translated from a known Latin homily, almost certainly in the first quarter of the twelfth century (Förster 1920: 58, Irvine 2000: 50).[13] In this homily, written in a southern dialect, the OE gender system is intact (Glahn 1918: 38–40). For instance, *cæstel* 'castle' and *mægeðhād* 'virginity' are consistently masculine (sg. nom. *ðēs cæstel, sē ilca cæstel*; acc. *pone cæstel*; gen. *þæs mægeðhādes*; dat. *ðyssen cæstele, intō sumen castele, fram þān mægeðhāde*), while abstract nouns made with the suffix *-nysse* are consistently feminine (acc. *ealle mōdiġnysse*; gen. *ēadmōdnysse* and *ēadmōdnyssen*, dat. *þære gālnysse, tō mīnre ēadmōdnysse*), and *godspell* 'gospel' is neuter (nom.-acc. *þiss godspell*, referred to as *hit*; dat. *on þyssen godspelle*). Rare departures from the LWS norm, such as neut. *þ betste dǣl* 'the best part' (p. 134, l. 15; LWS masc. *þone betstan dǣl*) probably reflect shifts in the gender of individual nouns, not erosion of the system as a whole.

Evidently, there was an isogloss in the southern Midlands, on one side of which the OE gender system had collapsed, while on the other it persisted more or less unchanged. Other twelfth-century documents can be located relative to that isogloss. For instance, the *Lambeth Homilies* belong to the more conservative area (cf. Morris 1868: xxxvi–xli, Allen 2008: 126),[14] while the *Trinity Homilies* clearly fall on the less conservative side of the boundary (cf. Morris 1873: xiii).

Extensive securely localizable documents from toward the end of the twelfth century help to fill out this picture. The *Orrmulum* was written at Bourne, about 25 km (16 miles) north of Peterborough, in the last decades before 1200 (Laing 1993: 135–6). It exhibits a complete absence of gender marking. The article is indeclinable *þe*, the old masc. and fem. nom. sg. form with *þ-* levelled in from the oblique forms; the singulars of the demonstratives are indeclinable *þatt* and *þiss*, the old neut. nom.-acc. sg. forms. In the singular the strong adjective ends in zero alternating

---

13. This is item 44 in the collection; items 48 and 49, extracts from the *Elucidarius* of Honorius of Autun, are of about the same date (Irvine 2000: 50 with references).
14. It seems increasingly clear that the *Lambeth Homilies* are localizable in the west Midlands; see, e.g., Laing 1992: 571 and passim, 1993: 111, Smith 2000: 132–3.

with -e according to phrasal rhythm, not grammatical function (Lehnert 1953: 31–9); i.e. the strong inflection has been abandoned. The only clear exceptions are a few examples of acc. sg. masc. *ænne* 'one', *nænne* 'no, none' (Lehnert 1953: 50, 51) and gen. sg. *āness* 'of one, of a'. The plurals of nouns are normally in -*ess*, the old default masc. nom.-acc. ending, though a handful of nouns have other endings; there is no correlation with original gender (ibid. pp. 56–8). The gen. sg. of nouns usually ends in -*ess*, the old default masc. and neut. ending (ibid. pp. 75–84).[15] These are virtually the only contexts in which an English dialect of that period *could* mark gender on a full noun phrase (Philippsen 1911: 73–4); thus a native learner of Orrm's dialect would have found it impossible to infer gender classes of nouns. (On a possible causal relationship between the simplification of inflection and the loss of gender see the following chapter.)

Vices and Virtues, which may be somewhat older than the *Orrmulum*, is clearly a text from Essex, since OE *y* is consistently reflected as *e* (e.g. in *senne* 'sin') and OE *ǣ* is often reflected as *ā* (e.g. *forlāten* 'renounced' (ptc.), *lāten* 'to leave alone', *lādde* '(that he) should lead', *dāle* 'part' on the first two pages of Holthausen's edition; cf. Laing 1993: 106). The OE inflections of the default determiner are fairly well preserved in this document, and so is the OE gender system (Philippsen 1911: 73–6). However, three innovations have occurred. *Đat* is used as a demonstrative with masc. and fem. nouns (ibid. pp. 73–4), as in the *Orrmulum* and in ModE. Many nouns have been shifted from one gender class into another (ibid. pp. 76–7); the pattern is complex and messy, though it seems clear that nouns in -*e* and abstract nouns tended to become feminine (ibid. pp. 77–83). Finally, uninflected *ðe* has begun to spread to all functions, though it is still in competition with inflected forms (ibid. pp. 104–6). The noun plural markers -*es* and -*en* have spread widely, but gen. sg. -*es* has not spread to feminines (ibid. p. 45).

The situation in western England is less clear. In the "AB language" of the *Ancrene Wisse* and the Katherine group of texts, adjectives do not retain the strong endings (d'Ardenne 1961: 217–18), while the default determiner has almost completely lost its feminine forms (ibid. p. 225) and has generalized *þet* as the stressed form for the direct cases (ibid. p. 224). Thus the only relics of gender marking are the use of unstressed *þet* with neuter nouns and the occasional use of masc. or fem. 3rd-person

---

15. The kinship terms in -*r* have endingless gen. sgs. regardless of gender (Lehnert 1953: 84). Phrases like *helle pīne* 'the torment of hell' might be interpreted as compounds (so ibid. p. 85); in any case, they are fixed collocations, and the productive gen. sg. of formerly feminine *helle* is *helles* (ibid. p. 86).

pronouns to refer to inanimate nouns (ibid. pp. 228–30). The noun plural markers -*es* and -*en* have spread widely, with no clear gender correlation, and gen. sg. -*es* has spread to feminine nouns, though it is not yet universal (ibid. pp. 204–10). It appears that the OE gender system has largely been lost in this dialect, which probably reflects the speech of northern Herefordshire or southern Shropshire (cf. Bennett and Smithers 1968: 402–3, Millett 1982: xvii–xviii, 2005: xi with references, Laing 1993: 24). But in the more conservative copy of Laȝamon's *Brut* (Cotton Caligula A ix, hereafter *Brut(C)*),[16] apparently composed at about the same latitude some 30 km (20 miles) to the east (Bennett and Smithers 1968: 145, Laing 1993: 70), the oblique sg. forms of the default determiner are still in regular use, as is strong dat. sg. fem. -*(e)re* and acc. sg. masc. -*ne*, mostly on quantifiers (e.g. *are* 'one (fem. dat.)', *ælcne* 'each (masc. acc.)', but occasionally on adjectives as well (Bennett and Smithers 1968: 343); a convenient collection of examples (made for syntactic purposes) can be found in Funke 1907, which contrasts Laȝamon's system with Orrm's. There are some examples of gender-marked forms that are etymologically incorrect (Jones 1988: 172–217, Shinkawa 2012), but the system as a whole is still in place[17]—and since the manuscript is clearly much later than the poem, the apparent errors need not reflect the poet's speech. Possibly, the isogloss noted above ran between the places where the "AB" authors and Laȝamon acquired their native dialects; conceivably, the *Brut* was composed in a more conservative register than the "AB" texts (as argued, e.g., in Stanley 1969). However, the likeliest reason is that the *Brut* was composed substantially earlier than the "AB" texts were. Some of the revisions in the *Ancrene Wisse* must postdate 1221 at the earliest (Millett 1992: 218–19, 2005: xl–xli); if they were made by the author (ibid. pp. xli–xlii), the original version need not be much older. The *Brut*, by contrast, could have been composed within, say, a couple decades of Wace's work, presented to Eleanor of Aquitaine in 1155—a

16. The two manuscripts of this work are different enough that they should not be analyzed together, as Jones 1988 does.

17. The discussion of Shinkawa 2012 is highly relevant and should be consulted *in toto* by interested students. He points out (pp. 18–19) that fluctuation in gender on the part of individual nouns in OE did not disrupt the system as a whole, and his interim summaries (pp. 69, 85, 97–8) make it clear that the same is still true of *Brut(C)* and even of *Brut(O)*. He concludes (p. 120) that a difference between formal and colloquial registers of the local dialect is unlikely to account for the variation in the text, and finally (pp. 118–19, 121) that unambiguous case-and-gender markers were not, in fact, being reanalyzed as pure case markers to any significant extent. In short, there is still a coherent system of genders in place in the *Brut*, and because that is true, deviations must be either lexically localized innovations or something outside the system.

hypothesis which has not received much attention, so far as I know, but perhaps should.[18]

By the end of the thirteenth century even southwestern texts, such as the *Legend of St. Kenelm* (Bennett and Smithers 1968: 96–107) have lost all trace of gender; only in the southeast did gender marking survive into the fourteenth century. In Kentish it is difficult to detect any erosion of the OE gender system. The *Ayenbite of Inwit*, written in Kentish and finished in 1340, is much like *Vices and Virtues*, except that unmarked *þe* is even more common; the marked forms of the definite article are in retreat, yet they are still used appropriately (see the extensive discussion of Glahn 1918: 62–90). This shows that the loss of gender in other dialects of English was by no means inevitable; it suggests, though it does not prove, that the loss might sometimes have occurred through dialect contact and spread roughly from northeast to southwest. That, in turn, suggests that contact with Norse might have had something to do with it, a hypothesis to which we shall have to return in Chapter 6.

4.2 The origin of the weak class I type *send, sent*

In a comprehensive and rigorous study Albert Marckwardt attempted to explain the spread of finite past *-te* and past participle *-t* to class I weak verbs whose stems ended in voiced sounds (Marckwardt 1935), e.g. *sente*, ptc. *sent* to OE *sendan* 'to send'. He refuted earlier hypotheses so thoroughly that only one is still worth discussing, and later hypotheses are few and unconvincing. It seems best to begin with a summary of the facts.[19]

The earliest example of such a form that Marckwardt was able to discover is *hē sænte* 'he sent' in an interpolation in the *Parker Chronicle* (in the entry for 959), which he dates tentatively to the last quarter of the eleventh century (Marckwardt 1935: 194; cf. Bately 1986: xxxix, 75). One other late OE example, *gebænte his boge* 'bent his bow', is cited by Wełna 2009: 24 from the *Life of St. Giles*. In *Peterborough1* Marckwardt

---

18. Madden's conclusion from Laȝamon's statement about Wace's book—*hē hā ȝef þare ædelen / Ælienor þe wes Henries quēne, þes hēȝes kinges*—namely, that Eleanor of Aquitaine must no longer have been Queen of England when Laȝamon wrote, reads too much into the passage, which merely says that Eleanor was Henry's queen at the time that Wace presented her with his book. I am grateful to Rolf Noyer for helpful discussion of this point.

19. Of the OE examples cited by Wełna 2009: 24 (at the top of the page), only *gebænte* is a past tense form; all the others are pres. indic. 3sg. Note that in the fourth example there is a clause boundary between *is* and *sent*; the latter is not a past ptc. So far as I can discover, recent research has not added substantially to the early examples found by Marckwardt.

notes ptc. *spilt* 'destroyed' (inf. *spildan*) in the entry for 1125; from other twelfth-century documents he quotes *ġewǽnte*, pl. *ġewǽnton* 'went' (inf. *wendan*), *ansente*, ptc. *ymbgert* 'girt about' (inf. *ymbgyrdan*), ptc. *onbylt* 'established' (inf. *onbyldan*), *aluste* (i.e. *alūste*) 'released' (inf. *ālīesan*), and a variety of examples in the Royal and Hatton manuscripts of the OE gospels (ibid. pp. 195–6). The table on the latter page shows that a large majority of the forms belong to *sendan* and *wendan*, and that all but one of the rest belong, or could belong, to class I weak verbs with roots ending in a sonorant plus -*d*- (ibid. p. 199). It seems clear that that was the original locus of the innovation, that it was firmly in place by 1200, and that the change began somewhere in the southeast or the southeast Midlands (ibid. pp. 197–8).

How the innovation occurred is a more difficult question. By a process of elimination Marckwardt establishes that it must have been an "analogical" (i.e., purely morphological) change. In fact, it had been suggested long before that the -*t*- of such class I weak pasts as *cēpte* 'kept' and *cyste* 'kissed' had been extended to *sente*, etc. as well. But such changes were then supposed to occur by "proportional analogy", and an analogical proportion such as *cēp…* : *cēpte* :: *send…* : X ("some form of *cēp*- is to *cēpte* as a parallel form of *send*- is to X"), yielding X = *sente*, cannot be constructed. Marckwardt therefore proposes an alternative. In the southern dialects, verbs such as *sendan*, *wendan*, *byldan*, etc. had pres. ind. 3sg. forms *sent* 'sends', *went* 'turns, goes', *bylt* 'settles, builds', etc.; verbs such as *myntan* 'to intend', *hentan* 'to seize', *gyltan* 'to be guilty', etc. had parallel forms *mynt*, *hent*, *gylt*, etc. Marckwardt's proportion is *mynt* 'intends' : *mynte* 'intended' :: *sent* 'sends' : X, yielding X = *sente* 'sent'. Luick 1914–40: 950 instead suggests that -*t*- first arose in the past participle by sporadic word-final devoicing and then spread to the finite past on the analogy of *cēpte*, etc.; but there was no categorical devoicing of word-final -*d*, and variable devoicing can hardly be the basis of a morphological innovation (see also the discussion of Marckwardt 1935: 205–16). Eliasson 1967: 211–12 points out that -*t*- appears only in past stems with short or shortened vowels (though not in all of those) and suggests a regular sound change: whereas OE *sendan* became *sēndan* in the tenth or eleventh century, its past *sendde* became *sente* (ibid. p. 215); but a sound change *dd* > *t* occurred in no other class of forms.

The relative merits of these scenarios cannot be discussed without considering whether proportional analogy is an adequate model of morphological change. On the one hand, it is true that native learners often appear to use proportional analogy to construct innovative forms; an obvious example is *beseeched* (replacing *besought*), which can be constructed by some such model as *preach* : *preached* :: *beseech* : X. On the other hand, any working historical linguist can produce a list of innovations that cannot have been created by proportional analogy; English examples include nonstandard *feets* and *drownded* and the increasingly acceptable *snuck*. We need to think in terms of rules instead of proportions, bearing in mind that rules will often give the same results as proportions, but not always.

It is hard to see how the rule that produced the *-t-* of *cēpte, cyste*, etc. could have been extended straightforwardly to produce *sente*, etc., for a simple reason. The suffix was underlyingly *-d-*, and it was devoiced to *-t-* in *cēpte, cyste*, etc. by the preceding voiceless consonant of *cēp-, cyss-*, etc.; but *send-, byld-*, etc. end in voiced consonants. On the other hand, it is just as hard to believe that the co-occurrence of *mynt* 'intends' and *mynte* 'intended' in the same paradigm could lead to past *sente* on the basis of *sent* 'sends', for an equally simple reason. The 3sg. present and past indicative and the past participle are normally the commonest forms of an OE verb, and *sendan* and *wendan*—the very common verbs in which the change almost certainly first occurred—together are many times as common in our texts as all the verbs in *-ntan* together; *sendan* alone is at least ten times as common as *myntan*, the commonest of the verbs in *-ntan*. Thus native learners should have been hearing pres. 3sg. *sent*, past 3sg. *sende*, and ptc. *send* many times as often as the corresponding forms *mynt, mynte, mynt*.

Before continuing this discussion we need to answer a question not usually addressed: was the past stem spelled *send-* pronounced differently from the present stem *send-* at the time when the change occurred? They are normally spelled identically; the *Dictionary of Old English Web Corpus* has one example of past *sendde*, but since there are more than a hundred examples of *-ndd-* like *blindde* 'blind', with no morpheme boundary between the *d*'s, we cannot infer that the past stem of these verbs exhibited a geminate stop in pronunciation. On the contrary: so far as we can tell, it was a standing rule of OE phonology that a geminate consonant could not occur next to another consonant. Such sequences must have arisen at the time of syncope (probably late in the 6th century), when *sændidæ* became *sænddæ*, *fyllidæ* became *fylldæ*, etc. (Ringe and Taylor 2014: 267–8), but apparently they were subsequently simplified. The question is, when? Strictly speaking we do not know, but the almost unanimous testimony of OE orthography suggests that it was long before the tenth century.

Yet the spellings of the *Orrmulum* show that, in Orrm's dialect in the late twelfth century, weak present stems in *-nd-* contained long vowels, while their finite pasts and past participles contained short vowels; for instance, we find infinitive *wendenn*, i.e. *wēnden* (Bennett and Smithers

1968: 175, l. 21) but past ptc. *sennd* (ibid. p. 177, l. 81). If both stems developed entirely by sound change, the lengthening of vowels before homorganic voiced sonorant-plus-obstruent clusters must have occurred before the simplification of geminates next to other consonants (as Eliasson seems to assume). But if that were true, we would expect to see spellings like *sendde* much more often in earlier OE documents. It is much more likely that the rule governing the vowel alternation of *fēdan* : *fedde*, *cēpan* : *cepte*, etc. was extended to verbs in -*nd*- and -*ld*-, yielding *sēndan* : *sende*, etc. It seems possible that the past tense suffix -*t*- was extended to these verbs at the same time as the vowel alternation, but since the vowel alternation also occurred in past stems such as *fedde*, with -*d*- rather than -*t*-, some other factor must also be operative.

Even a cursory inspection of the frequencies of verbs suggests what that other factor might be. Kodner 2020: 30–53 has shown that the frequencies of verbs in a language are so steeply uneven that the most common verbs in a corpus are likely to be common also in child-directed speech and therefore to be learned early (with occasional exceptions conditioned by the subject matter of the corpus). The other very common class I weak verbs of general meaning in our texts seem to be *hīeran*, *hīerde* 'hear', *fēran*, *fērde* 'go, travel', *wyrċan*, *worhte* 'work, make', *brīngan*, *brōhte* 'bring',[20] *þenċan*, *þōhte* 'think', and *settan*, *sette* 'set'.[21] Half these verbs are irregular, and in two-thirds the suffix is -*t*-; in *brōhte* it is underlyingly /-t-/. It seems possible that either the critical mass of verbs with -*t*- on the surface or the semantic parallel between *brīngan* and *sēndan* led native learners to remodel *sende* as *sente* by applying a rule that suffixed -*t*-. That could work only so long as the native learner's vocabulary was small; as it became large enough for the learner to work out the rules governing past tense formation and realize that many of these common verbs were irregular, the creation of *sente* would become less and less likely.[22] This possibility should be investigated rigorously in detail.

The spread of the new past formation in -*te* after 1200 has been out-

---

20. Strictly speaking, this verb has a strong present (without root-final palatalization) and a weak past, but that almost certainly would not have been obvious to a small child with a still limited vocabulary.

21. This estimate was arrived at by finding promising candidates in Jember and Kemmler 1981 and checking numbers of occurrences in the *Dictionary of Old English Corpus* online. The result is obviously a crude approximation of a careful statistical analysis, but for the formulation of an initial hypothesis it seems adequate. I exclude *cȳþan*, *cydde* 'make known, proclaim' because its meaning makes it an unlikely candidate for child-directed speech.

22. For an interesting discussion and exemplification of the consequences of increasing size of vocabulary in NLA see Kodner 2020: 128–48.

lined in great detail by Marckwardt; further information, supporting a spread of the formation from south to north, is furnished by Wełna 2009. Interested students should consult those papers.

4.3 The fate of late Old English -en

The OE inflectional endings -*en*, -*an*, -*on* all became /-ən/ when unstressed vowels merged as schwa; in addition, -*um* was usually replaced by /-ən/, though the survival of the adverbs *seldom* and (archaic) *whilom* shows that that was not simply the result of a sound change but reflects some other kind of acquisition error. However, though these -*en* (to use the ME spelling) were originally identical, they did not develop identically in the southern and Midlands dialects; final -*n* was lost, but not consistently, and the outcomes differed between one grammatical category and another.

Moore 1927 investigates the loss of -*n* in these endings statistically in great detail. His conclusions can be summarized as follows. He notes that -*n* was lost to some extent in all morphological categories, which shows that the loss began as a regular sound change. However, the loss must have been conditioned by what followed, since the result was, in every case, forms in -*n* competing with forms in which -*n* had been lost, and the distribution was altered differently in each category (and in each dialect) by subsequent "analogical" changes.

In the Neogrammarian paradigm of language change within which Moore worked, his hypothesis was the only one possible, and it could, in fact, be true. However, modern work in sociolinguistics suggests a plausible alternative. Even unconditioned sound changes are variable at first, the variation depending on register, rate of speech, and other nonstructural factors. Normally, the change goes to completion within a couple of generations. However, if variation persists, it seems possible that native learners could manipulate the variants, realigning the distribution of outcomes to conform to distinctions between morphological categories—and, in fact, -*n* survives better as a plural marker than as a case marker in all dialects (Kiparsky 1982: 91–3). It seems possible that we are witnessing such a process in the variable development of -*en* in late OE and early ME.

It seems likely that this nexus of changes was partly responsible for the loss of strong adjective inflection. Though masc. acc. sg. -*ne*, masc.-neut. gen. sg. -*es*, fem. gen.-dat. sg. -*re*, and gen. pl. -*re* were all distinctive, all the other strong endings had become -*e* or -*e(n)*; but all the weak endings were also -*e* or -*e(n)*, except for gen. pl. -*ene*. That could have given rise to confusion on the part of native learners. This possibility should be investigated in detail.

4.4 The origin of *she*

In *Peterborough2* there are half a dozen examples of *sċǣ* 'she', i.e. /ʃeː/, clearly the ancestor of ModE *she*. This form plausibly shares an origin with *schō*, which occurs in later texts written further to the north; it is possible that *schē* was remodelled to rhyme with the corresponding masculine *hē*,[23] though a more straightforward explanation will be suggested below. But the origin of *schō* has itself long been a subject of dispute. It seems best to start with a summary of the attested OE and ME pronouns meaning 'she', then discuss how each of the latter might have arisen.

In OE 'she' had become *hēo* except in Northumbrian, where it remained *hīo*, and in Kentish, where we find *hīo ~ hīa*; it is transparently the stem *hi- plus the nom. sg. fem. ending *-u. Of the ME forms (Moore, Beech, and Whitehall 1935: 19, Mossé 1952: 56–7, Bennett and Smithers 1968: xxxvi–iii), Kentish *hyē* is the regular sound-change reflex of the OE form. In the southwest and the southwest Midlands *hēo* > /høː/, variously spelled *ho*, *hue*, etc.; I will write it *hǒ* for convenience, though the manuscripts use no such diacritics. However, in the northern part of the west Midlands *ho* probably spells /hoː/, with a back vowel, since from northern Worcestershire northwards to southwestern Yorkshire *hoo* /uː/ is the form recorded from the seventeenth century onwards (Wright 1905: 273); such a form might have been an "adjustment" of *hǒ* because of contact with *schō*, but it need not be (Laing and Lass 2014: 232–3; see further below). In the AB dialect we find *ha*, a form which might originally have been maximally unstressed (Mossé 1952: 56) or might reflect remodelling (Bennett and Smithers 1968: xxxviii). In the north and the northeast Midlands forms with *h*- no longer occur in ME: usually we find *schō* in the north and *schē* in the east Midlands, but Orrm has *ȝhō*, with an orthographic sequence of consonants occurring word-initially in no other word in his vast composition, and similar forms occasionally occur elsewhere (e.g. *ȝē* in the *Bestiary*, a thirteenth-century text from western Norfolk; see Morris 1872: 1–25, Laing 1993: 67–8). The above summary is necessarily simplified; the distribution of spellings is somewhat scattered, partly because of the inconsistency of ME orthography. For further detail see the maps for SHE on map pages 76–7 of the *Linguistic Atlas of Early Middle English (LAEME)* (Laing 2013–).

23. This is no more surprising than the remodelling of *jūz* 'you (nom. pl.)' (cf. Gothic *jus*) as *jiz* to rhyme with *wiz* 'we', a change which certainly occurred in Proto-Northwest Germanic (see Ringe and Taylor 2014: 23 with references). To demand that *schē* must be explicable by sound change alone violates the UP. However, it *could* have arisen by sound change alone; see further below.

The most widely accepted explanation of *schō* and *ʒhō* attempts to posit a single origin for both. It is claimed that when *ēo* began to merge with *ē* in the east Midlands and the north, native speakers or learners found the resulting homonymy between 'he' and 'she' unacceptable and attempted to disambiguate by pronouncing *hēo* as (approximately) *hẹ̄ó*; that form subsequently developed into *hjō > /ço:/ (directly reflected in Orrm's *ʒhō*) > *schō* (see Britton 1991 with references). Almost all the literature focuses on the *phonetic* development posited, attempting to show that it was possible, or likely, that *ʒh* can plausibly be interpreted as /ç/, etc. Unfortunately, the premise on which this scenario is based is indefensible. For one thing, it is likely that *ēo* passed through a stage /ø:/ on its way to merger with *ē*, and that the difference between the east and the west Midlands is simply that the vowel was unrounded much later in the latter area (Luick 1914–40: 333); i.e. *hēo* > *hø̄* > *hē*. But there would be no danger of merger until the unrounding occurred—and by then there would no longer be a diphthong to be manipulated so as to preserve the distinction between *he* and *she*. More importantly, there is NO EVIDENCE that native speakers or learners are able to "stave off" an "unwelcome" regular sound change by this sort of manipulation; they can choose between competing variants, avoid using an ambiguous form, etc., but there are literally no PROVEN cases of preemption of a sound change for functional reasons. To explain *schō* by this scenario is, at best, explaining *ignotum per ignotius*; at worst, it is a gross violation of the UP. Starting from the default determiner, fem. nom. sg. *sēo*, does not obviate the problem. The one advantage of this hypothesis is that it explains Orrm's *ʒhō* (and occasional similar spellings elsewhere). What we need is a similar hypothesis that does not exhibit a fatal weakness.

In fact, Laing and Lass 2014 have solved the problem very neatly. They point out (pp. 213–15) that OE words with initial diphthongs can acquire an epenthetic initial *y-* in ME; that development is especially widespread in *yēde ~ yōde ~ yode* 'went'[24] < *ēode* and *yōw ~ yow* 'you (objective pl.)' < *ēow*, though it also occurs sporadically in other lexemes. This is not a regular sound change, but there is no doubt at all that it did occur. Since prevocalic /h/ is phonetically a voiceless version of the following vowel, it seems worth asking whether epenthetic *y-* ever co-occurred with *h-*, and occasional OE spellings strongly suggest that it did (ibid. pp. 215–16). If we start from OE *hịēo*, with an epenthetic /-j-/, we preserve all the advantages of the older hypothesis without invoking impossible behavior on the part of native learners or speakers; moreover,

---

24. It is sometimes suggested that these forms reflect OE prefixed * geēode*; but note that for the pronoun such a scenario is morphologically impossible.

since the regular sound-change outcome of *ēo* after /j/ might have been different from its outcome in other positions in any given dialect, we have a plausible source of /o:/ in various dialects (as Laing and Lass suggest). Since Orrm spells word-initial /j-/ with ȝ-, his unique *ȝhō* almost certainly reflects /hjo:/ or its further development /jo:/ or /ço:/, and a spontaneous change of an extremely rare phoneme /ç/ to /ʃ/ might actually be expected (Laing and Lass 2014: 218–19). For Orrm's dialect, at least, we can propose a regular sound change hypothesis on the basis of his reflexes of the three lexemes discussed in this paragraph. OE *ēode* has become *ȝēde*, with a front vowel, in Orrm's speech, but *hi̯ēo* has become *ȝhō* and *ēow* has become *ȝūw*, with back vowels. The most plausible conditioning that will account for the difference is whether the word was (usually) stressed or not (cf. Britton 1991: 9 with references): the verb, which must have been stressed most of the time, has the front vowel, whereas the pronouns, which must often have been unstressed, have back vowels (and *i̯ēow* > *ȝōw* > *ȝūw* is a plausible sequence of changes). If that is correct, the difference between *schō* and *schē* could also simply be the difference between an unstressed and a stressed variant.

The obvious alternative—namely, that *schō* reflects a borrowing of ON *sjá* 'this (nom. sg. fem.)'—is less attractive, not only because it cannot explain the *ȝhō* of Orrm's heavily Scandinavianized dialect, but also because there is no good reason why *á* should have been rounded in a northern English dialect (as observed in the *OED* entry for *she*).

Exercises

1. Here is a passage from the *Ayenbite of Inwit*, written in Kentish and finished in 1340, with a ModE translation.

   Huanne þe kempe heþ his velaȝe yveld and him halt be þe þrote, wel unneaþe he arist. Alsuo hit is of þan þet þe dyevel halt be þa zenne; and þervore bleþeliche he yernþ to þe þrote ase þe wolf to þe ssepe him vor to astrangli, ase he dede to Even and to Adam in paradys terestre. Þet is þe vissere of helle þet nymþ þane viss bi þe þrote and by þe chinne.

   'When the champion has felled his adversary and holds him by the throat, he rises with great difficulty. So it is with the one that the devil holds by the sin; and therefore eagerly he lunges at the throat, like the wolf (does) to the sheep, in order to strangle him, as he did to Eve and Adam in the earthly paradise. It is the fisherman of hell that takes the fish by the throat and by the chin.'

   Most of the articles in this passage are uninflected *þe*, but we also find *þan* and *þa* in the second sentence and *þane* in the third. Working from the table of inflections in 3.3, can you suggest what the genders of *viss* 'fish' and *zenne* 'sin' are? Given that *þan* is almost certainly masculine, can you suggest why it has the form that it does?

2. Take a look at the maps for SHE in the *LAEME* referenced in the last section and construct your own summary of the distribution of forms. Then consider the following sentences from ME texts. Can you suggest where each is most likely to have been written from the shape of the pronouns?

a. A leafdi wes mid hire fan biset al abuten, hire lond al distruet ant heo al povre.
   'A lady was beset by her foes all around, her land all destroyed and she thoroughly poor.'

b. Leizande sche saide to Blauncheflour, / "Com nou, se þat ilche flour!"
   'Laughing she said to Blancheflour, / "Come now, see that same flower!"'

c. Quen men til hir of husband spak, / scho said þat nan ne wald scho take.
   'When men spoke to her about a husband, / she said that she wanted to take none.'

d. Rymenhild undude þe durepin / of þe hus þer heo was in.
   'Rymenhild undid the door-pin / of the house that she was in.'

e. Ho watz me nerre þen aunte or nece; / my joy forþy watz much þe more.
   'She was nearer to me than aunt or niece; / my joy therefore was that much greater.'

5 Casemarking in Middle English

The previous chapter discussed the important inflectional changes that occurred in twelfth-century English, with the exception of changes in casemarking. This chapter will supply that omission and will follow the development of casemarking down to the end of the ME period. The demise of the dual pronouns will also be treated.

5.1 Accusative and dative

The personal pronouns are the only lexemes which are still casemarked in ModE. The case features of pronouns are necessarily still part of our language's morphosyntax; the development of the pronouns thus provides a framework within which the development of casemarking on other noun phrases can be understood.

As we observed in 3.3, the Anglian dialects of OE distinguished dative from accusative in all pronouns, including 1st- and 2nd-person pronouns; in the southern dialects accusative-dative syncretism had already occurred in the 1st- and 2nd-person pronouns, though the two cases remained distinct in the 3rd-person and interrogative pronouns, as well as in the determiners. In addition, nouns often, and strong adjectives always, distinguished between accusative and dative forms.

ModE pronouns have only a single objective form; there is no distinction between accusative (or direct object) and dative (or indirect object) forms. Otherwise, casemarking has been lost altogether. It might be supposed that the ModE system first arose by extending the dative-accusative syncretism of the 1st- and 2nd-person pronouns to all pronouns in the southern dialects, followed by further erosion of the system among other nominals. What actually happened was different and more complex.

In *Lindisfarne* the Anglian system of pronouns, with dative and accusative distinguished, is preserved intact and, for the most part, casemarking on nouns and adjectives survives with only minor changes, some of them phonological, such as the loss of word-final -*n* in unstressed syllables. Yet

the distinctive Anglian OE accusative forms of 1st- and 2nd-person pronouns do not appear in any text after the Conquest. Most remarkably, in
the *Hymns* of St Godric (Treharne 2010: 324–5 with references p. 835) we
find clear examples of accusative *me* and *us*, as well as a probable example
of accusative *þe* (in the prepositional phrase *wiþ þe*) in the longest hymn.
Those are the Anglian OE dative forms. Godric lived near Durham, deep
in the same Northumbrian territory that produced the *Lindisfarne* glosses,
and died before 1170. Since all the hymns are preserved in a manuscript
from the first quarter of the thirteenth century (Laing 1993: 163, 101),
and the longest hymn in slightly earlier manuscripts (ibid. pp. 47, 88), it
is unlikely that the text has been extensively revised by scribes whose usage
was very different. We can only conclude that the distinctive Anglian
accusatives must have been lost in the eleventh or early twelfth century,
though the almost complete absence of documentary evidence makes it
impossible to say exactly when or how that happened.

Since gender had been lost in the dialect of the *Lindisfarne* glossator
(see 4.1.2), it is obvious that loss of gender and loss of casemarking need
not go together. Yet in twelfth-century documents they often do go
together, as the discussion in the following section will show.

5.2 The Midlands isogloss

In the late additions to the *Peterborough Chronicle*—from an Anglian
area—the distinction between dative and accusative has collapsed completely. That is obvious for the 3rd-person pronouns in *Peterborough2*,
which contains not a single example of the distinctive masc. acc. sg. form
hine; the old dative *him* is used for all objects, exactly as in ModE. The
situation in the fem. is the same: the old dative *hire* is used for all objects,
e.g. in relating the adventures of Matilda the Empress:

> ... & sæhtleden wyd þemperice & bröhten hire intō Oxenford & iāuen hire þe
> burch.
> '... and (they) reconciled with the Empress and brought her into Oxford
> and gave her the castle.'

So also in the plural: *hem ~ heom*, the old dative form, is used for all
objects, while *hi*—originally ambiguous between nom. and acc.—is used
only for subjects. (1st- and 2nd-person pronouns do not occur in the passage.) As noted in 4.1.3, the determiners have not only lost the acc.-dat.
distinction but are uninflected altogether in *Peterborough2*. The adjective
has also lost its strong endings, including fem. dat. sg. *-re* and default
dative *-en* (OE *-um*), as well as masc. acc. sg. *-ne*; for instance, in the
entry for 1137 we find *mid miċel suinc* 'with great effort' (OE *mid miclum*

swince), and in 1138 we find *mid ormēte færd* 'with an immense levy' (OE *mid ormǣtre fierde*), while in the last year's entry the chronicler says

> *& te munekes innen dæis cusen ōþer of heomsælf*
> 'and the monks within a day chose another from among themselves'[1]
> (OE *& þā munucas innan dǣges curon ōþerne of him selfum*).

In noun inflection the dat. pl. had been unambiguously marked with *-um* in OE; dat. sg. *-e* was distinctive only for some masculine and neuter nouns (since others ended in *-e* also in the nom.-acc., while feminines usually exhibited *-e* also in the accusative and genitive). From the examples given above it can be seen that dat. sg. *-e* is usually absent in *Peterborough2* (though it does appear occasionally). The dat. pl. *-en* that we expect as the representative of OE *-um* is also absent, and accusative forms are used instead; for instance, in the entry for 1135 we read

> *pais he makede men & dēr*
> 'he made peace for men and animals'
> (OE *friþ hē fremede mannum & dēorum*),

in which the use of umlauted nom.-acc. pl. *men* shows that not just the loss of an ending but the use of a specifically nom.-acc. form in dative function is in question. In short, nominal inflection in *Peterborough2* is identical to that of ModE, modulo lexical details.

But even in *Peterborough1* the distinction between the accusative and dative cases is not consistently maintained. The entry for 1123 illustrates that neatly. In the passage describing the death and burial of the Bishop of Lincoln acc. *hine* is used repeatedly and correctly. In the following passage relating the dispute over who should be Archbishop of Canterbury pl. *hem* appears repeatedly, always clearly or at least plausibly dative. However, twice in that passage *swā hwām swā* 'whomsoever', which is dative in form, appears as the direct object of *cēsen* 'to choose', which took an accusative direct object in OE. Eventually, they chose William of Corbeil

> *& brōhten him tōforen se kyng, & se kyng him ġeaf þone ærċebisċoprīċe, & ealle þā bisċopas him underfēngen.*
> 'and brought him before the king, and the king gave him the archbishopric, and all the bishops accepted him.'

In those clauses the first and third *him*'s are direct objects, like *swā hwām swā*, and the one in the middle is an indirect object. Further examples of

---

1. In this passage *-sælf* is emphatic rather than reflexive. On the use of *self* in both functions in ME see Vezzosi 2007 with extensive references.

acc. *him* occur throughout *Peterborough1*. The situation is the same with forms of the default determiner. Masc. and neut. dat. sg. *þām* occurs only twice near the beginning, both times preceded by *tō* (*tō þām wolcne*, 1122; *tō þām kyng*, 1123), while fem. *þǣre* occurs only once, apparently in accusative function (*þā hwīle þe þā munecas sungen þǣre messe*, 1122); usually *þǣre* is a spelling of *þǣr* 'there' in this document (and it might conceivably be so in the passage just quoted; so Glahn 1918: 29). The distinctive masc. acc. sg. *þone* is used, but very often incorrectly (e.g. as fem. dat. sg. in *on þone lententȳde* 'in Lent', 1122). A remarkable passage in the entry for 1128 reads:

> *Hē dide ðone king tō understanden þet hē wolde mid alle forlǣten þone minstre*
> *& þet land & þǣr wunien mid him on Englalande & on ðone minstre of*
> *Burch,*
>
> 'He gave the king to understand that he wanted to relinquish the monastery
> and the land completely and live with him in England and in the
> monastery of Burg,'

in which the first example of *þone* is masc. acc., the second neut. acc., and the third neut. dat. Even nominative forms are used as datives; *tōforen se kyng* in the passage quoted above is not untypical. There are few strong adjectives in oblique positions in *Peterborough1*, but those that do occur end in *-e* or are endingless, e.g. at the end of the entry for 1123:

> *& swā myċel hearm þǣr wæs ġedōn swā nān man hit cūðe ōþer seċġen*
> 'and so much damage was done there that no man could describe it to
> another'

with uninflected *ōþer* for OE dat. sg. *ōþrum*, or *mid miċel unrihte* 'with great injustice' toward the end of 1124 (OE *mid miclum unrihte*). Once again we can only conclude that the writer of *Peterborough1* spoke more or less like the writer of *Peterborough2*, but had enough education to attempt to use the obsolete inflected forms, though he was not able to do so consistently or correctly.

As we saw in the last chapter, *Peterborough* falls to the northeast of an isogloss separating its genderless dialect from the more southwesterly dialects that retained the OE gender system.[2] It is reasonable to ask whether those dialects retained the distinction between accusative and dative as well, and it is easy to show that they did. In the early homily discussed in 4.1.4 at least the following forms of the 3rd-person pronoun and the determiners occur, all used correctly by late OE standards:

---

2. An extensive collection of data relevant to the following discussion is Greul 1934.

	masc.	neut.	fem.	masc.	neut.	fem.	masc.	neut.	fem.
sg. nom.	hē	hit	hēo	sē	þæt	sēo	þēs	þiss	þēos
acc.	hine	hit	hēo	þone	þæt	þā		þiss	
gen.	his		hire	þæs					
dat.	him		hire	þān				þyssen	þyssere
pl. n.-a.				þā				þās	
gen.				þǣre					
dat.				þān				þyssen	

The strong adjective endings are also mostly still in place; in addition to the phrases quoted in the preceding chapter, note *sumne cume* 'some stranger' (masc. acc. sg., OE *sumne cuman*), *intō sumen castele* (masc. dat. sg., OE *sumum*), *tō mīnre ēadmōdnysse* 'to my humility' (fem. dat. sg.), *on nānre ōðre* 'in the case of no other (woman)' (fem. dat. sg., OE *on nānre ōðerre*), etc. Dat. pl. *-en* (OE *-um*) is still normal on nouns, e.g. *æt ūres Drihtenes fōten* 'at our Lord's feet', *þan Hǣlende & his þēowen* 'for the Savior and his servants', etc. This is the LWS inflectional system, affected only by trivial sound changes and levellings.

Other twelfth-century documents group either with *Peterborough* or with the homily just discussed, though there are some complications; the most striking is that even the more conservative documents are abandoning the strong inflection of adjectives, which therefore often mark case indistinctly (if at all). But once again there is a clear contrast between the *Lambeth Homilies*, which clearly belong to the southwestern area, and the *Trinity Homilies*. Though clearly marked accusatives and datives can be found in both, and uninflected determiners (for instance) can also be found in both, the proportions are quite different in the two collections. A comparison of *Lambeth* XIII and *Trinity* XXVI—two very similar versions of the same homily—gives a reasonable picture of the situation. In the former we find

> *þā þe hē spec wið ðene hālie mon Abraham*
> 'when he spoke with the holy man Abraham',

with clearly marked masc. acc. sg. *ðene*; the latter renders the clause as

> *þǭ hē spac wið þe hǭli man Abraham,*

with an uninflected determiner. To *Lambeth*

> *nimeð ȝēme of twām þingen*
> 'takes notice of two things',

with the clear dat. pl. markers *-m* and *-en*, corresponds *Trinity*

> *nimeð ȝēme of twǭ þing*

with endingless acc. pl. forms instead; to *Lambeth*

> *on þēre feire forbisne*
> 'in the beautiful parable',

with a fem. dat. sg. determiner, corresponds *Trinity*

> *on þe faire forbisne*

with an uninflected determiner; etc.

Documents from late in the twelfth century exhibit a similar pattern. In the *Orrmulum* the accusative and dative cases have become a single objective case, exactly as in *Peterborough2* (Lehnert 1953: 109). On nouns and adjectives the objective is not marked; final *-e* occurs often, but its function is rhythmic rather than grammatical (ibid. pp. 32–42 and passim). The 3rd-person objective pronouns are the old datives *himm*, *hire*, *hemm*, except for inanimate sg. *itt*.

The situation in *Vices and Virtues* is more interesting. Among nouns dat. sg. *-e* largely survives, but the distinctive dat. pl. *-en* has mostly been abandoned, the nom.-acc. pl. forms usually appearing instead (Philippsen 1911: 39–40, 63, 70–1). The distinctive strong endings of adjectives also appear seldom (ibid. pp. 83–94). By contrast, well-marked sg. forms of the determiner are reasonably common: masc. acc. sg. *ðane*, masc.-neut. dat. sg. *ðan*, fem. dat. sg. *ðare*, all in competition with uninflected *ðe*; on the other hand, dat. pl. *ðan* has largely been replaced by *ðe*, exhibiting the same syncretism as in noun inflection (ibid. pp. 104–6). In the 3rd-person pronoun masc. acc. sg. *hine* is still found, but the old dat. sg. *him* in accusative function is more common (ibid. p. 111); in the plural a new form *hes* of uncertain origin is in competition with the old dative *hem* in accusative function (ibid. p. 114). In the fem. sg. *hes* is also the usual acc. form, inherited *hiē* appearing only twice; Philippsen notes that *hire* appears as an accusative only in reflexive function (ibid. p. 113), but that could be a statistical accident. What are we to make of this pattern? It is possible that the confusion of old accusative and dative forms is the work of a copyist, and that the original text exhibited no such changes; but it is also possible that *Vices and Virtues* was written in a dialect in which the collapse of the distinction was a change in progress (cf. Allen 2008: 128–9). The pattern is coherent: adjective inflection has been drastically simplified; the dat. pl. of nouns and the determiner has largely undergone syncretism with the nom.-acc. pl., but the dat. sg. is still marked; in the 3rd-person pronoun the dative forms have begun to encroach on the accusative, while a completely independent change has replaced the old fem. and pl. acc. with *hes*. The significance of this pattern will be discussed below.

The case system of the "AB language" of the West Midlands looks almost like a further development of the system of *Vices and Virtues*. Adjective inflection has been simplified; the dat. pl. is no longer marked, and while dat. sg. *-e* sometimes occurs on nouns preceded by preposi-tions, it is often absent (d'Ardenne 1961: 205–7). In the texts as we have them, pronouns usually have a single objective form, which is the old dative except in the neut. sg., and the determiner is most often uninflected; but as d'Ardenne notes (ibid. pp. 222, 224–6), there are occasional examples of *hine* and of inflected determiners, showing that the author's speech was more conservative. In *Brut(C)*, by contrast, the OE inflection of determiners, quantifiers, and the 3rd-person pronoun is still largely intact (as noted in 4.1.4 above): fem. dat. sg. is usually clearly marked, and though there is some interchange between (masc. acc.) *pane* and (dat.) *pan*, that could be the result of phonological developments or even of scribal error. Even strong adjective endings are still used, though not consistently; thus beside *umben longne first* 'after a long time' (l. 146) and *mid muchelure care* 'with great care' (l. 54) we also find *mid muchele worscipe* (l. 105).[3] By the early fourteenth century the distinction between accusative and dative had been lost completely, except in the southeast, but there it apparently persisted.

In short, the early ME dialects which have lost distinctive accusative and dative casemarking are the same dialects that have lost the gender system. The pattern of inflection found in *Vices and Virtues* suggests how those two developments might be connected. In that document the dat. pl. is no longer usually marked, adjective inflection has been simplified, inflected forms of the determiner are in competition with uninflected forms, and the accusative and dative have begun to merge in other inflec-tional paradigms; grammatical gender still exists, though a fairly large number of nouns have shifted their gender. It looks as if the erosion of nominal inflection preceded the final collapse of the gender system. In any dialect in which all the changes in progress in *Vices and Virtues* had gone to completion, the only markers of a noun's gender would have been whether its gen. sg. ended in *-es* and whether it was referred to by masc., fem., or neut. pronouns. It seems reasonable to suggest that such an outcome might have made noun gender too difficult to be learned consistently. On the other hand, the Kentish *Ayenbite of Inwit*, which preserves case and gender distinctions as late as 1340, shows that "gone

---

3. The table in Shinkawa 2012: 87 shows that masc.-neut. sg. *-en* is used much less often on strong adjectives than fem. *-re* or masc. acc. sg. *-ne*. It seems likely that this ending was affected by the variable loss of *-n* noted in 4.3; a special study of the question would be welcome.

to completion" has to be taken literally: unambiguous markers of gender and case occur at much lower frequency than in *Vices and Virtues*, yet the old system is still in place. Evidently, native learners were able to acquire it from relatively infrequent cues in child-directed speech.

5.3 The genitive

Unlike the dative case, the OE genitive survived in part. To some extent, it was replaced by prepositional phrases introduced by *of*. That development is sometimes attributed to the influence of French *de*, but the distribution of facts makes that unlikely; in particular, the *Orrmulum*, whose heavily Scandinavianized dialect shows little French influence, uses *off* just as freely as *Vices and Virtues*. A gradual extension of the semantic range of OE *of* by successive generations of native learners is all that is needed to account for the ME situation (cf. Allen 2008: 72–4).

The OE gen. pl. ending *-a*, n-stem *-ena*, and strong adj. *-ra* survived into the thirteenth century; it is still widespread in the "AB" language (d'Ardenne 1961: 207–9) and occurs with a restricted range of nouns in the *Orrmulum* (Lehnert 1953: 151–2). Increasingly, however, it was restricted to fixed phrases such as *alre kinge(ne) king* 'king of all kings', *alre þinge mæst* 'most of all things', except in the southeast. In early ME it is in competition chiefly with prepositional phrases introduced by *of*.

The masc. and neut. gen. sg. ending *-es*, on the other hand, became the usual gen. sg. marker on nouns. In *Vices and Virtues* it has not yet spread to feminine nouns, but in the "AB" language it has begun to take over, and in the *Orrmulum* the takeover is more or less complete. The latter document also yields some of the earliest unambiguous examples of *-es* as an agglutinative marker: whereas the gen. sg. of *mann* is *manness*, the gen. pl. is *menness*, i.e. the plural form *menn* with an additional marker of the genitive. (If the plural ends in *-es* there is no additional genitive marker, exactly as in ModE, and it is difficult to say exactly how that came about.) A different innovation is common to the *Orrmulum* and other twelfth-century texts: when several nouns are in apposition, only one is casemarked (Allen 2008: 139–41). Both dative and genitive were affected, but the innovation is more obvious in the genitive because the marker *-es* is clearer. Examples like *i Dauiþþ kingess chesstre* 'in King David's city', with gen. sg. marked only on the second noun, are commonplace in the *Orrmulum*.

These innovations, taken together, made it possible for native learners to reanalyze gen. *-es* (now no longer singular) as a clitic attached to phrases rather than an inflectional ending attached to nouns. However, such a reanalysis did not occur, or did not catch on in the speech community, for some two centuries. It clearly has not occurred in the *Orrmulum*, in which we still find *inn āness weress hēwe* 'in the likeness of a man', with gen. sg. marked both on the quantifier and on the noun, and even (exceptionally) *Dāuiþess kīngess kinnesmann*, with two nouns in apposition marked for gen. sg. (Allen 2008: 146–7). The first unambiguous instances of the reanalysis occur in the last quarter of the fourteenth century. Allen cites, from John of Trevisa's *Polychronicon* (1387),

> *but þe kyng of Fraunces men weren i-slawe*
> 'but the King of France's men were slain'

and from Chaucer's *Troilus and Criseyde* (I.15)

> *For I, that God of Loves servantz serve,*

—one of only three verifiable examples in Chaucer (Allen 2008: 153). As Allen has amply documented in more than a decade of work (ibid. pp. 152–4 with references), the clitic initially appears only on NPs composed of noun plus PP which are equivalent to a name or a title; the only actual difference between these NPs and the earlier ones is that now the PP can remain in place when the possessive marker is attached rather than being extraposed. But extraposed examples remain common; examples like the *dukes wyf of Tyntagail* 'the Duke of Tintagel's wife' routinely occur in Malory's work of the late 1460s (as observed already in Jespersen 1954: 287). The new construction won the competition in the sixteenth century and was extended to NPs of any length and complexity not too great to parse.

It has repeatedly been suggested that the clitic -*'s* is a reflex not of the OE gen. sg. ending -*es* but of the 3rd-person masc. gen. sg. pronoun *his*. Allen 2008: 223–73 investigates all the apparent evidence for that hypothesis and shows conclusively that it cannot be correct. Even a summary of her arguments is beyond the scope of this book; students should read Allen's book (which, in any case, is required reading for anyone working on the history of English morphology). Allen's main conclusions are the following.

1. All supposed OE examples of *his* in this function are better analyzed in other ways.
2. The syntactic distribution of the early ME examples (which occur in only two manuscripts) is indistinguishable from that of gen. sg. -*es*, so that *his ~ is* is most plausibly interpreted as a spelling of the gen. sg. ending.
3. The same is true of the late ME examples and continues to be true until the middle of the sixteenth century.

4. The use of a 3rd-person pronoun agreeing with the possessor, as in *Rebecca hir father* 'Rebecca's father', does not appear until the 1540s, long after the clitic had become usual; whether or not it reflects a genuine reanalysis of the latter in speech, it had died out again by 1700. During that entire period the clitic continues to be used.

For our purposes, this last phenomenon is too marginal and ephemeral to merit further discussion. However, the history of clitic -'s is important for linguistic theory, because it is the best documented counterexample to the erroneous contention that affixes cannot become syntactically independent functional items.

5.4 The dual pronouns

The OE 1st- and 2nd-person dual pronouns, inherited from PGmc., do not appear in *Lindisfarne*; in passages in which the WS gospels employ dual pronouns the *Lindisfarne* glossator regularly gives plural forms. Unfortunately, we cannot draw secure inferences from that fact, because he was glossing the Latin text word for word, and Latin has no duals.[4]

The dual pronouns were still in use in twelfth-century English; examples can be found in the *Orrmulum*, in *Vices and Virtues*, in Laȝamon, in the Katherine group, and in other early ME texts. The 1du. pronouns *wit* and objective *unc* (spelled *witt* and *unnc* by Orrm) retain their OE forms; so does 2du. *ȝit*, but its objective seems to have been influenced by the 1du., since beside inherited *inc* (e.g. in the Katherine group) we also find *ȝunc* (spelled *ȝunnc* by Orrm). These pronouns survived until perhaps the middle of the thirteenth century. The latest literary text in which they are used seems to be *Genesis and Exodus*, usually dated to about 1250 (Arngart 1968: 45). Unfortunately, the sole manuscript copy dates to ca. 1325 (Laing 1993: 25 with references), and it seems clear that the scribe did not always understand what he was copying; that is the most likely reason for his rendering of *ȝit* as "*ȝe it*" (Arngart 1968: 30–1). In later ME the dual is no longer a grammatical category.

Exercises

1. Here is a passage from *Lambeth* XIII and the same passage from *Trinity* XXVI (see above).

    Lambeth: Ðenne þes folkes larþew his sed wule sawen, he ahte to nimene

---

4. Lat. *duo* 'two' and *ambō* 'both' are inherited dual forms, but they trigger plural concord.

muchele ʒeme þet he hit sawe on bicumeliche eorðe & on rihte time,
on ðere monne heorte þe luveliche lusteð Godes wordes. Summe heo
ere ðon gode weoren; summe heo ðereþurh gode iwurðeð; & þet bið
bicumelic eorðe Godes wordes on to sawen. Ah þa ðe sunnen luveð &
forleten heom nulleð ne nane bileafe underfo, heo beoð unbicumelic
eorðe to þe sede of Godes weorde. Ævriche Sunendeie & oðre heʒe
daʒen is time to sawene þet halie sed þet is Godes word, & ðet in halie
chirche þer alle Cristene men aʒen to beon isomned togedere.

'When the people's teacher wants to sow his seed [i.e. preach God's
word], he ought to take great care that he sow it in suitable earth and
at the right time, in the heart of those men who listen to God's words
with affection. Some of them were good before that; some of them
become good thereby; and that is (always) suitable earth to sow God's
words in. But those who love sins and do not want to abandon them,
nor to accept any faith, they are (always) unsuitable earth for the seed
of God's word. On every Sunday and other high days is the time to
sow the holy seed that is God's word, and that in holy church where all
Christian men ought to be gathered together.'

Trinity: & þanne folkes lorþeawes his sed soweð, he oh to nime michel
ʒeme þat he hit sowe on bicumeliche eorðe & on rihte time, þere
mennes heortes hlisteð luveliche Godes lore þere me of Gode specð &
þere me God wurðeð. Þo ben bicumeliche eorðe Godes word on to
sowende. Ac þo þe luveð sinne & forleten nelleð, oðer bileved ne haveð
ne understonden Godes word noht, ben unbicumeliche eorðe to þe sed
of Godes wordes. Ech Sunedai & oðer hegh dai is riht time to sowen
þe holie sed þat is Godes word, & in chirche þer al chirche folc ohg to
ben gadered.

'And when (the) people's teachers sow his seed, he [*sic*] ought to take
great care that he sow it in suitable earth and at the right time, where
men's hearts listen with affection to God's teaching, where one speaks
of God and where one praises God. Those are (always) suitable earth
to sow God's word in. But those that love sin and do not want to
abandon (it), or have not believed nor understood God's word at all,
are (always) unsuitable earth for the seed of God's words. Each Sunday
and other high day is the right time to sow the holy seed that is God's
word, and in church where all church-folk ought to be gathered.'

It is clear (for various technical reasons) that neither of these texts
is a direct copy of the other, but it is clear that both are copies of an
earlier text. However, you can see from the disagreements between
them that the scribes did not copy slavishly; each produced a text that
makes sense, even though they do not agree. That raises a question
for the student of morphology: is the inflectional morphology of each

scribe a consistent system? Work through the texts and try to answer that question. Bear the following points in mind:

a. dative singulars (used after most prepositions, and also by themselves when a preposition would be required in ModE) end in *-e*, and dative plurals in *-en*;

b. in *Lambeth* the phrase *ðere monne* is a genitive plural 'of those men', but in both texts *ðere / þere* is also a possible spelling for 'there' or 'where';

c. the plural of nouns can end in *-es* or *-en*, but the plural of adjectives usually ends in *-e*;

d. while *þet* can correspond exactly to ModE *that* (in *Lambeth*), it can also be the neuter sg. corresponding to ModE *the*.

2. Here is a sentence from a thirteenth-century text. Can you suggest where it was written from the shape of the pronouns?

And alswo hi biknewe his beringe by þo sterre, swo hi nomen conseil bituene hem þet hi wolden gon forto hyne anuri, and þet hi wolden offri him gold and stor and mirre.

'And as soon as they recognized his birth by that star, they took counsel among themselves that they should go to honor him, and that they should offer him gold and frankincense and myrrh.'

6 Contact with Norse and French

This chapter will address the question of how far contact with Norse and with French can be held responsible for changes in English inflection. It will be seen that the impact of those two languages on English was quite different.

6.1 English and French: a typical contact situation

The influence of French on the morphosyntax of English in the centuries immediately following the Norman Conquest can be stated concisely: there was none. That is interesting because it can be shown that in other areas of the grammar and lexicon there was significant French influence, as the following summary indicates.

It seems clear that the phoneme /v/ was established in the east Midlands dialects of ME by French loanwords with initial *v-*; how that happened is discussed in Ringe and Eska 2013: 133–4 (see also Hickey 2015).[1] Word-initial /dʒ-/ likewise occurs exclusively in French words (and other, much later loans). It is well known that English was flooded by French loanwords between the Conquest and the Renaissance; what is less well known is that that process was very uneven, both geographically and temporally. In early twelfth-century documents the influx of French words is modest (cf. Dekeyser 1986), but around 1200 an interesting pattern begins to appear. In the *Orrmulum*, written in a heavily Scandinavianized dialect in the northeast Midlands, there are few French loans, in spite of

---

1. In northern documents one sometimes finds *w-* in place of *v-* (e.g. *woys* beside *voys* 'voice'), which suggests that in the north French word-initial /v-/ might have been borrowed as /w-/. South and west of the Thames the situation was more complicated. In those areas OE word-initial /f-/ had become [v-] some time in the eleventh century (Luick 1914–40: 933–4), so that French /v-/ could be borrowed as [v-]; the crucial question is how French word-initial /f-/ was borrowed in those dialects. Apparently, it was borrowed as [v-], to judge from *vigoure* 'figure' in *Kyng Alisaunder*, a southeastern text of ca. 1300 (see Bennett and Smithers 1968: 36, 276–7, 596).

the vast size of the work (some 19,000 lines); in the southwest Midlands *Ancrene Wisse* and Katherine group, by contrast, French loans are much more numerous. Even so, the French element in early thirteenth-century English is relatively modest; it was only about a century later that borrowing from French increased sharply, so far as surviving documents can tell us (see the chart in Durkin 2014: 33). By that point it is difficult to blame it on the direct effect of the Conquest (then well over two centuries past); what we seem to be witnessing instead is the effect of English having been drawn into the French culture area.

Why was inflectional morphology not altered by contact with French? It appears that the tightly integrated system of morphosyntax is the area of a language's grammar least accessible to foreign influence; for instance, King 2000 found that more than two centuries of intense English pressure on the French of Prince Edward Island (PEI) led to only modest influence on the syntax of the dialect, and none on inflection. That a similar pressure on post-Conquest English cannot possibly have been exerted by French is demonstrated by even a casual consideration of the demographic situation. If we accept the reasonable estimate of Treharne 2010: xxiii (some 25,000 Normans in a population of 1.5 million in the late eleventh century), speakers of French never amounted to as much as 2 per cent of the population of England, and most were scattered thinly over the landscape in manor houses. Moreover, as Clark has emphasized, many of the new Norman gentry came to England as landless young men without wives and children, and there is some evidence that a substantial number married Englishwomen, necessarily creating bilingual families (Clark 1992: 119–22 with references). Of course, the educated class spoke and wrote French at first, but the educated class was tiny, and much of it was sequestered in monasteries and cathedral chapters.[2]

It should also be noted that French loanwords are least common among the *basic* vocabulary of English. Durkin remarks that that "is what we should expect from a typical borrowing situation where there has not been language shift in the first language of a large proportion of a population" (Durkin 2014: 224). He goes on to point out that the number of less basic words borrowed from French was very large, however, and that they eventually had an impact on the derivational morphology of English (ibid. p. 224). We will need to examine that impact in detail in Chapter 10.

---

2. On the representation of multilingualism in Britain in medieval literature see Machan 2000.

6.2 English and Norse: intensive contact

The situation of the Norse immigrants who settled in England in the wake of the Scandinavian invasion of 865 was quite different, even though they were probably no more numerous than the later French settlers. The *Chronicle* says explicitly that they seized, settled, and farmed land in some districts of England (Bately 1986: 50–1, Townend 2002: 2). Where they settled can largely be determined from place names of Scandinavian origin in England. These are heavily concentrated in Yorkshire and the "Five Boroughs" (Lincolnshire, Nottinghamshire, Derbyshire, Leicestershire, and Northhamptonshire), with lighter concentrations in the far northwest and in and around Norfolk (Ekwall 1936, Townend 2002: 47–8 with references, Morse-Gagné 2003: 5–16, 21–73 with references; see the maps in, e.g., Campbell, John, and Wormald 1982: 162, Görlach 1986: 339, Richards 2000: 44, Warner 2017: 319). As Townend observes (2002: 47–8), many of these are names of farmsteads and even of fields, and it is inconceivable that Anglo-Saxon farmers would have given Norse names to such features just because the new landlord was Scandinavian. The thickly clustered names are evidence of fairly dense Scandinavian settlement (see Kastovsky 1992: 322–4 with references). Linguistic evidence of other kinds suggests that the areas of densest settlement were Yorkshire and areas immediately to the west and northwest—the latter mostly settled by Norwegians in the tenth century—plus, by some criteria, Lincolnshire (Samuels 1989: 106–11 with references).

It stands to reason that there must have been some Norse–English bilingualism in late Anglo-Saxon England, and there is indirect evidence for that in a poem called *The Battle of Brunanburh*, written to commemorate an English victory of 937 and inserted into the *Chronicle* for that year (Dobbie 1942: 16–20). A noun *cnear* 'longship' occurs in l. 35, and the compound *nægledcnearrum* 'in nail-fastened longships' in l. 53. It looks like an ordinary West Saxon OE noun; in particular, the diphthong *ea* is exactly what is expected before *r* followed by a further consonant (Campbell 1962: 56, Hogg 2011: 84–5, Ringe and Taylor 2014: 180–1, the last with many examples). But the word does not occur in any earlier OE document, and there are no cognates in other West Germanic languages; it was obviously borrowed from ON to denote a specifically Scandinavian type of ship. But consider the inflection of the source word in early ON (Noreen 1923: 273):

	sg.	pl.
nom.	*knǫrr*	*knerrer*
acc.	*knǫrr*	*knǫrro*
gen.	*knarrar*	*knarra*
dat.	*knerre*	*knǫrrom*

The underlying shape of the stem is, in fact, /knarr-/, but a more than superficial acquaintance with the language would have been required to figure that out. On the other hand, a solid knowledge of OE and a practical understanding of cognations between the two languages would have been required to construct a "correct" OE *cnearr* on the basis of obvious cognates (e.g. ON *barn* = OE *bearn* 'child', *varð* = *wearþ* 'I/(s)he became', etc.).[3] Evidently, whoever first came up with OE *cnearr* was a competent bilingual.

How long ON was spoken in England is difficult to determine and in any case must have varied somewhat by geography, social class, etc. (see the discussion of Townend 2002: 189 with references).[4] What is clear is that the entire area of Norse settlement eventually became English-speaking. In other words, community-wide language shift on a very large scale is known to have occurred. The influence of Norse on English must be judged in light of that secure inference.

6.3 Norse lexemes and morphosyntax in English

English has borrowed so many words from French that the French element in the ModE lexicon is immediately obvious. Loans from Norse are fewer and much less conspicuous, yet by some measures they are actually more significant. The discussion in Philip Durkin's *Borrowed Words* gives a good idea of the situation. The charts in Durkin 2014: 24–7 show that, in terms of raw numbers, there is no comparison: in the entire ModE lexicon there are some 6,000 direct loanwords definitely from French ("French only"), but only about 200 from Norse ("early Scandinavian"). But the raw numbers do not tell the whole story. Durkin's remarks are worth quoting at some length:

> However, it should be noted that these raw numbers . . . do not reflect qualitative differences in impact on the vocabulary of modern English. . . . It will be noted that, for example, in these charts the total of loanwords from Japanese comes next after the total from early Scandinavian. However, Japanese has (so far at least) contributed no words to English which form part of the basic vocabulary of modern English, whereas early

---

3. Sequences *arC* and *ærC* do occur in West Saxon OE, but only as a result of metathesis or dialect borrowing, and they are therefore rare; see Ringe and Taylor 2014: 85, 197–8, 252, 340–1 with references for details.
4. The speculations of Samuels 1989: 113–14 are merely possible, as he admits.

> Scandinavian contributed several, including even the third-person plural
> personal pronoun *they*. (Durkin 2014: 28)

The last sentence encapsulates neatly what is unusual about Norse loanwords in English: they skew heavily toward the basic vocabulary in a way
that even French loanwords do not. As Durkin points out, if one looks
only at the 100 most frequent words in the *British National Corpus*,

> the Scandinavian contribution significantly exceeds that from French and
> Latin combined:
> Scandinavian: *they, their, to get, to take, to give, like, to want*
> French: *people, very*
> French and/or Latin: *just, to use.* (Durkin 2014: 40)

Other experiments with basic wordlists gives similar results. On the
ModE version of the Leipzig-Jakarta list of 100 words most resistant
to borrowing (on the average, across a wide range of languages) there
are eight Norse loans but only four French (Durkin 2014: 41–2 with
references). In a typical ModE version of the Swadesh 200-word list,
constructed so as to include a maximally basic and maximally cross-
cultural vocabulary, there will be about a dozen words of French origin
and about fifteen of Norse origin. In northern ME the Norse lexical
element was much more extensive (Björkman 1900–2, Samuels 1989:
110–11, Durkin 2014: 182–6; for the OE period cf. Kastovsky 1992:
320–36, with an in-depth discussion of the historical and sociolinguistic
situation). In other ME dialects Norse words also occur, but in far fewer
numbers; they can be explained as dialect borrowings from the area of
Scandinavian settlement (see the extensive discussion of Dance 2003).

But there are also Norse elements in the grammatical machinery of
English, especially the "function words". Most famously, ModE *they*
(oblique *them*, possessive *their*) was transferred into English from ON;
it obviously reflects ON pl. masc. nom. *þeir*, dat. *þeim*, gen. *þeira* rather
than OE pl. nom. *hī(e)*, dat. *him ~ heom*, gen. *heora*. The innovative
pronoun appears first in areas of Scandinavian settlement and spreads
visibly from there over the temporal course of ME, as Morse-Gagné 2003:
119–53 documents in detail with numerous references to earlier work. In
general, the nominative form is borrowed first and the objective form last,
for reasons that are still unclear.

An additional Norse pronoun that never spread beyond the area of
Scandinavian settlement is attested once on the Aldbrough sundial, whose
inscription reads:[5]

5. I have dotted letters which are damaged but appear to be partly legible in
   photographs. Okasha's system is more conservative and makes more distinctions (see

ULF [H]ET ARŒRAN CYRICE FOR HĄNUM & FOR GUNWĄRĄ
SAULA (Okasha 1971: 47, Townend 2002: 190)

The most natural interpretation of the inscription is

'Ulf had (the) church raised for himself and for Gunnvǫr's soul.'

Hánum is the early ON pronoun corresponding to OE masc. dat. sg.
him, but unlike the OE form, it is not used reflexively; 'for himself' is *sér*
in ON (so already Page 1971: 178). In other words, the ON pronoun
is being used in a purely English grammatical pattern; the family that
commissioned the monument, whose names are obviously Scandinavian,
was speaking English, not Norse, but with more Norse pronouns than
we might have expected. Whatever process brought *they* into English
evidently could bring other pronouns too.

Other functional items were also transferred from ON into English;
Richard Dance's short list of items not usually borrowed, such as numerals
and place adverbs (Dance 2003: 289–91), gives a good idea of the penetration of English by Norse function words. Perhaps most striking is *at* in its
use to introduce infinitives, replacing OE *tō* in the core area of Scandinavian
settlement. Interestingly, *til* appears in its place in a more peripheral area,
again reflecting the use of a Norse item in an English pattern: ON *til* corresponds to OE *tō* in introducing prepositional phrases, but not infinitives
(Samuels 1989: 110). Many northern dialects of ME have ON *til* and *frā*
in place of OE *tō* and *fram*. The relative particle *sum* is especially prominent
in the *Orrmulum*. The ON loan *both*, replacing OE *bēgen*, should probably
also be considered a functional item, as should the conjunction *though*.

The items listed above are the hard evidence proving that contact
between OE and ON was exceptionally intensive, because they are dis-
tinctively Norse forms found as functional items in ME dialects. There
is some other evidence for the grammatical penetration of English by
Norse, but it is less decisive; it will be discussed in 6.5. Before addressing
it, we must consider what the process of transfer of Norse items into
English might have been, given that it was obviously not garden-variety
word-borrowing.

6.4 The process of transfer

In older discussions one sometimes sees the suggestion that northern ME
after the Scandinavian invasion was a creole language. That suggestion

Okasha 1971: 45), but she agrees on the probable reading. The inscription might
read [L]ET, but the meaning would be the same.

is now universally rejected (cf. Görlach 1986, Thomason and Kaufman 1988: 306–15, Kastovsky 1992: 327). If "creole" has any precise meaning, it means a pidgin language—i.e. a rudimentary language evolved by adults speaking different languages who need to communicate in a hurry—which has been learned natively by children. Creole languages usually exhibit radical simplification in their inflectional morphology and syntax. Such languages do exist; Tok Pisin is a well-documented example. But as DeGraff 2009 has emphasized, even many languages that exhibit the simplification typical of creoles need not have passed through a pidgin stage; they can ultimately be the results of imperfect second-language learning by adults. Since northern ME does not even show the level of simplification typical of creoles, it obviously never passed through a pidgin stage.

Another hypothesis—namely, that northern ME reflects a kind of "koiné", or compromise dialect, resulting from an amalgam of OE and ON—rests on an assessment that ON and OE might have been mutually intelligible. As any experienced linguist will be aware, the question of mutual intelligibility is often complex, so this possibility requires some discussion. However, I should say at the outset that I am not entirely convinced. Potential evidence falls into several categories, as follows.

The anecdotal evidence collected by Townend (Townend 2002: 150–71 and passim, conveniently condensed and accurately summarized in Warner 2017: 376–7) seems to me inadmissible simply because there are too many uncertainties involved (Gneuss 1993: 129–31). For instance, statements in much later Icelandic sources that the languages of England and Scandinavia were "the same" early in the tenth century can rest only on oral history, a notoriously poor preserver of details, and a good storyteller might well omit references to interpreters and bilingualism in order to streamline the story and make it more effective.

Structural differences of a kind that would impede easy communication have, in my opinion, been downplayed too much. That the enclitic definite article of later ON, one of the more dramatic differences between the languages, had not yet developed (Warner 2017: 376 with references) is true, but there were other marked differences between the OE and ON inflectional systems. The suggestion that ON, which is adequately attested only later, might have been much more similar to OE in the ninth and tenth centuries is shown to be mistaken by reconstruction of the relative chronologies of changes in OE and ON (cf., e.g., Ringe and Taylor 2014, Noreen 1923, Krause 1948). Especially disruptive on the English side were the early loss of word-final *-z and of most word-final syllables containing short *a throughout West Germanic (Ringe and Taylor 2014: 43–6), WGmc. changes of long vowels in word-final syllables (ibid. pp. 58–60) and further changes in northern WGmc. (ibid.

pp. 152–4), the WGmc. replacement of the past indicative 2sg. form of strong verbs (ibid. pp. 67–9), and the northern WGmc. syncretism of plural finite verb forms under the form of the 3pl. (ibid. pp. 158–60)—all changes which were centuries in the past by the ninth century.

It also matters whether we are talking about adults well beyond the developmental window for NLA or young people for whom the window has not quite closed. In the case of adults, I think it might be significant that the late Dieter Kastovsky shared my skepticism regarding the mutual intelligibility of OE and ON (Kastovsky 1992: 328–9). He was especially concerned with inflectional morphology; moreover, he was a native speaker of a language (German) with significantly more inflectional morphology than modern English or any modern continental Scandinavian language. His statement (op. cit.) that native speakers of German can expect to understand no more than about half of a Dutch conversation strikes me as highly relevant.[6] I think it is worth asking whether not enough attention has been paid to the specific impact of inflection on communication in assessing potential mutual intelligibility between adults.

For adolescents and young teenagers the situation can be very different. Bettelou Los (personal communication), a native speaker of Dutch, reports that at the age of eleven she was able to learn to understand German broadcasts simply by listening to them for hours. Maria Bittner once demonstrated to a group of linguists that she had acquired an apparently native command of Greenlandic—a language with a very complex morphology, structured very differently from that of any European language—in spite of the fact that she first encountered the language at the age of thirteen.[7] But that is the sort of experience that gives rise to competent bilingualism, not to koiné formation.

Of course, it is also true that OE and ON shared many obvious cognates, especially in their basic vocabularies. Whether that made the languages similar enough to encourage some sort of compromise in which both sides participated is really the point at issue. I will suggest below that it should have had rather different consequences.

If northern late OE or early ME was neither a creole nor a koiné, how did the transfer of grammatical items from Norse to English occur? The

6. I unwittingly performed a similar experiment while still a teenager. I had learned to read OE, more or less, and attempted to read prose narratives in ON. My understanding was fragmentary at best. I recommend the experiment to any student who has learned OE but not (yet) ON. The reverse experiment should also be attempted, of course.

7. The occasion was a dinner after an invited talk at some point in the 1990s. Bittner discussed a Greenlandic affix whose function is pragmatic and quoted Greenlandic newspaper articles from memory.

appearance of ON functional items in ME resembles the appearance of ModE *about*, *back*, and similar prepositions and adverbs in PEI French (King 2000). As King has shown, they were borrowed into the local French dialect as a result of more than two centuries of unrelenting social and political pressure from English. But the influence of Norse on medieval English was clearly greater, since even basic 3rd-person pronouns were transferred from the one language to the other. The period in which Norse could have been politically dominant in the area of Scandinavian settlement extends at most from 865 (the year of the great invasion) to 954 (the year when Eric Bloodaxe was driven out of York), i.e. less than a century;[8] social dominance might have endured somewhat longer in outlying areas, but it seems clear that nothing like the PEI scenario is realistic for medieval England. It should be remembered that medieval Scandinavian society was relatively egalitarian, and there is no reason to believe that Scandinavians treated English people in their midst any differently from the way they treated each other.

On the other hand, the community-wide shift from Norse to English, which we know must have occurred, offers a plausible context for the transfer of Norse grammar and vocabulary into English (Townend 2002: 204–10). It is widely documented that most adults who must learn a foreign language learn it imperfectly, and a major source of imperfections is their inability to suppress the grammar of their native language, so that they import native grammar, including function words, into the nonnative language that they are trying to speak.

There might be further evidence for such a development; unfortunately, it involves the vexed question of the pres. indic. ending *-(e)s*. The data are clear enough. The OE paradigm of the present indicative in the Anglian and the southern dialects can be exemplified by *bindan* 'tie':

		Anglian	*West Saxon*
pres. ind. sg.	*1*	bindu	binde
	2	bindes	bintst
	3	bindeþ	bint
pl.		bindaþ	bindaþ

---

8. The later period during which England was governed by Svein Forkbeard, Cnut, and Cnut's sons (1013–42) is also often mentioned in this connection; but it seems clear that the eleventh-century Danish kings ruled England with and through English earls, and that no significant additional use of ON in England can be demonstrated. Whether those northern Englishmen of Scandinavian descent who were still speaking ON found that their language suddenly enjoyed greater prestige in England is probably unknowable, but that it might have been able to exert renewed social pressure on OE seems unlikely.

The ME situation around 1300 is surprisingly different. The southern dialects have undergone no sigificant morphological changes, but the Midlands and northern dialects have. Simplifying slightly, we can give the paradigms as:

		northern	Midlands	southern
pres. ind. sg.	1	bind	bīnde	bīnde
	2	bindes	bīndest	bintst
	3	bindes	bīndeþ	bint
pl.		bindes	bīnden	bīndeþ

The Midlands innovations will be discussed in Chapter 7; for the moment, we need to consider the northern forms. Obviously, OE -þ has been replaced by -s both in the 3sg. and in the pl. Probably the earliest attestation of -s for -þ in a verb ending occurs in the runic inscription on the Urswick Cross of Lancashire, which ends with the request *gebidæs þer saulæ* 'pray for the soul (of him)' (LWS *ġebiddaþ þǣre sāwle*; Page 1973: 150–1). Though it has traditionally been dated to the middle of the ninth century, there is no hard evidence, and, in fact, the unexpected *æ* for *a* in the ending suggests merger of unstressed vowels and therefore a later date (see the discussion in Kroch, Taylor, and Ringe 2000: 383–4 with references). *Lindisfarne* exhibits endings in -ð and in -s side by side. The replacement was not the result of a regular sound change, because nouns in -þ were never affected either in *Lindisfarne* (consistently *mōnað* 'month', *ġigoð* 'youth') or later (northern ME *mōneþ*, *ȝouþ*). That -s appeared first in the 2pl. by a combination of phonological dissimilation and levelling from the 2sg., as suggested by Blakely 1949, is highly implausible, among other reasons because OE had not distinguished person in the plural for centuries.[9] But the ending cannot have been imported straightforwardly from Norse either; cf. the corresponding ON paradigm:

		singular	plural
pres. ind.	1	bind	bindom
	2	bindr	bindeð
	3	bindr	binda

The suggestion that the identity of 2sg. and 3sg. in ON led to levelling in English does not help much, because if that was the motivation we should expect the 3sg. ending to have been levelled into the 2sg., not the other

---

9. Of course, ON did (see immediately below), so such a development could conceivably have occurred among speakers of Norse learning English; but there are more straightforward hypotheses involving Norse influence, as the following discussion shows.

way round.[10] That the ON reflexive clitic -sk might have been borrowed as an active ending (Samuels 1989: 112) is likewise implausible, given the great difference in function between the two. Perhaps the least unlikely explanation is that northern late OE and ME -s in verb endings reflects Scandinavian mispronunciation (Kroch, Taylor, and Ringe 2000: 378–80). In ON [θ] occurred only word-initially; in other positions inherited *þ had merged with the fricative allophone of *d as [ð]. The merger was already underway in Denmark in the sixth century and in Sweden in the eighth, to judge from confusion between the runic letters representing the inherited consonants (Noreen 1923: 162); it ought to have been complete by the middle of the ninth. No doubt some Scandinavians had no trouble reproducing OE word-final -þ [θ], but others could have found it difficult, and in that case they would have to choose between [ð] and [s] (the latter was voiceless in all positions in ON). This is not necessarily more surprising than the inability of most speakers of ModE to pronounce word-initial [ŋ] (e.g. in Vietnamese names). If that is what really happened, -s in these endings would be a "smoking gun" revealing imperfect adult learning, since native learners never fail to learn how to pronounce common grammatical endings. Unfortunately, proof is likely to remain elusive.

If we accept the likely explanation of adult language shift as the source of Norse function words in English, we have some further explaining to do. There must have been gifted language learners and competent bilinguals in the Danelaw, but the ON grammatical elements in ME cannot reflect their speech; they must reflect the speech of Scandinavians who learned OE much less well. Why should the bad English of Scandinavian settlers have become dominant in some areas? Moreover, the Scandinavianisms of adult speech cannot have been perpetuated unless they were learned natively by children. Under what circumstances could that have occurred?

The persistence of Scandinavianized English is explained in part by a perceptive observation of Matthew Townend (Townend 2002: 183; cf. also Thomason and Kaufman 1988: 303): because OE and ON shared so many basic words, it must have been possible in some situations for a speaker of ON to make himself understood in OE, even if his English grammar was haphazard and his speech was peppered with Norse function words. Such a situation could actually have militated *against* learning OE well, even if a speaker of ON had been able to do so: why go to all that trouble if you can make yourself understood anyway? Moreover, gifted language learners are fairly rare in any community, and there is no

10. Note also that the ON ending was almost certainly some sort of rhotic, not [z], by the time of the Scandinavian invasion, pace Samuels 1989: 111 with references.

obvious reason why they should also be community leaders; the faulty OE of the majority, probably including the leaders in many communities, was likely to win out.

But if there were significant numbers of English families surviving in any community, we might expect the children of Scandinavian settlers to have learned OE from English children, with the result that their parents' faulty OE would have left no linguistic descendants. If there was a critical mass even of OE-speaking adults in a community, the children of the Scandinavian settlers could have learned OE natively from them (as Los's experience, quoted above, shows). In Norfolk and in most of the Five Boroughs one or both of those things must have happened often, since the ME of those areas does not appear to have been "Scandinavianized". Scandinavianized English must instead have arisen in communities where English settlement was negligible by the time the shift from Norse to English occurred—or where the original English settlers had shifted to Norse completely at least two or three generations before—so that the children were constrained to learn their parents' Scandinavianized English. There must have been such settlements in the far northwest of England, where settlement was very sparse before Norwegians began to arrive in the tenth century, but there may also have been some in the thickly Scandinavian-settled areas of Yorkshire and even northern Lincolnshire (cf. Thomason and Kaufman 1988: 284, though their dialectal characterization of "Norsified English" needs a thorough review by ME dialect specialists).

When ON grammatical items were learned natively, their status was transformed: they were now simply English dialect peculiarities. Since mutually intelligible dialects can borrow virtually anything from one another, it is no surprise that some Norse items—most obviously *they* and its caseforms—spread into dialects which had never experienced any direct Norse influence. It must be true that the entire "package" of Scandinavianized grammar spread most easily to other communities where only Norse had previously been spoken (Thomason and Kaufman 1988: 285), but that amounts to a difference of degree, not of kind.

6.5 Other probable consequences of Norse-to-English language shift

Section 6.3 discussed the clearest linguistic consequences of the community-wide shift from ON to OE. There are some other characteristics of ME dialects that can also be attributed to that shift with varying degrees of plausibility.

Two recent pieces of scholarly work suggest further areas of grammar in which ON might have influenced OE through language shift. Warner 2017: 321–5, 338–45 examines in great detail the development of the distinctive OE inflection of class II weak presents, in which most endings were preceded by a syllabic *-i-* (see 3.1.3). It seems clear that that peculiarity was abandoned early in areas settled by Scandinavians but persisted much longer in the west Midlands and the south. What happened can be illustrated by a partial paradigm of OE *lofian* 'to praise' and its ON cognate *lofa* compared with the same verb in two ME dialects, the southwestern dialect on the left and the northeastern dialect of the *Orrmulum* on the right:[11]

	southwestern ME	Old English	Old Norse	Orrmulum
infin.	lovien	lofian	lofa	lofenn
pres. indic.				
1sg.	lovie	lofie	lofa	lofe
2sg.	lovest	lofast	lofar	lofesst
3sg.	loveþ	lofaþ	lofar	lofeþþ
3pl.	lovieþ	lofiaþ	lofa	lofenn
pres. subj.				
3sg.	lovie	lofie	lofe	lofe
3pl.	lovien	lofien	lofe	lofe(nn)
pres. iptv. sg.	love	lofa	lofa	loff

(Note that in late OE all the unstressed vowels merged in /ə/, usually written *e*, so that the inflection of class II weak presents became more or less identical to that of other regular verbs, modulo *-i-*; levelling on that basis explains the endinglessness of even old weak class II imperatives in the *Orrmulum* (Thüns 1909: 16).)

It is clear that the grammatical endings in the northeastern dialects, here exemplified by that of Orrm, are English, not Norse, but, like the ON endings, they have no *-i-* before them. They are approximately what an adult native speaker of ON might be expected to produce in trying to speak OE, and they appear as early as *Peterborough2*. Though finite forms of the present stem scarcely occur in that document, occasional infinitives show that the change is already underway: we find *uuerrien* 'to make war on' in the entry for 1135, but *äxen* 'to ask' (OE *āscian* ~ *āxian*), *polen* 'suffer, hold out (in a siege)' (OE *polian*), and *rīxan* 'reign' (OE *rīcsian*) in 1140. In later eastern Midlands, northwestern Midlands, and northern texts the change is virtually complete. Of course, it is not *impossible* that the endings of other regular verbs were simply levelled into class II weak

---

11. It is more usual to illustrate the OE paradigm with *lufian* 'to love', but that verb has no ON cognate.

presents, without any input from adult second-language learners of OE (as Warner admits); but the fact that the new system of inflection more closely resembles that of ON, together with the geographical correlation between the new system and the area of Scandinavian settlement, makes this a plausible case of ON interference.

Another plausible case for contact-induced change has been made by Millar 2000. He observes that whereas OE had a single functional item, the default determiner, used for both 'that' and the definite article, ON distinguished the two; and since the functional split between ModE *that* and *the* is first clearly attested in the heavily Scandinavianized *Orrmulum* and apparently spreads from north to south, it is reasonable to ascribe the split to contact with ON, among other factors (Millar 2000: 331–8, summarizing a long and complex discussion). Once again, it cannot be denied that such a change *could* have occurred spontaneously, as it did in Romance languages (for instance, Lat. masc. *ille*, fem. *illa* 'that' is the source of the Italian definite article *il*, *la*, but also of the demonstrative *quello*, *quella* 'that', compounded with the emphatic particle *ecco*). But again, the correlation of dialect geography and potentially ON grammar is reasonably persuasive, even if it is not clinching.

A third instance, though also plausible, is perhaps not quite as good. Kroch, Taylor, and Ringe 2000 show that whereas the more southwesterly dialects of early ME exhibit clausal word order that is obviously a direct continuation of the OE pattern, the more northeasterly dialects have a stricter V2 pattern like that of ON (cf. Walkden 2014: 68–9 with references). However, ON is adequately attested only from the twelfth century, and there is no guarantee that it was already strictly V2 in the ninth or tenth. There is some evidence that early OHG had a system like that of OE but became more strictly V2 later (Walkden 2014: 69–71 with references); such a development could have occurred independently in ON and/or northern ME, especially since a strict V2 system is simpler and easier to learn.

Other potential cases of Norse interference are still less easy to demonstrate. The previous two chapters have outlined some of the simplifications that English grammar underwent in the late OE and early ME periods, especially the loss of grammatical gender and of most of the case system; and since those simplifications apparently occurred first in the north and the northeast Midlands and spread from there to the southwest, bypassing the far southeast of the country, it would be natural to ascribe them to Norse-to-English language shift as well (a point explored at length by Warner 2017). However, a look at the details argues caution. We saw in Chapters 4 and 5 that the collapse of the concord system does not seem to have been identical in *Lindisfarne* and in the early ME documents: in the former the case system was not affected, while in the latter loss of gender and loss of case seemed to go together and the erosion of the case system might even have occurred first in some dialects. An attribution of all the simplifications to Norse-to-English shift would be more convincing if the effects of the shift were identical in all areas. Of course, they *need* not have been, but since they apparently were not, much more work will be required to give the hypothesis of interference a firm grounding in the facts—if relevant facts survive.

A further candidate for simplification through imperfect second-language acquisition is the streamlining of strong verb inflection in northern ME. OE strong verbs of the first five classes, with the exception of 'eat' and 'come', had two finite past stems, one for the pres. indic. 1&3sg. and another for all other forms (see 3.1.1, 3.1.2). In the southern and Midlands dialects that organization of strong verb stems persisted until late ME. In northern ME, by contrast, all strong verbs have only a single finite past stem; the simplification has already occurred by ca. 1300, when we first have northern documents long enough to give us adequate evidence. The pattern is so pervasive that it can be exemplified even by extracts of northern texts reproduced in handbooks. For instance, in the extracts from the *Cursor Mundi* (possibly composed before 1300) in Bennett and Smithers 1968 we find *quen þe flōd rās* 'when the flood rose', l. 289 (OE 3sg. *ārās*) beside *þār rās o þām thrē wandes yong* 'there rose from them three young shoots', l. 282 (OE pl. *ārison*); in the selections from Barbour's *Bruce* reproduced in Mossé 1952 we read *saw he* 'he saw', l. 457 (Anglian OE *hē sæh*) beside *thai saw* 'they saw', l. 473 (Anglian OE *hīe sēgon*), etc. But in this case the distribution of the new system does not coincide with the area of Scandinavian settlement; for instance, the northeast Midlands dialect of the *Orrmulum* is heavily Scandinavianized, yet the OE four-stem system of strong verbs persists unchanged. Once again examples are common enough to be exemplified by handbook extracts. The passages in Bennett and Smithers 1968 include *annd all þatt hīrde-flocc hemm sahh* 'and all the company (sg.!) of shepherds saw them', l. 103 beside *annd forrþrihht summ þeȝȝ sæȝhenn himm* 'and as soon as they saw him', l. 73, with the OE forms preserved except for the effects of sound change; other past indic. pl. forms in the selections include *þeȝȝ wurrden* 'they became', l. 74 (OE *hīe wurdon*), *whatt teȝȝ sūngenn* 'what they sang', ll. 104, 107 (OE *sungon*), *fundenn* '(they) found', l. 129 (OE *fundon*), etc. If contact with Norse is responsible for the northern simplification of the strong verb paradigm, why does Orrm's dialect, which provides our earliest examples of *they*, not exhibit the simplification?

The simplification of adjective inflection probably owes nothing to Norse interference. Except in the southeast, the strong inflection of adjectives is in rapid retreat already in early ME documents; the most plausible scenario for its obsolescence is that native learners had begun to use the weak inflection in all circumstances—an innovation plausibly not disfavored because the strong vs. weak distinction was functionless anyway, so that no confusion could result—and the (now universal) endings -e and -en were vulnerable to phonological erosion (see 4.3).

A pervasive problem besetting suggestions of Norse interference is that there is nothing specifically Norse about some of the simplifications; on the contrary, the structure of ON replicated that of OE point for point in many ways. Like OE, ON had three concord classes, or genders, and four cases, and their functions were very similar. ON strong verbs of the first five classes typically had two finite past stems, just like the corresponding OE verbs. The double inflection of OE adjectives was likewise replicated in ON. Any difficulty speakers of ON might have had in learning the OE system must have resulted from the fact that the details of the two systems were sometimes different. In those cases the argument for interference has to depend on the correlation between simplification and demonstrable Scandinavianization, which holds reasonably well for some simplifications, but not for all (cf. Fernández Cuesta and Rodríguez Ledesma 2007: 129–31). On the other hand, at the coarsest level of resolution, simplifying innovations appear to spread from the north and northeast to the southwest and south (with the southeast typically resisting to the last), and that is why the hypothesis of simplification as a result of contact is difficult to exclude (cf. Görlach 1986: 340–2 and especially Warner 2017).

The most general considerations also cut both ways. It must never be forgotten that, though adult non-native language learners make plenty of mistakes, so do native language learners (i.e. small children) in the first few years of NLA—and native-learner errors have a much better chance of becoming linguistic changes than non-native errors do. On the other hand, the evidence for extensive language shift from ON to OE in northeastern England is as good as could reasonably be expected for any period of the distant past, so that interference phenomena are much more likely in the relevant English dialects than in most other languages.

The discussion of these problems will probably go on forever, and given the limited facts at our disposal, it should.

Exercises

1. Recall that as the ON pronoun *they* spread through England the nominative (subject) form was usually borrowed first and the objective form last. Here are short passages from several fourteenth-century ME

documents. Arrange them in rough geographical order in light of that
pattern of borrowing.

a. He preyd . . . þat swych a veniaunce were on hem sent, / are þey
    oute of þat stede were went, / þat þey my3t ever ry3t so wende /
    unto þat tyme twelvemonth ende.
    'He prayed . . . that such a punishment might be visited on them,
    / before they left that place, / that they should keep going just like
    that / for a whole year.'

b. For joie þai wepe wiþ her ei3e / þat hem so sounde ycomen sei3e.
    'For joy they wept with their eyes / that saw them returned in such
    good health.'

c. Ofte hy sseaweþ and di3teþ ham þe more quainteliche and þe more
    honesteliche vor to maki musi þe foles to ham.
    'Often they display and adorn themselves all the more elegantly
    and respectably in order to make the fools marvel at them.'

d. Thai wrote all þe werkes wroght at þat tyme,
    in letturs of þere langage, as þai lernede hade:
    Dares and Dytes were duly þere namys.
    Dites full dere was dew to the Grekys,
    a lede of þat lond, and logede hom with.
    'They wrote all the works made at that time,
    in letters of their language, as they had learned:
    Dares and Dictys were their proper names.
    Right noble Dictys belonged to the Greeks,
    a person of that land, and dwelt with them.'

e. Þe nedy and þe naked, nymmeth hede how hii liggeth,
    and casteth hem clothes, for so comaundeth Treuthe.
    'The needy and the naked, take heed how they lie,
    and throw them clothes, for so commands Truth.'

f. The toune enveremyt thai in hy / and assalit with sa gud will— /
    for all thair mycht thai set thartill— / that thai thame pressit fast of
    the toune.
    'The town they surrounded in haste / and assailed with such good
    will— /
    for they put all their power into it— / that they pressed them of the
    town hard.'

g. And heere þe freris wiþ þer fautours seyn þat it is heresye to write
    þus Goddis lawe in English and make it knowun to lewid men.
    And fourty signes þat þey bringen for to shewe an heretik ben not
    worþy to reherse, for nou3t groundiþ hem but nygromansye.
    'And here the friars with their supporters say that it is heresy to
    write God's law in English like that and (so) make it known to

laymen. And (the) forty diagnostics that they adduce to identify a heretic are not worth rehearsing, for nothing underpins them but black magic.'

2. Here are fifty words still in common use in ModE that were unproblematically borrowed from French in the Middle Ages.[12] Choose any ten of them, look them up in the *Oxford English Dictionary (OED)* online, and find the first date of their attestation in English. (If there is more than one word so spelled, the parentheses after the word will indicate which item to consult.)

Note that in the *OED* "c" means "about" (Latin *circa*), while "a" means "before" (Latin *ante*). The most common meaning of the modern word might not be the first meaning attested; you should record the date of the word's first attestation in any meaning (usually in the first subsection of the article, but not always—you should scroll down to make sure). When you have completed your list of words and dates, read the discussion at the end of this exercise and consider how the words you chose fit into the larger pattern of French loanwords in English. If you are part of a class studying the history of English morphology, a group discussion might be useful and instructive; if you have divided the words among yourselves so as to get complete coverage, so much the better.

aunt	face (n)	pay (v1)
beef (n)	family	plate (n)
boil (v)	flower (n)	pocket (n)
boot (n3)	forest (n)	poison (n)
branch (n)	fruit (n)	poor (adj)
brush (n2)	fry (v)	price (n)
button (n)	fur (n)	push (v)
cattle	garden (n)	rent (n1)
chain (n)	grain (n1)	river (n)
chair (n1)	join (v1)	roast (v)
coat (n)	lake (n4)	rock (n1)
coin (n, meaning	money (n)	roll (v2)
II)	mountain (n)	save (v)
cousin (n)	move (v)	table (n)
dig (v)	oil (n1)	uncle (n)
dinner (n)	onion (n1)	valley (n)
easy (adj)	paint (v1)	wait (v1)

12. These were selected from the first twelve sections of Buck 1949, not a definitive etymological dictionary but a useful and reliable quick reference. I have tried to select only frequently used words with relatively basic meanings.

Some of the dates of first attestation given by the *OED* require comment. Normally the date of the manuscript is given; sometimes the inferred date of composition is given, introduced by a black wedge. Occasionally, this makes a difference. Both the *Brut* and the *Owl and the Nightingale* are dated c1275, but there is strong circumstantial evidence that they were composed before 1200; the date of *King Horn* is likewise probably much earlier than the manuscript of c1300. On the other hand, the *Ancrene Wisse* is probably not much earlier than the earliest manuscript of c1225 (see the discussion in 4.1.4). The overall picture is that twelfth-century loans are probably not quite as rare as the raw dates suggest, though they are still a small minority of the total. Two of the words appear to go back to OE but probably do not; in both cases it appears that the word was reborrowed in the period after the Conquest. *Rock* appears in OE only in the compound *stānrocc*, and only in early glossaries; there is then a gap until the thirteenth century, which is effectively proof of reborrowing. A similar pattern, though not quite as dramatic, appears with *table*. *Lake*, on the other hand, might have had a continuous history from late OE to the present, though the evidence is not quite conclusive.

How does the distribution of these words compare with the more comprehensive account of Durkin 2014: 258–63?

7 Middle English verb inflection

The ModE system of verb inflection, which is simpler than verb inflection in other European languages (except continental Scandinavian), took shape in the ME period. Some of the relevant changes were phonological; they will be mentioned only briefly here. The more important morphological changes are the subject of this chapter.

An excellent summary of ME verb inflection in detail can be found in Fulk 2012: 71–90; the fact that Fulk writes from an OE perspective, more or less, makes his discussion especially useful to a student of historical linguistics. All the points made below are further exemplified in Fulk's discussion.

7.1 The northern system

As we saw in 6.4, all the forms of the pres. indic. in the northern dialects had the ending *-es* except the 1sg., and, in fact, *-es* spread to the 1sg. variably as well. The subjunctive endings *-e* and *-en* were lost by sound change, both in the present and in the past. A single stem had been generalized in the past, and the endings 2sg. *-e* and pl. *-en* were likewise lost by sound change. The infinitive ending *-en* had been lost, but in the strong past participle *-en* survived, possibly first in forms in which it was followed by number-and-case endings, with early levelling into the endingless form. The present participle typically ended in *-and*. The stem formation of preterite-present verbs was also simplified, so that there was typically only a single present stem (cf., e.g., Mossé 1952: 82–3). Thus the northern ME verb system was similar to that of ModE, though the single past stem that had been generalized in strong verbs was not invariably the same one that survives in standard ModE.

7.2 The south and the Midlands: verb endings

In the dialects to the south the situation was very different. South of the Thames the OE system survived with little change into the fourteenth century. The southern ME paradigm of *vīnde(n)* 'find' will illustrate:

	present	*past active*	*past passive*
infinitive	vīnde(n)	—	
inflected inf.	vīndene	—	
participle	vīndinde, -inge	—	yvounde
indicative			
sg. 1	vīnde	vǭnd	
2	vintst	vounde	
3	vint	vǭnd	
pl.	vīndeþ	vounden	
subjunctive			
sg.	vīnde	vounde	
pl.	vīnden	vounden	
imperative			
sg.	vīnd	—	
pl.	vīndeþ	—	

These are the OE forms as affected by (mostly) regular sound changes (note that *ou* spells *ū* in ME). Only two changes of other kinds affected southern ME verbs. In the first place, OE i-umlaut in the syncopated forms of the pres. indic. was gradually eliminated. For instance, the pres. indic. 3sg. of OE *understandan* 'understand' was *understent*, but in the fourteenth-century Kentish *Ayenbite of Inwit* the corresponding form is *onderstant*; in place of Kentish OE *helt* 'holds' (Early West Saxon *hielt*, Late West Saxon *hylt*) we find *halt*, etc. Secondly, the Midlands forms with syllabic endings 2sg. *-est*, 3sg. *-eþ* (reflecting the Anglian OE paradigm) gradually spread into the south. The *Brut* is an early document from the southern area, which, for the purposes of verb inflection, includes the southwestern Midlands, but it shows both i-umlaut and syncopated endings already in retreat (Böhnke 1906: 3–6). In the "AB" dialect i-umlaut no longer operates in these forms, and contracted endings appear chiefly when the verb root ends in *t* or *d* (d'Ardenne 1961: 234–5); the same is true of the *Ayenbite*.

In one other point the southern dialects continued to be conservative. Recall that class II weak verbs had present-tense endings with an additional syllabic *-i-*, which were maintained in the southern dialects. Here are the present-stem paradigms of two weak verbs, *hēren* 'hear' and *ondswerien* 'answer', in the "AB" dialect (cf. d'Ardenne 1961: 234–5):

infinitive	hēren	ondswerien
participle	hērinde	ondsweriende
indicative		
sg. 1	hēre	ondswerie
2	hērest	ondswerest
3	hēreþ	ondswereþ
pl.	hēreþ	ondswerieþ
subjunctive		
sg., pl.	hēre, -en	ondswerie, -en
imperative sg.	hēr	ondswere

After a heavy syllable the sequence -*ie*- contracted to -*ī*-; thus the corresponding forms of 'look' (OE *lōcian*) were inf. *lōkīn*, ind. 1sg. *lōkī*, pl. *lōkīþ*, etc. The dialects of the north and the northeastern Midlands eliminated this distinction early, plausibly because of Norse interference (see 6.5).

The Midlands dialects exhibit an interesting levelling: the pres. indic. pl. ends in -*en* rather than in inherited -*eþ*. The source of the new ending is clear enough. The past indic. pl., pres. subj. pl., and past subj. pl. all already ended in -*en* (see above); the most economical hypothesis, either for a native learner or for a linguist, is that -*en* was the default plural ending, since the categories in which it occurred did not all share any feature or bundle of features except "plural".[1] Yet the present indicative—the default tense-and-mood category—did not exhibit the default plural ending. The change rectified that anomaly. The fact that in the preterite-present verbs, many of which occurred frequently, -*en* was already the plural ending in the pres. indic. probably gave added impetus to the change; for some native learners it could even have been a trigger for the change.[2] Surprisingly, the new ending did not spread to the plural of the imperative, which remained -*eþ* in the Midlands.

Roger Lass has observed an interesting pattern in the development of -*en*, which marked both the infinitive and the finite plural (except the iptv. pl.) in the Midlands dialects (Lass 1992: 97–8). In both categories the -*n* tended to be lost (and then the preceding schwa as well), but the loss was not the same across the categories. In Chaucer more than three-quarters of the plural forms end in -*en*, while the proportions of infinitives

---

1. The imperative pl. did end in -*eþ*, like the pres. indic. pl., but that clearly did not inhibit the change. Possibly the imperative was too marginal to the system to exert much influence on native learner perceptions and analyses.
2. A parallel change occurred in Middle High German; in that language the present indicative 3pl. -*ent* was replaced by default -*en* (Paul, Moser, and Schröbler 1969: 186).

in *-en* and in *-e* are more or less even. In the early fifteenth century the proportions of plural forms with and without *-n* have become more or less even, while three-quarters of the infinitives are now endingless. By late in the century infinitives are usually endingless, and most of the examples with *-n* are *be(e)n* 'be', but about a quarter of the plural forms (now mostly present plural, see below) still end in *-n*. It looks as though the rate of change in this period might be more or less the same, with loss of *-n* in the infinitive starting out ahead in the fourteenth century and staying ahead. That would be interesting in light of the constant rate hypothesis, proposed for various types of change by Anthony Kroch (Kroch 1989). A rigorous statistical analysis of the relevant data will be needed to resolve this question.

A puzzling development affected the present participle suffix in the south and the Midlands. Along the margins of the area—roughly in eastern Kent and Essex, the coast of Suffolk and Norfolk, Lincolnshire, Lancashire, and the counties bordering Wales—the OE ending survived, spelled *-ende* or *-inde*. In most of the area, however, we find *-inge* instead. This does not seem to be the result of a regular sound change; contamination with derived nouns in *-ing(e)* is the most likely explanation, but exactly how that occurred is not recoverable.

7.3 The south and the Midlands: stem formation of strong verbs

In one respect the Midlands were just as conservative as the south: the formation of past stems hardly changed at all before the fifteenth century; in particular, most strong verbs of the first five classes continued to exhibit both a default finite past stem and a special stem for the endingless past indic. 1&3sg. With the southern paradigm of 'find' given above compare the east Midlands paradigm:

	present	*past active*	*past passive*
infinitive	finde(n)	—	
inflected inf.	findene	—	
participle	findinge	—	(y)founde(n)
indicative			
sg. 1	finde	fǭnd	
2	findest	founde	
3	findeþ	fǭnd	
pl.	finde(n)	founde(n)	
subjunctive			
sg.	finde	founde	
pl.	finde(n)	founde(n)	

imperative

sg.	find	—
pl.	findeþ	—

(In the north, by contrast, all finite past forms of this verb are typically represented by the monosyllable *fand*.)

Exemplifying this pattern in any single document or group of documents is often a challenge, for an interesting reason. In any sufficiently large corpus (of any language) the frequencies of lexemes follow "Zipf's Law": the most frequent word is much more common than the next most frequent, which in turn is substantially more common than the third, etc. As you go down the list, with each lexeme less frequent than the last, the differences in frequency become less and less marked; if you plot numbers of examples on the vertical axis and list the lexemes by rank on the horizontal, the curve described by their frequencies falls very steeply at first, becomes progressively less steep, and eventually levels off in a very long tail of infrequent words (the vast majority). To collect enough examples of verbs to construct anything like a full paradigm, you need to concentrate on the most frequent verbs in a suitably large corpus. But unfortunately, the forms of a single verb's paradigm also obey Zipf's Law: in an English corpus, pres. and past 3sg. forms and past participles typically provide an actual majority of the examples, while some of the forms we might be most interested in, such as the past 2sg. and the imperative pl., are quite rare.[3] Circumventing these limitations requires a carefully constructed strategy such as the following.

I collected ModE strong verbs from among the most frequent 400 lexemes collected by Andrea Ceolin from the *Corpus of Contemporary American English* (*COCA*; Davies 2008–). Of the 18 or 19[4] verbs thus collected, 8 had never had two different finite past stems (namely, *become, come, grow, hold, know, let, stand*, and *take*). I looked for examples of the others in two reasonably large bodies of text by single authors from the end of the fourteenth century: namely, the Chaucer corpus and *Sir Gawain and the Green Knight*. For Chaucer there is an old concordance in the public domain (Tatlock and Kennedy 1927, reprinted 1963); it might not be accurate enough for statistical work but is more than adequate for simply finding verb forms. For *Sir Gawain* the glossary in the edition of Tolkien and Gordon is useful. Chaucer's extensive works yield plenty of material, and it turns out that *Sir Gawain* is just

---

3. See Kodner 2020: 42–8. I am grateful to Jordan Kodner for helpful discussion of this problem.
4. Though *lose* and *help* are not strong verbs in ModE, *helpen* was strong in early ME, and in usage *lose* largely continues ME *lēsen*, which was strong.

long enough to provide diagnostic examples of at least four relevant verbs.

Chaucer normally maintains the two-stem finite past system of these verbs. There are multiple examples of *hē fǫnd* and of *they founde(n)*, and 2sg. *thou founde* occurs at *Troilus and Criseyde* III.362; both 3sg. *bigan* and pl. *bigonne(n)* are frequent, as are 3sg. *ran* and pl. *ronne(n)*; 3sg. 'saw' is variously *saugh* and *seigh*, but cf. pl. *sawe they* (*Man of Law's Tale* 218), *thy blisful eyen sawe* (ibid. l. 845), and 2sg. *thow sawe* (ibid. l. 848); 3sg. *spak* but pl. *spēke(n)*, etc. However, it seems that Chaucer must also have been at least somewhat familiar with a dialect that exhibited only one finite past stem (the northern pattern), since we occasionally find such forms as *they saugh* (*Friar's Tale* 1539) and *thou spak* (*Pardoner's Tale* 753). We even find the more conservative and less conservative systems exemplified together at least once:

> *and whan that they him fǫnd in this array,*
> *they bounde him fast and putten out his ÿen.* (*Monk's Tale* 3259–60)

This suggests that there was already variation between the older and newer systems in the London English of Chaucer's generation (unless, of course, the newer forms were introduced into the text by fifteenth-century scribes).

Sir Gawain, from the opposite end of the Midlands area, naturally provides less material, but enough to show that the author's verb system, like Chaucer's, was on the cusp of change—and in this case scribal corruption is unlikely. We read *hē þat wan* 'he who won' (l. 70), *hē wan* 'he got' (l. 2231), pl. *þay hym wonnen* 'they conveyed him' (l. 831); *Gawan, þat sate bi þe quene* (l. 339), pl. *sēte(n)* (5x). But beside *hē fonde* (ll. 694, 716), pl. *þay founden* (l. 1704), we also find *þay fonde* (l. 1329) and subjunctive sg. *þēr hē hit eft fonde* 'where he could find it again' (l. 1875); pl. *runnen* (ll. 66, 1703), but also *vncoupled among þo þornes / racheʒ þat ran on race* '(they) uncoupled among those thorns / hounds that ran headlong' (ll. 1419–20).

In the fifteenth century this simplification went to completion. That century is the period in which London English, and the dialects of the eastern Midlands generally, begin to dominate the written record, so that we are constrained (for the most part) to observe what happened in those dialects. But the story which the record tells is both clear and interesting. Texts long enough to furnish adequate material include the *Book of Margery Kempe*, John Capgrave's *Abbreviation of Chronicles*, and the works of Thomas Malory. By chance, Kempe, who was born about 1373, and Capgrave, born in 1393, both came from Lynn in northwestern Norfolk; Capgrave's work survives in what appears to be an autograph manuscript of 1462 or 1463, while the lone manuscript copy of Kempe's spiritual autobiography was apparently written by a scribe from northern Norfolk in the 1440s.[5] Malory is most plausibly identified with a knight of Newbold Revell in Warwickshire, who was born in or a little after 1410, served in the Earl of Warwick's armies in the Wars of the Roses, and apparently pursued a life of violent crime. His Arthurian romances seem to have been written in prison shortly before his death early in 1471 (Vinaver 1971: v–vi); they were published by Caxton in 1485, but a better text also survives in a manuscript of about the same date (ibid. pp. ix–x).

Though Kempe was born thirty years or more after Chaucer and lived some 140 km (88 miles) to the north, the verb system of her book is organized much like the famous poet's, though of course there are differences of detail. An extensive list of forms, more or less exhaustive for strong, preterite-present, and irregular verbs, can be found in Meech and Allen 1940: xxvii–xxxi; examples can be found easily by searching the selections from *Kempe* in the *Penn–Helsinki Parsed Corpus of Middle English (PPCME2)* (Kroch and Taylor 2000). For many verbs we are not able to construct full paradigms, but when we can we usually find two finite past stems for strong verbs of the first five classes, just as in Chaucer. However, also as in Chaucer, there are levellings in both directions. For instance, the finite past 3sg. of *abyde(n)*[6] 'abide, stay' is *abood* (*& sche abood not so long in Rome*, Meech and Allen 1940: 94), while the plural varies between inherited *abedyn*[7] (*& so þei abedyn þer xiiij days in þat lond*, ibid. p. 110) and *abood* (*The pilgrimys þei . . . durst no lengar abydyn in Leycytyr but went x myle thens & abood þer . . .*, ibid. p. 114). Conversely, while the past plural of *breke* is *brokyn* (*for þei sworyn gret othys & brokyn þe comaundment of owr Lord God*, ibid. p. 101), the singular varies between inherited *brakke* (*þat hir thowt hir bakke brakke a-sundyr* 'so that it seemed to her that her back broke in two', ibid. p. 21) and levelled *broke* (*in-to þe tyme þat it broke owte*, ibid. p. 69), the modern standard form. There are also innovations of other kinds. Though inherited *halpe*, pl. *holpyn* survive in Kempe, we also find *helpyd*, the weak past that would eventually prevail in this verb's conjugation. The most interesting innovation is 2sg. *fondist*, e.g.

---

5. Students who are interested in medieval languages and literature are strongly advised to read Meech and Allen 1940: vii–xi, xxxii–xxxviii, xliv–xlv, which describe and analyze in detail the very diverse pieces of evidence that allow us to make reasonably certain statements about the *Book of Margery Kempe*. Of course, we are seldom so lucky; in this case we have evidence of almost every kind that we could have.

6. The infinitive ending in this document is variously spelled *-yn*, *-en*, *-e*, and zero.

7. Inherited short *i* is very often spelled *e* in *Kempe*.

. . . & perfor mystrost me not. Þu fondist me nevyr deceyvabyl . . .
'therefore do not mistrust me. You have never found me deceptive . . .' (ibid.
p. 76)

Since the past pl. of *fynde* is *fowndyn*, we might expect to find **fownd(e)*
as the 2sg.; the form we actually find is evidently 1&3sg. *fond* (i.e. *fǫnd*,
< OE *fand*) plus the weak past indic. 2sg. ending *-est*.

Not surprisingly, the situation in Capgrave's *Chronicles* is similar. For
instance, *began* with a sg. subject is common, and in the excerpts in the
PPCME2 there are two examples of pl. *begun(ne)* (e.g. *Sone aftir þe feest
þei went to Londoun and þere begunne a parlement*, Lucas 1983: 153). But
there are also two examples of pl. *began* (*In þis ȝere began at Rome to regne
to emperoures*, ibid. p. 53; *In þese dayes began þe too ordres of Prechoures
and of Menowres*, ibid. p. 113). The fact that in both the latter cases the
subject follows might seem to show that in such clauses the verb defaults
to the sg. form, but the examples of the finite past of *fynde* show that the
use of the old sg. form was more general than that. Though there are four
instances of inherited pl. *founde* in the *PPCME2*'s selections (e.g. *Whan it
was ondo, þei founde a grete tabard of wrecchid cloth*, ibid. p. 140), there are
more instances of sg. *fond* used with a pl. subject, some with the subject
preceding (e.g. *Whan þat was reysid þei fond a oþer lich it, and þan þe þirde*
'When that one was raised they found another like it, and then the third',
ibid. p. 73).

In Malory the simplification of strong past inflection has gone much
further. In the *PPCME2* excerpts the past of *begin* is always *began*, no
matter what the subject is, and though *fond* occurs only with a sg. subject
in those passages (*I fond nobody at home*, Vinaver 1971: 8; *and told the
knyghte how he fond her*, ibid. p. 55), *found(e)* occurs with subjects of both
numbers (*The meanwhyle com in kyng Arthure with an egir countenans
and founde Ulphuns and Brastias on foote*, ibid. p. 19; *the beste that ever y
founde*, ibid. p. 39; *and in a chirch they founde one*, ibid. p. 45; *Found ye
ony knyghtes about this swerd?*, ibid. p. 8). In fact, perusal of Kato 1974,
a complete concordance of Malory's works, shows that for every strong
verb there is an overwhelming preponderance of one finite past stem
with all subjects, the majority stem typically occurring dozens of times
while the alternative occurs only once or only a few times. Thus *began(ne)*
occurs more than a hundred times, finite *begon* only once; *founde* well
over 200 times, *fond* only four times, etc.

It is difficult to know what to make of these patterns of variation.
Taylor 1994 investigates variation between strong and weak past stems
for individual verbs—a different variation, to be sure, but likely to exhibit
many of the same patterns—and finds that in the fifteenth-century *Paston*

Letters there was almost no variation at all (Taylor 1994: 146). That shows that at least some individuals exhibited very little variation in past tense stem formation, and it follows that individual variation cannot simply be a general default hypothesis. For Capgrave's autograph manuscript written in prose it is a likely hypothesis (though he might have adopted non-native forms from his sources if he did not find them jarring); for *Kempe* and *Sir Gawain*, each transcribed by a copyist who spoke the author's dialect not long after the composition of the work, it is reasonably likely (especially since most of *Sir Gawain* is not rhymed). For Chaucer it is not likely at all, given the artistry of his verse, as Taylor emphasizes (op. cit.). The variation in Malory is as lopsided as in the *Paston Letters*, suggesting that there was no variation in his speech, and that anomalous forms either are errors or were introduced by a copyist.

By the generation of Sir Thomas More (born 1478) the simplification was complete: for instance, in his *History of Richard III* the past of *fynde* is always *found(e)*, regardless of subject.

7.4 Weak verbs

The most important ME development in weak verb inflection was the gradual relegation of (the descendants of) OE weak class I to "irregular" status as the default weak class II steadily gained membership and began to dominate the lexicon. Up until some time in the fourteenth century, the important distinction between the two classes was that the default class had finite past stems in *-ede*, with a vowel between the root and the past tense suffix, while weak class I did not. But the consonant clusters in weak class I past stems triggered various changes in the vowels of their verb roots, especially shortening, so that there was often also a difference in root vocalism between a class I weak present and its past. No such changes affected any weak class II forms. Thus by 1400 OE *hȳdan, hȳdde* had become *hīde(n), hidde*; OE *cēpan, cēpte* had become *kēpe(n), kepte*; OE *lǣdan, lǣdde* had become *lę̄den, ladde* and was being adjusted to *lę̄de(n), ledde*, etc.

Beginning early in the fourteenth century in London English, but earlier in the north, the fully unstressed vowel schwa /ə/ began to be lost, variably at first, in various environments by regular sound change. Lass 1992: 128–30 discusses the (messy) evidence for the progress of this change in our texts and its impact on weak verb inflection. Once the loss was more or less complete, the only remaining reflex of OE weak class I inflection was the vowel alternation, if any, in the root syllable of the verb; thus ModE *keep, kept*, with an alternation, reflects OE weak class I *cēpan, cēpte*, while *hope, hoped*, with no alternation, reflects OE weak class II *hopian, hopode*. But there was also a fairly steady leakage of class I weak verbs into class II, beginning already in OE (Lass 1992: 128), so individual ModE verbs do not always reveal their original class by their pattern of inflection.

7.5 Minor classes of verbs

As might be expected, the maximally irregular *be, do, go*, and *will* maintain many of their OE irregularities in ModE simply because they are very common and are learned early in NLA; Lass 1992: 139–43 gives a good summary of their development. The most interesting change was the replacement of early ME *yēde ~ yōde* by *wente*, originally the past of *wendan* 'turn'. The earliest citation of the latter in the *OED* is actually in Chaucer, for whom it is the most usual past of this verb (ibid. p. 143), but many much earlier examples occur in the selections in Bennett and Smithers 1968. The problem is that the ME present *wende(n)* can also mean 'go', so that we have a case of verbs in competition; only when *yēde ~ yōde* is no longer usual, as in Chaucer, can we say for certain that it has been replaced by *wente*, yielding a different suppletion for the most basic verb. The inherited past remained in competition for a long time, even in the north; for instance, the *OED* cites *ȝoid* from Gavin Douglas's late fifteenth-century Scots adaptation of the *Aeneid*. An attempt to pin down the facts in greater detail might be interesting, though there is no guarantee that the material is sufficient to yield firm conclusions.

Good summaries of the ME forms of preterite-present verbs can be found in Mossé 1952: 82–3 and Fulk 2012: 86–7. By far the most important thing about them is that several of them (as well as *wille(n)*) developed into ModE modals, while the rest were eventually lost. Warner 1993 is the most detailed and informative treatment of the history of these verbs. He establishes that many of them already shared some syntactic features in OE (Warner 1993: 110–34), but also that the class seems to split morphologically in ME, with *schal* 'owes; ought to; shall' and *mōt* 'is allowed to; is obliged to' exhibiting no nonfinite forms, like ModE modals, while the remainder have at least infinitives, even if they did not in OE (ibid. pp. 144–8). The development of (most of) this class of verbs into true modals occurred only later, in the decades around 1500 (Warner 1993: 198–206); for our purposes the most important development was the loss of nonfinite forms of most of these verbs, and of *will*.

7.6 The trajectory of change

Taylor 1994: 150–2 observes that a large majority of the shifts of strong verbs into the default weak class occurred in the thirteenth through fifteenth centuries. Changes of inflection within the strong verb system are spread over roughly the same time period, though earlier in the north and skewed toward the end of the period further south. Taylor also observes (p. 155) that the appearance of new Scandinavian loanwords in ME texts peaks within the same period (see the chart in Durkin 2014: 43, which locates the peak more precisely in the thirteenth century). That might seem to suggest that the inflectional changes, like the loanwords, are ultimately the result of language contact—though as Taylor points out (p. 154), the long delay between the Scandinavian settlement and the phenomena under discussion has yet to be satisfactorily explained. Krygier 1994: 250–2 seems confident that contact with French led to the shift of many verbs into the default weak class, but as we have seen, the known demographics of early ME make such a hypothesis very unlikely.

It seems fair to say that the jury on the causes of these changes is still out; a much more comprehensive study will be needed to establish any hypothesis about changes in ME verb inflection. Among the questions that need to be asked are: how much of the pattern is an artefact of which documents survive from which dialect areas at which dates? How can we explain the apparent time lag in the appearance of Scandinavian loanwords in written English? Will the same explanation work for the late appearance of simplifications in verb morphology? Do population densities and population movements have anything to do with it? The first task, of course, is to assemble the data in finer detail than has ever been attempted before. I hope that at least some students who are reading this book will be among those that answer these and other relevant questions.

Exercise

Many OE strong verbs simply fail to survive. That is not surprising: lexical replacement is one of the universal types of language change, and strong verbs have no special status as lexemes. Of those that do survive, some remain strong (though in some cases the inherited classes have morphed into new classes), while others have become weak verbs (default or otherwise).

The following is a list of OE strong verbs that survive more or less straightforwardly in ModE (sometimes only as literary archaisms), regardless of whether they are still strong in ModE. I have omitted those whose development was complex and tangled, such as *forlēosan* 'lose' and *hōn* 'hang'. On the other hand, I have included *tacan* 'take', an ON loanword which appears at the end of the OE period, and three verbs whose shapes have been at least influenced by ON: *cuman*, whose ModE past *came* is Norse in form, and *ġiefan* and *beġietan*, whose ModE representatives *give* and *get* owe at least their initial stop /g-/ to ON. The ModE descendant of the OE verb is usually its translation, or among its translations; where that is not the case, the ModE descendant has been added in parentheses.

Do the following with the verbs in this list. First determine how the finite past and participle of each are formed in ModE; in most cases that should be easy if you are a fluent speaker, though in a few cases the forms you use might be different from those of other speakers. Then consider how each subclass of OE verbs has developed *as a class* in ModE. Make as many generalizations as you can and attempt to state an overall pattern. There is more than one way to divide the OE strong classes into sub-classes; if you prefer a different classification, and especially if a different classification makes it possible to posit a more coherent pattern of development, say what classification you prefer and what its advantages are.

Class I.
>*ābīdan, ābād, ābidon, ābiden* 'wait (for)' (*abide*)
>*bītan, bāt, biton, biten* 'bite'
>*drīfan, drāf, drifon, drifen* 'drive'
>*glīdan, glād, glidon, gliden* 'glide'
>*grīpan, grāp, gripon, gripen* 'seize' (*gripe*)
>*rīdan, rād, ridon, riden* 'ride'
>*rīsan, rās, rison, risen* 'rise'
>*sċīnan, sċān, sċinon, sċinen* 'shine'
>*slīdan, slād, slidon, sliden* 'slide'
>*smītan, smāt, smiton, smiten* 'daub, smear' (*smite*)
>*spīwan, spāw, spiwon, spiwen* 'spit' (*spew*)
>*strīcan, strāc, stricon, striċen* 'stroke' (*strike*)
>*wrītan, wrāt, writon, writen* 'write'
>*wrīþan, wrāþ, wripon, wripen* 'wrap' (*writhe*)

Class IIa.
>*brēowan, brēaw, bruwon, browen* 'brew'
>*ċēosan, ċēas, curon, coren* 'choose'
>*ċēowan, ċēaw, cuwon, cowen* 'chew'
>*crēopan, crēap, crupon, cropen* 'crawl, creep'
>*flēogan, flēag, flugon, flogen* 'fly'
>*flēon, flēah, flugon, flogen* 'flee'
>*frēosan, frēas, fruron, froren* 'freeze'
>*hrēowan, hrēaw, —, —* 'regret' (*rue*)

lēogan, lēag, lugon, logen 'lie, tell a lie'
rēocan, rēac, rucon, rocen 'smoke, reek'
sċēotan, sċēat, sċuton, sċoten 'shoot'
sēopan, sēap, sudon, soden 'boil, seethe'

Class IIb.

būgan, bēag, bugon, bogen 'bend, turn' (*bow* /baʊ/)
sċūfan, sċēaf, sċufon, sċofen 'push, shove'
sūcan, sēac, sucon, socen 'suck'
sūpan, sēap, supon, sopen 'swallow, gulp' (*sup*)

Class IIIa.

bindan, band, bundon, bunden 'tie, bind'
climban, clamb, clumbon, clumben 'climb'
clingan, clang, clungon, clungen 'stick together' (*cling*)
drincan, dranc, druncon, druncen 'drink'
findan, fand, fundon, funden 'find'
beġinnan, begann, begunnon, begunnen 'begin'
grindan, grand, grundon, grunden 'grind'
sċrincan, sċranc, sċruncon, sċruncen 'shrink'
sincan, sanc, suncon, suncen 'sink'
singan, sang, sungon, sungen 'sing'
slincan, slanc, sluncon, sluncen 'slink'
spinnan, spann, spunnon, spunnen 'spin'
springan, sprang, sprungon, sprungen 'jump, burst forth' (*spring*)
stincan, stanc, stuncon, stuncen 'smell (intr.)' (*stink*)
stingan, stang, stungon, stungen 'stab' (*sting*)
swimman, swamm, swummon, swummen 'swim'
swingan, swang, swungon, swungen 'beat' (*swing*)
windan, wand, wundon, wunden 'wind, wrap'
winnan, wann, wunnon, wunnen 'struggle' (*win*)
wringan, wrang, wrungon, wrungen 'twist, wring'
birnan, barn, burnon, burnen 'burn (intr.)'
irnan, arn, urnon, urnen 'run'

Class IIIb.

beorcan, bearc, burcon, borcen 'bark'
ċeorfan, ċearf, curfon, corfen 'cut, carve'
feohtan, feaht, fuhton, fohten 'fight'
steorfan, stearf, sturfon, storfen 'die' (*starve*)
weorpan, wearp, wurpon, worpen 'throw' (*warp*)
delfan, dealf, dulfon, dolfen 'dig' (*delve*)
helpan, healp, hulpon, holpen 'help'
melcan, mealc, mulcon, molcen 'milk'
meltan, mealt, multon, molten 'melt, burn up'

swelgan, swealg, swulgon, swolgen 'swallow'
swellan, sweall, swullon, swollen 'swell'
ġieldan, ġeald, guldon, golden 'pay' (*yield*)
ġiellan, ġeall, gullon, gollen 'shout, yell'
ġielpan, ġealp, gulpon, golpen 'boast' (*yelp*)

Class IIIc.

breġdan, bræġd, brugdon, brogden 'brandish' (*braid*)
berstan, bærst, burston, borsten 'burst'
perscan, pærsċ, purscon, porsċen 'thresh'

Class IIId.

spurnan, spearn, spurnon, spurnen 'kick, reject' (*spurn*)
murnan, mearn, murnon, — 'mourn'

Class IV.

brecan, bræc, bræcon, brocen 'break'
beran, bær, bæron, boren 'carry, bear'
teran, tær, tæron, toren 'tear'
sċieran, sċear, sċēaron, sċoren 'cut, shear'
stelan, stæl, stælon, stolen 'steal'

Class IV, irreg.

cuman, cōm, cōmon, cumen 'come' (crossed with ON *koma*)

Class V.

cnedan, cnæd, cnædon, cneden 'knead'
metan, mæt, mæton, meten 'measure' (*mete*)
specan, spæc, spæcon, specen 'speak, talk'
tredan, træd, trædon, treden 'walk (on), tread'
wefan, wæf, wæfon, wefen 'weave'
wegan, wæġ, wægon, weġen 'move, carry, weigh'
wrecan, wræc, wræcon, wrecen 'drive (out), avenge' (*wreak*)
ġiefan, ġeaf, ġēafon, ġiefen 'give' (crossed with ON *gefa*)
beġietan, beġeat, beġēaton, beġieten 'get' (crossed with ON *geta*)

Class V, irreg.

etan, æt, æton, eten 'eat'
sēon, seah, sāwon, sewen 'see'

Class V, j-presents.

biddan, bæd, bædon, beden 'ask (for)' (*bid*)
liċġan, læġ, lægon, leġen 'lie (down)'
sittan, sæt, sæton, seten 'sit'

Class VI.

bacan, bōc, bōcon, bacen 'bake'
dragan, drōg, drōgon, — 'pull, draw'
faran, fōr, fōron, faren 'go, travel' (*fare*)
gnagan, gnōg, gnōgon, gnagen ~ gnæġen 'gnaw'

grafan, grōf, grōfon, grafen 'dig' (*grave*)
hladan, hlōd, hlōdon, hladen 'load' (*lade*)
forsacan, forsōc, forsōcon, forsacen 'reject, give up' (*forsake*)
sċacan, sċōc, sċōcon, sċacen 'shake'
sċafan, sċōf, sċōfon, sċafen 'shave'
tacan, tōc, tōcon, tacen 'take' (ON loan)
wadan, wōd, wōdon, waden 'walk, wade'
wascan, wōsċ, wōscon, wasċen 'wash'

Class VI, contracted.

flēan, flōg, flōgon, flagen ~ flæġen 'skin, flay'
slēan, slōg, slōgon, slagen ~ slæġen 'hit, kill' (*slay*)

Class VI, j-presents, all more or less irreg.

swerian, swōr, swōron, sworen 'swear'
hebban, hōf, hōfon, hafen ~ hæfen 'lift' (*heave*)
sċieppan, sċōp, sċōpon, sċapen 'create, make' (*shape*)
hliehhan, hlōg, hlōgon, —— 'laugh'
stæppan, stōp, stōpon, stapen 'step'

Class VI, irreg.

standan, stōd, stōdon, standen 'stand'

Class VIIa.

lǣtan, lēt, lēton, lǣten 'let (go), allow'
rǣdan, rēd, rēdon, rǣden 'advise, read'
ondrǣdan, ondrēd, ondrēdon, ondrǣden 'dread'
slǣpan, slēp, slēpon, slǣpen 'sleep'

Class VIIb.

fealdan, fēold, fēoldon, fealden 'fold'
healdan, hēold, hēoldon, healden 'hold'
feallan, fēoll, fēollon, feallen 'fall'
sealtan, sēolt, sēolton, sealten 'salt'
wealcan, wēolc, wēolcon, wealcen 'roll' (*walk*)
weaxan, wēox, wēoxon, weaxen 'grow' (*wax*)
blāwan, blēow, blēowon, blāwen 'blow'
cnāwan, cnēow, cnēowon, cnāwen 'recognize, know'
crāwan, crēow, crēowon, crāwen 'crow'
māwan, mēow, mēowon, māwen 'mow'
sāwan, sēow, sēowon, sāwen 'sow'
þrāwan, þrēow, þrēowon, þrāwen 'turn, twist' (*throw*)
bēatan, bēot, bēoton, bēaten 'beat'
hlēapan, hlēop, hlēopon, hlēapen 'leap'
hēawan, hēow, hēowon, hēawen 'chop, cut down' (*hew*)
flōwan, flēow, flēowon, flōwen 'flow'
glōwan, glēow, glēowon, glōwen 'glow'

grōwan, grēow, grēowon, grōwen 'grow'
hlōwan, hlēow, hlēowon, hlōwen 'moo, low'
rōwan, rēow, rēowon, rōwen 'row'

Class VIIb, j-present.

wēpan, wēop, wēopon, wōpen 'weep, cry'

8 Toward Modern English

By about 1500 English inflection had settled into its modern pattern, for the most part; that is clear from the invaluable summary of Görlach 1991: 79–94. The prose of Sir Thomas More and the verse of Sir Thomas Wyatt, produced between 1510 and 1540, are even more immediately intelligible to the modern educated reader than Malory's narratives; the unfamiliar details are mostly lexical. This chapter will discuss a number of notable developments of detail that occurred between the sixteenth and twentieth centuries inclusive; section 8.2.1 will reach back into ME, but most of the development that it outlines occurred in Early Modern English (EModE), between ca. 1500 and 1700. Fuller information on virtually every topic (and several not treated here) can be found in Lass 1999.

8.1 Early Modern English verb inflection

8.1.1 The past tenses of irregular verbs

As we saw in the previous chapter, by about 1500 all strong verbs had evolved single finite past stems. However, the finite past stem was not the same for every verb in every dialect; most notably, strong verbs which have /æ/ in the finite past in standard ModE had /ʊ/ (> /ʌ/) in some dialects, and occasionally vice versa (Lass 1999: 166–75). For instance, though the finite past of *begin* is usually *began* in EModE, the *PPCEME* (Kroch, Santorini, and Delfs 2004) gives at least one example of finite *begun* from quite late in the period:

> . . . *those of our friends of the House of Commons that were in Town, and that were the most zealous with us in setting up Sir Peter King, begun to press us to accommodate the matter and not to make division,* . . .
> (SPENCER-1700-E3-P2,2.4,257.29, letter of the Earl of Sunderland to the Duke of Newcastle, November 4, 1708)

In some cases the proportions of competing finite past tenses are more nearly equal; for instance, in the *PPCEME* there are 12 examples of *sang* and 12 of finite *sung* by my count. Most remarkably, in the excerpts from the diary of Samuel Pepys, written by a single Londoner over about a decade (the 1660s), there are two of each (Ringe and Yang, forthcoming). It appears that a competition between finite past tenses of some strong verbs existed not only in English overall and in the speech community of London, but even (for some verbs) in the speech of some individuals. By the early eighteenth century the competition was largely over in standard ModE, but nonstandard alternatives survive to this day in areas of the English-speaking world relatively insulated from cosmopolitan speech. Jean Ritchie of Perry County, Kentucky (1922–2015), in her rendition of *Little Musgrave* (Childe ballad no. 81), sings:

> *Then he cast off his hose and shoes, set down his feet and he run,*
> *and where the bridges were broken down he smote his breast and he swum.*

Yet in the preceding stanza she also uses *ran* (to rhyme with *man*, so Ritchie's use of the standard form might be forced).

The survival of finite *sung*, *sprung*, and *rung* throughout the seventeenth century, even in standard English, might have had an interesting consequence for English verb inflection, as argued in Ringe and Yang, forthcoming. Within the sixteenth century regular *stringed* was replaced by irregular *strung*, and *sticked* was replaced by *stuck*; in the following century *digged* was replaced by *dug*. The first of those "irregularizations", at least, is not surprising if Yang's "tolerance principle" (TP) hypothesis is correct. Though full discussion is beyond the scope of this book, the idea behind the TP is simple enough. Native learners (i.e. small children) are not presented with full paradigms of verbs in the adult speech that they hear, because of the Zipfian distribution of forms (Kodner 2020: 42–8); they need to infer which they have not heard. One might expect that, for each lexical class of verbs that a three- or four-year-old might posit, the majority inflection, or even the plurality inflection, would be generalized; for instance, since roughly half the ModE verbs in *-ing* have finite pasts in *-ung*, while the other classes are small (only *ring*, *sing*, *spring* with pasts in *-ang*; only *brought*; and regular pasts like *winged* are few and heard extremely seldom), we might expect to find *brung* and *sung*, for instance, catching on as finite pasts in standard ModE. That is not happening; apparently, a supermajority is needed to trigger such a development, and Yang 2016 proposes a formula for defining such a supermajority. It turns out that in the sixteenth century, when finite *rung*, *sung*, and *sprung* were still common, pasts in *-ung* to verbs in *-ing* did have a supermajority, so that the creation of *strung* is actually unremarkable. *Stuck* must have arisen by another process (see Ringe and Yang, forthcoming, for details); but once *stuck* and *struck* (replacing *stroke*, also by a complex and messy process) were in common use, the replacement of *digged* by *dug* can also be explained by the TP. It seems clear that the TP can be useful in explaining the occurrence of unexpected innovations in inflection, though it also seems clear that other processes, especially lexical analogy, are involved too.

In 3.1.6 there is a table of OE verb classes arranged by size. Here is a comparable table for ModE. Modals have been omitted, since they are no longer full verbs syntactically; so are regular verbs with strong past participles, which are now usually optional. All other irregular verbs are included, including the classes that reflect OE weak class I.

ModE verb subclasses by size	*no. of classes*	*no. of verbs*
uniquely inflected verbs	32	32
pairs of identically inflected verbs	10	20
membership 3–6	7	32
membership 7–9	3	24
membership 11–19	3	42
membership very large	1	very numerous

(The raw material for this table is given in the Exercise. Note that many partially similar unique verbs, pairs, and small classes are lumped together in the Exercise.) The number of classes is smaller than in OE, the average membership of the small classes is smaller, and there are fewer unique verbs (though if modals, *ought*, and verbs with optional strong past participles had been included, the number of uniquely inflected verbs would be 43, not many fewer than the 47 of OE). Though ModE still has many more irregular verbs than, say, Spanish, the system as a whole is less elaborate than it was in OE.

8.1.2 Pres. indic. 3sg. -eth and -s

Early in the fourteenth century pres. indic. 3sg. *-(e)s* was restricted to the north and the northern Midlands, roughly north of a line running from Chester to Lichfield to Nottingham to the northwestern corner of Norfolk on the southern shore of the Wash (see the map in Moore, Meech and Whitehall 1935). That distribution probably already reflected some spread from the area in which the ending must have arisen. Subsequently *-(e)s* continued to spread southward at the expense of inherited *-(e)th*. The course of that spread is difficult to chart, because the northern ending was resisted in southern English writing; Sir Thomas Wyatt, writing between about 1520 and 1542, still uses -eth consistently,[1] and "-th seems to have been written long after it stopped being said" (Lass 1999: 163). In fact, even Rudyard Kipling (1865–1936) is capable of using -th in order to get a rhyme, e.g. in his jingle about the mongoose and the cobra:

> *At the hole where he went in*
> *Red-Eye called to Wrinkle-Skin.*
> *Hear what little Red-Eye saith:*
> *"Nag, come up and dance with death!"* (Kipling 1894: 174)

Lass (1999: 163) suggests very plausibly that after some time in the first half of the seventeenth century -th probably no longer occurred in London speech.

What we can do is observe the spread of -(e)s in spite of that resistance. To quote Lass (ibid. p. 163), "Forms in {-s} first occur in fourteenth-century London texts, but are rare . . .; they increase gradually during the fifteenth century, and explosively in the next two. By about 1600 {-s} is probably the norm." However, he goes on to note that Shakespeare uses both in verse, exploiting the fact that -eth yielded an extra syllable for most verbs whereas -s usually did not. For further details (and some interesting statistics) see Lass 1999: 162–5.

8.1.3 The demise of the subjunctive

Already by the early fifteenth century the subjunctive was poorly marked in Midlands English, as a table of regular indicative and subjunctive endings demonstrates:

	indicative	subjunctive
1sg.	-(e)	-(e)
2sg.	-(e)st	-(e)
3sg.	pres. -(e)th ~ -(e)s, past -(e)	-(e)
pl.	-(e(*n*))	-(e(*n*))

As the parentheses indicate, both -*n* in verb endings and word-final schwas were rapidly being lost. As a result, the subjunctive could be distinguished from the indicative reliably only in the 2sg. and the pres. 3sg., in which it was marked by *absence* of the usual indicative ending. The only clear exceptions were the subjunctive forms of *be*: namely, pres. *be*, past *were*. The former was different from all the indicative forms (except in those

---

1. Wyatt is especially useful because one of the two major manuscripts containing his poetry, the Egerton Ms., was in his personal possession and exhibits corrections in his own hand; see, e.g., Muir 1950: 255.

dialects which used *be* as indic. pl.), while the latter was different from all the indic. sg. forms.

Under the circumstances the use of the subjunctive must have been fairly difficult for native learners to acquire accurately. It is therefore no surprise that the subjunctive has largely been lost in ModE. Past subj. *were* is still common in American and some British speech, nearly always as a counterfactual (e.g. *If I were a rich man . . .*); an endless pres. 3sg. also occurs, at least in American English, in a type of clause introduced by *that* (e.g. *It is very important that he take his temperature every day*), and *be* occurs instead of *is* in the latter context (. . . *that he be honest*), which appears to show that the "base form" of the verb is what is being used (Aarts 2012: 8). Such clauses exhibit a number of syntactic peculiarities which make it uncertain whether their verbs should still be called subjunctives; for extensive discussion see Aarts 2012.[2] In other contexts, such as conditional clauses, pres. subj. *be* now sounds either archaic or dialectal, and the same is true of endingless pres. 3sg. subjunctive forms (*If the Lord be willin' an' the crick don't rise . . .*).

8.1.4 The rise of modals

The development of some preterite-present verbs and *will* into genuine modals is discussed in detail in Warner 1993: 156–206. Warner's analysis makes it clear that semantic and pragmatic properties of individual verbs led to their reanalysis as modals, with reanalysis of *must* and *shall, should* probably well ahead of the others. He notes (p. 189) that indicative and subjunctive forms of *shall* are already indistinguishable by some point in the ME period; thus there seems to be some connection between the loss of the subjunctive and the rise of modals, though it does not seem to be particularly straightforward. By 1500 nonfinite forms of *can, could* no longer occur in standard written English prose (though they continue to occur in outlying dialects, occasionally in verse, and in the usage of grammarians); the last citation of a nonfinite form of *may, might* seems to be from the 1550s, and a construction *had would* limps on into the seventeenth century (Warner 1993: 198–201).[3] Finally, the gradual loss of *wit* 'know', going to completion early in the seventeenth century, led to a complete correspondence in the distributions of preterite-present morphology and modal semantics (ibid. pp. 204–5). In ModE the missing

---

2. I am grateful to Bettelou Los for the reference and for helpful discussion.
3. The history of the construction *might could* 'might be able to', current in the vernacular of the southeastern USA, is not known to me, and I have not been able to find any discussion of it.

nonfinite forms of modals must be supplied by phrases with other verbs, e.g. *to be going to, to be able to, to have to.*

8.1.5 Continuous *be* and passive *be*

The ModE auxiliary-and-verb complex can be diagrammed as follows, where in each parenthesis the material following "+" is inflectional morphology applied to whatever follows next:

TENSE (MODAL) (have + PASTPTC) (be + PRESPTC) (be + PASTPTC) VERB.

"Tense" is likewise inflectional morphology applied to whatever follows next. Only the tense morphology and the main verb are obligatory. Verb phrases including all the optional items are not common, but they are not far-fetched either; plausible examples are easily constructed, e.g.

> To judge from its thickness, that stratum of rock <u>might have been being laid</u> down for several million years.

in which *might* is formally the past of the modal *may.* As can be seen from this example, *have* followed by a past participle indicates an anterior (or "perfect") tense, *be* followed by a present participle indicates a continuous ("progressive") tense, and *be* followed by a past participle marks a passive verb phrase. The first and last of those three were inherited from OE. Continuous *be* is more recent, but examples can be found in Chaucer (e.g. *were dwelling* near the beginning of the *Legend of Thisbe* in the *Legend of Good Women*). By the sixteenth century the construction was essentially the modern one, with one exception: *is being* does not appear until the late eighteenth century (Warner 1993: 63). Some authors continued to elide passive *be* after continuous *be*, so that *was building* could also mean *was being built*; an example of that construction occurs early in *Ivanhoe* (published 1819) by Sir Walter Scott (born 1771). By the middle of the nineteenth century the modern system in every detail appears to be firmly in place in all the standard Englishes.

8.2 Early Modern English pronouns

8.2.1 Second-person pronouns and pres. indic. 2sg. -est

ModE personal pronouns distinguish number in the 1st and 3rd persons (*I* vs. *we*; *(s)he, it* vs. *they*), but not in the 2nd, for which the only standard form is *you*, both sg. and pl. That is a relatively recent development. In ME the inherited system, with number and case distinguished in the 2nd person as well, is still in place; for instance, Chaucer typically employs the forms of the following paradigm (given here in the spellings that eventually became standard):

	1st person	2nd person
sg. nom.	I	thou
obj.	me	thee
pl. nom.	we	ye
obj.	us	you

The same distinction is observed in the possessive adjectives, 2sg. *thy* contrasting with 2pl. *your.*

The earliest attestation of a 2pl. used to address a single person seems to be from *Havelok*, a thirteenth-century narrative poem from Lincolnshire that survives in a manuscript of about 1300 (Laing 1993: 136, Fulk 2012: 264):[4]

> *But þe k[n]aue, þat litel was,*
> *he knelede bifor þat Iudas,*
> *and seyde, "Louerd, merci nov!*
> *Manrede, louerd, biddi you:*
> *Al Denemark I wile you yeue,*
> *to þat forward þu late me liue.*
> *Here Hi wile on boke swere*
> *þat neuremore ne shal I bere*
> *ayen þe, louerd, shel[d] ne spere,*
> *ne oþer wepne bere þat may you dere.* . . . (Smithers 1987: 16, ll. 481–90)

This "plural of respect" can only be an imitation of French practice, and its use in English is inconsistent. That is still the case in Chaucer, late in the fourteenth century. For instance, early in the *Knight's Tale* the spokeswoman for the group of ladies that greets Duke Theseus with weeping begins by addressing him in the 2pl.:

> *Lord to whom Fortune hath yiven*
> *victorie, and as a conqueror to lyven,*
> *nat greveth us youre glorie and youre honour,* . . .

but then lapses into the 2sg.:

> *Som drope of pitee, thurgh thy gentillesse,*
> *upon us wrecched wommen lat thou falle.*

---

4. This is the earliest example adduced in Mossé 1952: 94; it is referenced at Lass 1999: 148.

Two centuries later Shakespeare's characters are much more consistent in making the distinction, though it never became as hard-and-fast as the French distinction between *tu* and (sg.) *vous* (see Lass 1999: 148–53 for extensive discussion with numerous examples and references). But by Shakespeare's day a second change was already well advanced: objective *you* had begun to be used in place of nominative *ye*; for example, both are used as nominatives in the opening scene of *Richard III*, which is largely a conversation between the royal brothers Gloucester and Clarence. (Gloucester, when he is not bothering to be polite, addresses the constable Brackenbury with the old singular pronoun: *Her husband, knave! Wouldst thou betray me?*) Why *you* should have encroached on *ye* is not so obvious; it seems likely that unstressed forms, both probably /jə/, led to confusion on the part of native learners (cf. Lass 1999: 153–4). From fairly early in the seventeenth century *you* seems to be the usual form for both numbers and both cases.

When *thou* fell out of use, the verb forms in *-(e)st* that went with it also became obsolete; though there are occasional uses of *you* with *-(e)st* (Lass cites one from a letter of Sir Thomas More), they are very rare. This is cogent proof that person-and-number features are copied from the subject onto the finite verb at some abstract level. Of course, the loss of *-(e)st* simplified ModE verb inflection even further, leaving only pres. ind. 3sg. *-(e)s* as a person-and-number ending.

8.2.2 Case-marking on pronouns

Case continues to be well marked on pronouns (except *you*) in standard ModE; the distinction between nominative and objective forms inherited from early ME largely survives. As noted in 5.1, the objective sg. forms reflect the OE dative sg. forms, except for *it*, which reflects the OE accusative sg., identical with the nom. sg. The old genitive forms of the 3rd-person pronoun have become possessive adjectives, parallel to the 1st- and 2nd-person possessive adjectives found already in OE (Lass 1999: 147).

However, a few changes of detail have occurred. As Lass (ibid. p. 147) notes, the forms *mine* and *thine*, originally used in all environments where not followed by a consonant within the same noun phrase, were restricted to predicate position in the seventeenth century; parallel predicative forms *ours, yours, hers*, apparently formed with gen. sg. *-s*, had appeared already in the early thirteenth century (to be joined by *theirs* when northern texts become available; see the *OED* entries). Up until about the middle of the sixteenth century *his* was the possessive both of *he* and of *it* (as in OE); at that time a new possessive *its* was formed with the clitic *-s*, and over the course of about a century it became the regular possessive of *it* (Lass

1999: 147–8). There may have been a much earlier precedent for this development. Though ModE *who* and *whom* are the direct descendants of OE masc./fem. nom. sg. *hwā* and dat. sg. *hwām*, *whose* is not the regular sound-change reflex of OE *hwæs*; instead it appears to be the old nom. sg. plus *-s*. Surprisingly, it appears already in *Vices and Virtues* (as *hwos*), and though it competes with *hwas* and *hwes* (the direct descendants of *hwæs*, depending on the dialect) until late in the fourteenth century, innovative *whos* is Chaucer's only form and is more or less universal thereafter. However, the possibility that *whos* resulted from levelling the vowel of *who* into *whas*, and not from a new construction *who* + *-s*, cannot be discounted entirely.

Already in early ModE the use of nominative and objective personal and interrogative pronouns began to be modified, though the contrast does not seem to be breaking down. Examples of *me* as a predicate after *be* can be cited from Shakespeare, e.g.

> *Oh, the dogge is me, and I am my selfe.*
> (*Two Gentlemen of Verona* II, iii, 22, as cited in the *OED* s.v. *me*)

That usage is now more or less universal in colloquial English (*it wasn't us, it was him*, etc.); those of us who are middle-aged or older were taught to say *it is I*, but hardly anybody does. This appears to reflect a reanalysis of the objective forms as postverbal. More surprisingly, the case assignment of conjoined pronouns has been modified in various ways. In Jane Austen we find

> *Anne and me are to go . . .*
> (*Sense and Sensibility* II, ii, 31, as cited in the *OED* s.v. *me*)

with objective *me* as part of a conjoined subject. In the modern Philadelphia vernacular some conjoined objects have shifted in the other direction; *between you and I*, for instance, is universally used. It is likely that this began, at least, as a hypercorrection; I have never heard **between you and we*, for instance, and if only the replacement of *me* by *I* is in question, hypercorrection is likely (as Bettelou Los observes; cf. Lasnik and Sobin 2000: 367).

Finally, objective *whom* now has a restricted pattern of occurrence and is slowly passing out of use. The *OED* s.v. *who* cites examples of *who* as grammatical objects from as early as the fifteenth century, and they become steadily more frequent over time; especially frequent is the use of *who* for objects fronted out of prepositional phrases, e.g. *Who are you talking to?* In my own speech *whom* almost always is, or can be, replaced by *who* except in one construction: namely, the fronting of an entire prepositional phrase: *To whom are you talking?* is a more formal equivalent of the last sentence cited, but *To who . . .?* sounds strange to me. It seems clear that many speakers of English do not have a native command of *whom*, using it only when attempting to speak formally; the discussion of Lasnik and Sobin 2000 is highly relevant.

Strictly speaking, the changes discussed in the last few paragraphs are syntactic changes; I mention them here because they have consequences for our understanding of ModE casemarking.

8.3 The development of contracted *-n't*

Lass 1999: 179–80 summarizes the history of contractions in English, with references; the chief points are the following. Cliticization of an auxiliary verb, or of main verb *be* or *have*, onto a subject enters the written record sometime in the sixteenth century; spellings such as *I've* and *they'll* appear in early editions of Shakespeare, and there are passages of verse in which written *I am*, for instance, must be read as monosyllabic *I'm*. Cliticization of *not* onto one of the same verbal items is apparently attested only metrically in Shakespeare; Lass 1999: 180 cites *Othello* IV, ii, 161, where *cannot* must be read as *can't*. Actual spellings with *-n't* become common only in the 1660s. But it seems clear that in speech the cliticization of negatives must have begun much earlier. Though the vowel of *won't* probably ultimately reflects levelling from past *wolde* (> *would*), as suggested by Lass, the phonology strongly suggests that the contraction *wol not* > *won't* occurred in the fifteenth century (Luick 1914–40: 373); at any later time the result probably would not be what we actually find.

These contractions would seem to be mere phonology, but the details of ModE contractions with *-n't* suggest that something further has happened. Zwicky and Pullum 1983 assess the grammatical status of contracted *-n't* according to a range of criteria that usually distinguish clitics from inflectional morphemes and conclude that *-n't* has become a negative inflectional ending. Their strongest arguments are the facts that contractions with *-n't* are moved as single constituents in ModE syntax (*Haven't you been there?* vs. *Have you not been there? / *Have not you been there?*), that *-n't* cannot cliticize to a clitic (**I'dn't be doing this if . . .* vs. *I'd've done so*), that *-n't* appears only on a very restricted set of items, some of which are very idiosyncratic (e.g. *ain't*), and that in such a contraction as *can't* the modal and the negative cannot be interpreted separately. Of course, in some grammatical theories, such as DM, the difference between clitics and inflectional affixes is a relatively superficial matter, but it is undeniable that there is some difference, and it appears that *-n't* is no longer a clitic. How and when it became an affix remains to be investigated in detail.

8.4 Latinate plurals

Finally, a word should be said about the attempt to borrow Latinate plurals into ModE. Late in the sixteenth century educated speakers of early ModE began to borrow Latin and Greek nouns in some numbers with their (nominative) case endings intact, and some of those nouns sometimes have Latin and Greek plural forms in ModE. It would be natural to suppose that the plurals were borrowed at the same time as the singulars, but the historical record, as revealed in citations in the *OED*, is much more complex, as a few examples will demonstrate.

Some relevant nouns are used reasonably often in both singular and plural. They typically exhibit a Latinate plural and a default ModE plural in competition throughout much of their history in English, so far as we can tell from *OED* quotations. For instance, *cactus* was first applied to the genus of plants which it now denotes in 1752. The *OED* quotes no instances of pl. *cacti*, but that is now the commonest plural on the web (as Greg Ward observed to me some years ago); yet *cactuses* is quoted from as early as 1832 and remains in contention. Pl. *incubi* was in (rare) use in ME, and sg. *incubus* appears in Chaucer, but *incubusses* is attested from 1653. *Formula* first appears late in the sixteenth century; the Latinate plural *formulae* is quotable from 1798, the default plural *formulas* from 1837, and both remain common in print. In at least two cases the default plural definitely has the upper hand. *Forum* was at first used in English by Capgrave to denote the Roman forum, and in that meaning a default plural *forums* appears in 1647; the broader meaning is attested from 1735, and *forums* in that meaning from 1858; the *OED* offers no examples of the Latinate plural *fora*. *Antenna* is probably used more often in the plural than in the singular; *antennae* appears first in 1646 and *antennas* in 1826, but only the latter is used as the plural of the device for detecting and retrieving radiomagnetic communications (*OED* s.v., sense 4)—a clear case of an innovative use triggering default inflection, but also an indication that *antennas* is the more productive plural.

Nouns of this type which are used much more often in the plural exhibit a somewhat different development in ModE. Pl. *data* is quoted from 1630, sg. *datum* not before 1807; yet already in 1645 a plural *datas* is attested, implying the reanalysis of *data* as a singular count noun, and that plural continues to occur sporadically right down into the twenty-first century. The corresponding singular is attested as *a data* in 1807, but in the meantime a mass noun *data* had made its appearance (first in 1702), and it is now by far the most commonly used form.[5] *Phenomena* (or, in older records, *phænomena*) is similar: the Greek plural is quoted first from 1583, to be followed by *phenomenas* in 1635 and *phenomenons* in 1693; the singular *phenomenon* was in use by the middle of the seventeenth century, but *phenomena* is also used as a collective singular from 1708 onward. The history of *medium* is only modestly different. The singular is quotable from 1573, pl. *mediums* from 1641, pl. *media* not until 1817, but only the latter seems to be used of news organizations. However, by 1923 it had evolved into a singular collective too, and there is even a pl. *medias* attested from 1927. Not all predominantly plural Latinate nouns have undergone such a development, but the ones that have not are special cases. *Alumni* and *alumnae* are not in competition with default plurals, but that is partly because they are quasi-collectives, usually denoting organizations of ex-students; moreover, by nature they are mostly used by ModE speakers with a higher education, most of whom (though not all) use also the singulars *alumnus* and *alumna*. *Bacteria* also has no competition, but it is still a scientific term used primarily by the educated. (In North America, at least, the vernacular equivalent is *germs*.)

In short, the historical record reveals that the attempt to borrow Latinate plurals into ModE has largely been a messy failure, and there was never any period during which it was an unequivocal success. That is not surprising. Everything we know about language contact suggests that it is difficult for native speakers to borrow foreign inflection into their native language. Under conditions of community-wide bilingualism such borrowing can succeed, but there was never more than a tiny minority of speakers of English that had even a good passive command of Latin or Greek.

Exercise

Below is a list of ModE irregular verbs, arranged in inflectional classes; I have tried to posit coherent classes and to list similar classes near one another, though other classifications and arrangements might be no worse. The forms mostly reflect my standard American English speech. Compounds are not normally listed unless the simple verb is archaic. You may find that your pronunciation differs from mine, and you may judge that some other classification is preferable; if so, work with your own pronunciation and your own analysis of classes.

The purpose of this exercise is to continue examining how the classifi-

---

5. In addition, the technical surveying term *datum* 'baseline' appears in 1795, and a plural *datums* is quoted from 2004.

cation of English verbs has changed over time, this time beginning from the endpoint of the development. You should first go through the list and cross off the verbs which were strong verbs in OE and appeared in the preceding exercise. You will find that (a) ModE classes 19 through 25 are completely accounted for; (b) few strong verbs have wound up in classes 1 through 9 and 26 through 28; but (c) classes 10 through 18, though clearly strong in ModE, contain quite a few verbs that were not strong in OE (or even that did not exist in OE). A few of those developments were described and a hypothesis to explain them was advanced in 8.1.1 above, but many others remain to be investigated in detail.

Now choose one of the following ModE classes or groups of classes:

a. class 1;
b. classes 2 through 5;
c. classes 6 through 9;
d. classes 10 through 13;
e. classes 14, 17, 18, and 27.

Using the *OED* (online, if you have access to it), find the etymology of each of these verbs that is *not* straightforwardly descended from an OE strong verb. If the verb was inherited from OE, consult one of the standard grammars to find what class it belonged to. Then describe the origin of each of the classes that you chose, making all the generalizations that seem appropriate.

1. Past and ptc. with no affix, e.g. *hit, hit, hit.*
    bet, burst, cast, cost, cut, fit (intrans.), *hit, hurt, knit* (intrans.), *let, put, quit, set, shut, slit, split, thrust, wet; bid* (modern meaning 'place a bid'), *rid, shed, spread.*
2. Pres. with /iː/, past and past ptc. with /ɛ/.
    bleed, breed, feed, lead, meet, plead (legal language, otherwise reg.), *read, speed.*
3. Pres. with /iː/ or /uː/, past and past ptc. with /ɛ/ or /ɑ/ and /-d/.
    flee (past *fled*); *shoe* (past *shod*).
4. Pres. with /iː/, past and past ptc. with /ɛ/ and /-t/.
    creep, deal, dream (also reg.), *feel, keep, kneel* (also reg.), *leap* (also reg.), *mean, sleep, sweep, weep; leave (left), bereave* (reg., but also past ptc. *bereft*).
5. Pres. with /uː/, past and past ptc. with /ɔ/ and /-t/.
    lose (lost).
6. Pres. with /-d/, past and past ptc. with /-t/.
    bend, build, gird, lend, rend (archaic), *send, spend.*
7. Past and ptc. with /-t/ or /-d/.
    burn, dwell, learn, smell, spell, spill, spoil.

8. Pres. with /ɛ/, past and ptc. with /oʊ/ and /-d/.
   sell, tell.

9. Past in /-ɔt/.
   beseech (also reg.), *teach; catch, bring, think, seek, buy.*

10. Past and ptc. with /ʌ/.
    cling, dig, fling, sling, slink, spin, stick, sting, string, swing, win, wring, strike; hang.

11. Past with /æ/, ptc. with /ʌ/.
    begin, drink, ring, shrink, sing, sink, spring, stink, swim; run.

12. Past and ptc. with /æ/.
    sit, spit (the latter also under 1 above).

13. Pres. with /aɪ/, past with /oʊ/.
    a. Ptc. with /ɪ/ and /-ən/.
    drive, ride, rise, smite, strive, thrive (also reg.), *write.*
    b. Ptc. with /oʊ/.
    shine, stride.
    c. Reg., but past also with /oʊ/.
    abide, dive.

14. Pres. with /aɪ/, past with /ɪ/.
    a. Ptc. with /ɪ/ and /-ən/.
    bite, hide.
    b. Ptc. with /ɪ/, no suffix.
    light, slide.

15. Pres. with /i:/, past with /oʊ/, ptc. with /oʊ/ and /-ən/.
    freeze, speak, steal, weave.

16. Pres. with /u:/, past with /oʊ/, ptc. with /oʊ/ and /-ən/.
    choose.

17. Pres. with /eɪ/, past with /oʊ/, ptc. with /oʊ/ and /-ən/.
    break, wake (the latter also reg.).

18. Pres. with /ɛ:/, past with /ɔ/, ptc. with /ɔ/ and /-n/.
    bear, swear, tear, wear.

19. Pres. with /ɛ/, past with /ɑ/, ptc. with /ɑ/ and (variably) /-ən/.
    get, tread.

20. Pres. with /eɪ/, past with /ʊ/, ptc. with /eɪ/ and /-ən/.
    forsake, shake, take.

21. Pres. with /aɪ/, past and ptc. with /aʊ/.
    bind, find, grind, wind.

22. Pres. with /aɪ/, past and ptc. with /ɔ/.
    fight.

23. Past with /u:/, ptc. with /oʊ-n/.
    blow, grow, know, throw; fly.

24. Past with /uː/, ptc. with the vowel of the pres. plus /-n/.
    draw; slay.
25. Unique strong verbs.
    forbid, forbade /fɔɹbˈæd/, *forbidden*
    give, gave, given
    eat, ate /eɪt/, *eaten*
    come, came, come
    fall, fell, fallen
    see, saw, seen
    lie, lay, lain
    beat, beat, beaten
    hold, held, held
    shoot, shot, shot
    stand, stood, stood
26. Unique weak verbs.
    hear, heard /hɹ̩·d/, *heard*
    make, made, made
    say, said /sɛd/, *said*; also pres. 3sg. *says* /sɛz/
    have, had, had; also pres. 3sg. *has* /hæz/
27. Weak verbs with strong past ptcc. (often optional or increasingly adjectival).
    mow (mown), sew (sewn), show (shown), sow (sown); hew (hewn), strew (strewn); saw (sawn); shear (shorn).
28. The same with irreg. phonology:
    do, did, done; also pres. 3sg. *does* /dʌz/

I omit the suppletive verbs *go* and *be*, as well as the modals, whose very special histories have been discussed above.

Section C

Derivational morphology

9 Inherited derivational patterns

9.1 Old English relics

Much of this section will be unfamiliar to a native speaker of ModE; that shows how much the derivational morphology of English has changed over the past fourteen centuries or so. I will here discuss OE derivational patterns—some no longer productive even in OE—that survive only in isolated examples, if at all, in later stages of the language. Much further information can be found in Kastovsky 2006: 216–46.

OE inherited from PGmc. a range of ways of forming nouns from strong verbs that involved putting the verb root in one or another of its ablaut grades and adding a vowel that would allow the result to be inflected as a noun. Most of these patterns were unproductive already in OE, and only occasional examples survive in ModE. What is interesting is that those survivals are often still clearly derived from the relevant verbs, even if the process of derivation is opaque. Some examples are still completely transparent. For instance, OE *drinc* '(a) drink' was derived from *drincan* '(to) drink', and similarly *slæp* 'sleep' from *slæpan*, by inflecting the root as a masculine noun according to the default pattern. Their descendants still fit well into the ModE pattern of "zero derivation" (even though not every basic verb can give rise to a noun by that process; it works with *bind, tie, break, drive, go*, etc., but not with *come, weep, sit*, etc.). But even the ModE descendant of OE *sang ~ song*, derived from *singan* with a different ablaut grade of the root, is unproblematically associated with its verb by native speakers, though the vowel alternation is unique. The same is sometimes true of other OE survivals—for instance, the ModE descendant of OE *talu*, related to *tellan*, though the meanings of both have shifted in the meantime ('count, recount' in OE; 'tale' and 'tell' in ModE).[1] Examples with fossilized suffixes are similar. For instance, OE *dæd* (Anglian *dēd*)

---

1. It is not clear which of these words was derived from the other, either synchronically in OE or historically in Proto-Northwest Germanic.

'deed' was probably still obviously derived from *dōn* 'do', and the same might be true of their ModE descendants for some speakers, though the derivational relationship was already idiosyncratic in OE. Evidently, it is not necessary for a derivational pattern to be productive, or even regular, for native speakers to be aware of it. On the other hand, it is clear that native learners do not normally make isolated relationships like these the basis of larger productive patterns; they might attempt to do so at first, but they soon desist in the absence of reinforcement from what they hear spoken around them.

More striking (to a historical linguist) are patterns that were reasonably extensive in OE but have left little trace in the modern language. A substantial class of OE masculine abstract nouns was constructed by putting a verb root in the zero grade and affixing *-i-, which umlauted the vowel of the root and triggered the Verner's Law alternation (VL); typical examples are *cyme* 'approach, arrival' ← *cuman* 'come', *sleġe* 'stroke, slaughter' ← *slēan* 'strike, slay', *cwide* 'speech' ← *cweþan* 'say', etc. The only survival of this class in ModE is *breach* < *bryċe* (← *break* < *brecan*; cf. Kastovsky 2006: 204). A substantial class of feminine abstracts was formed from adjectives with -*u*, likewise with i-umlaut. Typical examples are *strenġu* 'strength' and *hǣlu* 'health'; only *hǣtu* 'heat' survives. As the ModE translations suggest, this type lost a competition with a parallel type in -*þ*, on which see 9.2. A class of OE nouns which has disappeared altogether are the n-stem agent nouns. When derived from strong verbs or preterite-presents these exhibited zero grade of the root and VL, e.g.:

boda 'messenger' ← *bēodan* 'announce'
heretoga 'general' (lit. 'army-leader')[2] ← *tēon* 'pull, lead'
cuma 'stranger, guest' ← *cuman* 'come'
wita 'wise man, counsellor' ← *witan* 'know'

But they could also be derived from other verbs, in which case they exhibited the root shape of the verb, e.g.:

dēma 'judge' ← *dēman* 'judge'

A similar group of agent nouns were fossilized present participles; many were already restricted to verse in OE, but some were in general use, e.g.:

2. I do not agree with Schroeder and Carr that this compound *must* originally have been a Gothic loan translation of Gk. στρατηγός /strateːgós/ (στρατός 'army', ἄγειν /ágeːn/ 'to lead'; Carr 1939: 5–6). Kluge and Seebold 1995 s.v. *Herzog* suggest that it might actually be older ("gemein-g[ermanisch]."), though they also admit that it could be a West Germanic innovation.

wealdend 'ruler' ← *wealdan* 'rule'
hǣlend 'savior' ← *hǣlan* 'heal, save'

These classes were ultimately replaced by agent nouns in *-er*, on the origin of which see 9.2.

There were three large groups of class I weak verbs that were still clearly derived in OE. One group was derived from strong verbs, using the finite past 1&3sg. form as a base, with i-umlaut and VL; many examples were causative, though others had meanings much like the verbs from which they were derived or had been specialized semantically. Typical examples include:

bærnan 'burn' (trans.) ← *birnan* 'burn' (intr.)
drenċan 'give (someone) a drink' ← *drincan* 'drink'
fēran 'go, travel' ← *faran* 'go, travel'
fiellan 'cause to fall, fell' ← *feallan* 'fall'
lǣdan 'lead' ← *līþan* 'go'
leċġan 'lay' ← *liċġan* 'lie'
rǣran 'raise, rear' ← *rīsan* 'rise'
settan 'set, seat' ← *sittan* 'sit'
snǣdan 'cut' ← *snīþan* 'cut'

García García 2012 argues convincingly that this type was no longer productive in OE. Another clearly derived type of class I weak verbs are factitives, meaning 'make (someone or something) X', where X is the meaning of the adjective from which the verb is derived. Typical examples include:

cȳþan 'make known' ← *cūþ* 'known'
fyllan 'fill' ← *full* 'full'
ġierwan 'prepare' ← *ġearu* 'ready'
hǣlan 'heal, save' ← *hāl* 'healthy, whole'
trymman 'strengthen, confirm' ← *trum* 'strong, firm'
wierman 'warm, make warm' ← *wearm* 'warm'

Whether this type was still productive in OE is not clear. In addition, quite a few class I weak verbs were derived from nouns and other major words. Typical examples include:

ċīepan 'buy, sell, trade' ← *ċēap* 'merchandise, bargain'
dǣlan 'divide, distribute' ← *dǣl* 'part'
dēman 'judge' ← *dōm* 'judgment'
fēdan 'feed, nourish' ← *fōda* 'food'
fremman 'make, do, accomplish' ← *fram* 'forward' (adv.)
ġelīefan 'believe' ← *ġelēafa* 'faith'
nemnan 'name' ← *nama* 'name'
timbran 'build' ← *timber* 'timber, building'

All these types survive in ModE only as relics. Of course, the derivational relationship can still sometimes be perceived—in addition to the examples adduced above, *bleed* is still obviously connected to *blood*, and *breed* might still be connected to *brood* for some speakers—but by no means always; for instance, how many speakers of ModE connect the verb *defile* with *foul*? But in any case the survivors are now relics, without a systematic relationship to their derivational bases.

9.2 Old English patterns of suffixation that remained productive

A number of OE derivational patterns survived into ME, and some have survived into ModE. They constitute the native system of derivation. This section will discuss a few of the more important examples.

As was observed in 3.1.6, class II weak verbs could be derived from nouns and adjectives productively in OE. That was arguably a case of "zero derivation" (cf. Kastovsky 2006: 211, 242–4); it will be discussed in detail in 12.1. Though a large number of the OE examples have been lost, examples that survive are not hard to find, for instance:

āgnian 'own, possess' ← *āgen* '(one's) own, property'
andswarian 'answer' ← *andswaru* 'answer'
endian 'end' ← *ende* 'end'
lufian 'love' ← *lufu* 'love'
openian 'open' ← *open* 'open'
þancian 'thank' ← *þanc* 'thought, favor, thanks'
wundrian 'wonder, be amazed at' ← *wundor* 'wonder'

This pattern of OE verb derivation remains fully productive in ModE.

One other verb-forming suffix retains at least some productivity. PGmc. had evolved a suffix *-inō-, forming class II weak verbs (Ringe 2017: 324), by resegmentation (Marchand 1969: 271 with references); in West Germanic it was used to form transitive verbs from nouns and adjectives (Ringe and Taylor 2014: 131), of which at least one ancient example survives in ModE: namely, *fasten* < OE *fæstnian* 'to make fast' (cf. Old Frisian *festnia*, Old Saxon *fastnon*, OHG *festinōn*).[3] Marchand 1969: 271–3 lists and discusses numerous examples from the thirteenth century on, most of which appear to have been formed from adjectives (e.g. *redden*)—the modern productive pattern.

---

3. Marchand's derivation of the OE verb from *fæsten* 'fortress' fits neither its meaning nor the pattern of cognation among West Germanic languages. In fact, his derivation might be inadmissible, even on formal grounds: OE 'fortress' is underlyingly /fæstenn-/, so that the expected shape of a derived verb would be *fæstennian*.

Several OE noun-forming suffixes remained productive in ME and later (cf. Kastovsky 2006: 238–41). The most spectacular example is *-ness*, which formed feminine abstracts from adjectives in OE. Though the origin of the suffix is murky (Ringe and Taylor 2014: 131–2), it had become exuberantly productive in OE by about the year 900; Cosijn 1888: II.28–32 lists scores of examples. It is still fully productive in ModE. As with all fully productive derivational patterns, old examples have been replaced continuously with new ones, so that comparatively few of the early OE examples survive; but Cosijn's list includes, e.g., *clǣnness, lustfulness, gōdness, hāliġness, īdelness, sċearpness, stilness, swētness,* etc., all of which are immediately intelligible in ModE.

The history of feminine abstracts in *-þ(u)* has been more complex. A number of OE examples survive in ModE, sometimes disguised by regular sound change, e.g. *strengþ(u)* 'strength', *lengþ* 'length', *hīehþ* 'height', *fylþ(u)* 'filth, rottenness' (*fūl* 'unclean, rotten'), *cȳþ(þu)* 'kith, kinship, acquaintance' (*cūþ* 'known'), *wrǣþ(þu)* 'anger, wrath' (*wrāþ* 'angry, wroth'), *myrġþ* 'mirth' (*myrġe* 'merry'), *trīowþ* 'trust, covenant' (*trīowe* 'trustworthy'; ModE *true, truth*); *hǣlþ* appears in late OE as an alternative to *hǣlu* (see 9.1). What is surprising is that many of the common ModE examples are ME or even early ModE innovations (Marchand 1969: 349; see the *OED* s.vv.). *Warmth* first appears in the twelfth-century *Lambeth Homilies, wealth* in the thirteenth-century *Proverbs of Alfred, dearth* in the *Cursor Mundi; depth* is not attested before Wycliffe, late in the fourteenth century. *Breadth* is first attested in 1523, replacing *brede* (< OE *brǣdu*), which survives only in outlying dialects after the 1550s; *width* does not appear until 1570, and in the mid-eighteenth century Samuel Johnson is still stigmatizing it as "vulgar", advising his readers to use *wideness* (< OE *wīdness*) instead. *Growth*, exceptionally derived from a verb root, appears first in Surrey's verse in the early sixteenth century. Other examples have occasionally been ventured but have not become part of standard ModE. On the strength of the earlier examples, Marchand (ibid. p. 349) says that *-th* remained productive in ME, but it seems clear that it did not enjoy anything like the productivity of *-ness*. *Health, depth,* and *breadth* replaced examples of the alternative OE formation in *-u* or their descendants, and could conceivably be regarded as late outcomes of the OE competition between those two formations; but it seems more accurate to say that *-th* has been marginally productive, probably helped along by lexical analogy (*depth, breadth,* and *width* being in part modelled on inherited *length*, for example).

Yet a third pattern of productivity appears in the history of ModE *-ing* (the noun suffix, not the participle suffix, on which see 7.2; cf. Marchand 1969: 302–4). OE had a pair of parallel formations: feminine abstract nouns in *-ung* were formed mostly from class II weak verbs, while those in *-ing* were formed mostly from class I weak verbs; in early ME *-ing* was generalized. The OE suffixes were fully productive; not only has *-ing* remained so, it has become part of the inflectional morphology of the language, forming from every English main verb a noun which, if the verb is transitive, can govern a direct object (e.g. *taking bribes is illegal*).

All three of these suffixes illustrate something further about derivational formations. Though their productive function is the formation of abstract nouns, various individual examples have become specialized in more concrete meanings. A phrase such as *several standard lengths of tubing* can mean actual pieces of tubing of standard length (as well as several different lengths in which tubing is standardly manufactured); one can say *landing an army on a hostile shore is very difficult*, but also *put in at the next landing*, in which the word means a place where a boat can be landed. Even *-ness* exhibits an occasional concretization: though *kindness* usually means 'being kind', in *their many kindnesses to me* it means 'act of kindness'. This shows that specific examples even of fully productive formations can acquire a lexical life of their own, so to speak, enabling their meanings to "drift" away from the productive meaning of the formation. The classic discussion of this phenomenon is Jackendoff 1975.

A further point about productive formations (also discussed by Jackendoff, op. cit.) is that they can occasionally be blocked if a less derived alternative already exists. The classic instance in ModE is **gloriousness*, which should be derivable from *glorious* by productive rule but is not because the more basic noun *glory* is already in existence (or, from the native speaker's point of view, has already been learned; see Aronoff 1976: 43–5, Carstairs-McCarthy 2018: 98–9).

An OE noun-forming suffix that has become almost fully productive in ModE is masculine *-ere*. Unlike the suffixes discussed above, *-ere* was not an inherited Germanic morpheme; it reflects borrowing of Latin *-ārius* into Proto-West Germanic as **-ārī*, which in the northern dialects became **-ǣrī* by regular sound change, whence early OE **-æri* (by regular shortening of fully unstressed long vowels) > *-ere* (by regular merger of fully unstressed front vowels; see Ringe and Taylor 2014: 138, 149–50, 298–300, 332–5). Of course, the suffix was not borrowed by itself; languages do not normally borrow pieces of foreign words. Rather, Latin words in *-ārius* and their derivational bases were both borrowed; then the suffix was extracted from those pairs by native learners and used to coin new words, at first probably by narrow lexical analogies, eventually becoming productive when enough such words had been created. Few of the original pairs of loanwords can be expected to survive in the daughter languages, but one probably does: Latin *monēta* 'coin' was borrowed as Proto-West Germanic *munit (OE *mynet*, OHG *muniʒ*) and its derivative *monētārius* 'mintmaster, person authorized to coin money'[4] was borrowed as Proto-West Germanic (PWGmc.) *munitārī (OE *mynetere*, OHG *muniʒāri*, Meid 1967: 81–2). In early OE this suffix was only modestly productive; frequently encountered examples include *bōcere* 'scholar' and *fiscere* 'fisherman'. Note that the former, like virtually all the Latin examples, is clearly derived from a noun (*bōc* 'book'); the suffix denoted professions and was often appended to a noun that characterized the profession in question. However, already in OE it could be added to verb stems; typical examples are *wrītere* 'scribe' and *cwellere* 'executioner' (*cwellan* 'kill'). Though both those terms were (at least sometimes) names of professions, -*ere* had begun to be more widely applied before the end of the OE period; perhaps the most striking example is *wlæffettere* 'stammerer', which, like its ModE translation, is an agent noun indicating that the referent habitually or regularly performs the action of the verb from which it is derived. ModE -*er* has become a productive deriver of agent nouns; Marchand 1969: 273–81 gives numerous examples (including examples of more evolved uses) with incidental information about when they first appear in the written record.

Mention should also be made of the pseudoparticiple suffix -*ed*, which is used to form adjectives meaning 'having / provided with (the noun to which the suffix is appended)'. A typical ModE example is *bearded* 'having a beard'; it looks like a past participle, but there is no verb *beard* meaning 'provide with a beard'. Pseudoparticiples are ancient, and cognate formations occur widely in IE languages (e.g. Latin *barbātus* 'bearded', formed directly from *barba* 'beard'). As usual, few of the OE examples survive—ModE *bearded* is probably not a direct descendant of OE *gebearded*, since the modern word does not seem to be attested before the late fourteenth century—but the derivational type has remained productive. On the use of this suffix in compounds see 9.4 below.

In addition to suffixes which were just suffixes as far back as we can trace them, a number of second members of compounds have become suffixes in the attested Germanic languages. This is a typical development in derivational morphology. An important example that might already have become a suffix long before the separate prehistory of English began was a masculine noun in *-i- (see 9.1 above) formed from PGmc. *skapjaną

---

4. This was an important and (of course) lucrative position in late Roman and sub-Roman Gaul, and subsequently in the Frankish kingdom. For instance, St Eligius, the famously honest bishop of Noyon on whom King Dagobert I relied for advice, began his meteoric career as an apprentice to a goldsmith and mintmaster at Limoges (Fletcher 1997: 145).

'make, fashion, create'; it must originally have been *skapiz and meant 'creation; thing made', but its meaning seems to have shifted very early to 'shape; condition' (Ringe and Taylor 2014: 132). In OE it survives as the suffix *-scipe*, which forms abstract nouns from other nouns;[5] an OE example which is still common in ModE is *frēondscipe* 'friendship'. A few other OE and ME examples survive, but *-ship* did not become very productive until early ModE; it is most often added to nouns denoting persons, e.g. *championship, dictatorship, fellowship, kinship* (Marchand 1969: 345). As usual, some of these nouns have evolved in other directions semantically; a prominent modern group denotes skills characteristic of a profession, e.g. *workmanship, salesmanship* (ibid. p. 346).

Two examples which were still second members of compounds in OE have undergone a similar evolution. Unlike *-scipe*, *hād* was still an independent noun meaning 'condition, state, rank, station (in life)', and its compounds must still have been semantically transparent, at least in part; typical examples are *cildhād* 'state of being a child, childhood' and *munuchād* 'monastic life, state of being a monk'. Its descendant *-hood* has never been very productive, though there is a steady trickle of new examples century after century, e.g. *brotherhood, boyhood, spinsterhood*; most examples still indicate conditions of human life, though *statehood* (for instance) represents an extension of use, and there are even a few examples formed from adjectives, such as *falsehood* and *likelihood* (Marchand 1969: 293). OE *dōm* 'judgment; jurisdiction' was likewise an independent word, and some of its (fairly few) compounds were still transparent; for instance, *wīsdōm* meant 'wise judgment', therefore 'wisdom', and *cynedōm* 'royal authority; kingdom' could then, as now, mean the territory in which the authority of a king was recognized.[6] But already in OE *-dōm* had begun to encroach functionally on *-hād* (e.g. in *þēowdōm* 'servitude, slavery'); the most striking illustration is the coexistence of *martyrdōm* and *martyrhād*, both innovations made to a Latin loanword[7] (of which the former eventually won the competition). A few examples, such as *campdōm* 'military service', show that development in other directions had also begun. For many centuries *-dom* was only modestly productive, denoting areas of jurisdiction (e.g. *Christendom*), in some cases also the offices that exercise authority over them (e.g. *earldom*), status (e.g. *stardom*), and communities of humans, often with a pejorative tinge (e.g. *whoredom*). In recent centu-

---

5. Also related is *gescēap* 'shape', but it is a different formation.
6. On the early OE form of this word see 9.4. The usual OE word for 'kingdom' was *rīce*.
7. The native OE term seems to have been *cȳþere*, literally 'proclaimer, testifier', a typically felicitous loan translation of Greek μάρτυς /mártys/ 'witness (to one's faith)'.

ries it has become more productive, but few of the products are frequent in speech or writing; Marchand 1969: 262–4 gives a comprehensive summary with references.

Other common productive suffixes that began their careers as second members of compounds are the adjective-forming suffixes *-ful* (originally the adjective *full*) and its antonym *-less* (OE *lēas* 'free from'[8]); *-fold* (as in *threefold*) and *-ward* (as in *southward*) were already only suffixes in OE but appear to have been independent words in prehistory. See Marchand 1969: 291–2, 324–5, 351–2 for discussion.

By far the most productive suffix of this etymological type is *-ly*. It was originally a neuter noun, PGmc. **līką* > PWGmc. **līk* > OE *līċ* 'body', and it formed compounds meaning 'having the shape / appearance of (the first member)'. A few examples are pan-Germanic; the OE representative of one such family is *lēoflīċ* 'lovable, pleasant, beautiful, precious', originally **'having a lovable / dear appearance'[9] (Gothic *liubaleiks*, OHG *lioblīh*, modern *lieblich*; see Ringe 2017: 327). By the early OE period it had become a very productive adjective suffix, added both to nouns (e.g. *eorþlīċ* 'earthly') and to adjectives (e.g. *rihtwīslīċ* 'righteous'), denoting qualities characteristic or typical of the referent of the base word. It is still an adjective suffix in ModE; among the common examples listed in Marchand 1969: 329–31 whose creation spans the whole attested history of English[10] are *friendly, worldly, manly, cowardly, scholarly, leisurely*, etc., as well as the set *daily, yearly, hourly*, etc. indicating regular repetition in time. But *-ly* has become most productive as the regular means of forming adverbs from adjectives—so productive that, like *-ing*, it could be considered an inflectional morpheme. This was the result of a series of lexical accidents that was just beginning in OE. The productive suffix forming adverbs from adjectives was *-e* in OE (see 3.3), and of course adjectives in *-līċ* formed adverbs in *-līċe*. But there are a few OE adverbs in *-līċe* for which no adjective in *-līċ* can be cited. A fairly common example is *bealdlīċe*, for which the only adjective attested is *beald* 'bold' (though there is also an adverb *bealde*); a less common pair is *hwæt* 'sharp, bold, quick', *hwætlīċe* 'quickly', for which we can cite neither an adjective **hwætlīċ* nor an adverb **hwate*. Of course, the OE corpus is so small—about a million and a half words of text—that we can never be completely certain that such gaps are not accidental, but there are enough of them to suggest that

---

8. This was a completely different word from *lǣssa* 'less'; the two are not even etymologically related.

9. ModE *lovely* is a descendant of OE *luflīċ*, a related but not identical formation.

10. I see no reason to suspect backformation from adverbs after the OE period, pace *OED* s.v. *-ly*, suffix1.

before the end of the OE period native learners might already have been beginning to extract *-līċe* as an adverb-forming suffix. In ME the number of such adverbs increased substantially, until the suffix became almost fully productive in that function; the approximately cognate ON suffix *-līga* might have contributed to that development.

9.3 Old English prefixes

By far the commonest OE prefix was *ġe-*; it seems to have acquired multiple functions, with the result that it was becoming functionless in many words already in OE. In southern ME it survived in its function of perfectivizing verb forms, especially past participles, typically spelled *i-* or *y-* (e.g. *sumer is icumen in* 'summer has come in / begun' at the beginning of the well-known thirteenth-century round). In ModE it survives only as the fossilized initial vowel of a few words, e.g. *enough* (< OE *ġenōg*) and *aware* (< OE *ġewær*). Also very productive, but with a well-defined meaning, was *un-*, which made negative adjectives (and derived adverbs) productively in OE (e.g. *unblōdiġ, unboren, unclǣne, unfrēondlīċe,* etc.) and has continued to do so ever since.

Otherwise prefixes were mostly affixed to verbs and to nouns derived from such verbs in OE, and many of them resembled OE prepositions and adverbs (see Kastovsky 2006: 235–8). Such verbs are usually called "compound" verbs, but since their first elements do not always occur independently, it seems just as reasonable to regard those elements as prefixes. A restricted number of prefixed verbs survive in ModE. A representative list might include:

> *abide, alight, arise, awake(n), become, befall, beget, begin, behold, bequeath, beseech* (to *seek*), *beset, forbear, forbid, forget, forgive, forsake, forego, foresee, foretell, mistake, overcome, overflow, override, overwinter, understand, undertake, uphold, upset, withdraw, withhold, withstand.*

There are also more or less archaic examples, such as *betake oneself* and *bespoke* 'made to order', the latter originally a past participle. Three-quarters of the examples adduced above are inherited from OE (though the /g/ of *beget, forget,* and *forgive* shows that they have been adjusted to fit base verbs borrowed from ON[11]), and many others first appear in early ME: *beseech* first appears in *Lambeth, withhold* in *Vices and Virtues, undertake* in the *Orrmulum* (replacing OE *underfōn* with a corresponding compound of ON *taka*), and *uphold* and *withdraw* in *Ancrene Wisse.* The

---

11. However, the /g/ of *begin*, which has no ON cognate, must have been levelled from *began, begun.*

remaining examples have more interesting histories. *Foretell* is first attested in the *Cursor Mundi*, but it is a more or less straightforward replacement of OE *foreseċġan*, the descendant of which occurs in the same text and survives in normal usage as *foresay* down to about 1600 or so. *Mistake* first appears in the late fourteenth century, more or less simultaneously in the works of Wycliffe, Trevisa, Gower, and Chaucer; it replaces *misnimen*, which appears first in the AB language and is clearly a compound of OE *mis-* and *niman* 'take'. The simple verb *tacan*, an ON loanword, is already current in late entries in the more northerly recensions of the *Chronicle*, including *Peterborough*, but *nim* survives in relatively central dialects of English into the early fifteenth century, so that its final supersession by *take* in London English is roughly contemporary with the appearance of *mistake*. *Upset* appears in the fifteenth century (and does not acquire its modern meanings until the late eighteenth).

Most of these prefixes seem to have enjoyed limited productivity in ME and later, not unlike the suffix *-hood*, but a few have enjoyed a more active life. Perhaps the most surprising example is *be-*, which is (in part) a prefix systematically changing the thematic relationships of a verb; for instance, one can *spatter paint on a wall* or *bespatter a wall with paint*. That function seems to have been present already in OE, to judge from the relation between *smierwan* 'to smear (something on something else)' and *besmierwan* 'to (be)smear (something with something else)'; the prefix has remained productive at low frequency throughout the history of the language, in this and perhaps in other functions (see Marchand 1969: 146–8). Considerably more productive, or at least more salient, is *mis-* 'bad, badly', the descendant of PGmc. **missa-* (cf. Gothic *missadēþs* 'misdeed, sin'). In addition to the few surviving OE examples (*misdǣd* 'misdeed', *mishīeran* 'mishear', *mislǣdan* 'mislead'), there has been a steady stream of new ones, mostly verbs or derivatives of verbs (*mishandle, misunderstand, misconceive, misgovern, misbegotten, misapprehension, misconduct,* etc.), though there are a few others (e.g. *misfortune*; see Marchand 1969 176–7). As Marchand notes (ibid. pp. 176–7), this prefix was reinforced by Old French loanwords with the prefix *mes-* (e.g. *misadventure, mischief*; see the *OED* s.v. *mis-*, prefix2).

Finally, the verb prefix *un-*, indicating reversal of an action, as in *undo, untie*, remains fully productive in English. This is not the same prefix as the negative *un-* of ModE *unhappy*, OE *unclǣne*, etc. The latter was *un-* already in PGmc. (cf. e.g. Gothic *unhrains* 'unclean'), but the reversative prefix was *on-* in OE (e.g. in *onbindan* 'to untie') and **andi-* in PGmc. (cf. Gothic *andbindan*); that the two have become homonymous in ModE is sheer accident.

This is the most convenient place to note that a number of ModE prefixed adverbs, such as *today* and *away*, have developed from earlier prepositional phrases. Whether univerbation had already occurred in OE is not always clear, because in OE manuscripts the correlation between blank spaces and word boundaries is much less than perfect. OE *on weġ* was plausibly still two phonological words, but *tōdæġ* might or might not have been. An example which clearly had been univerbated is *tōgædere* 'together', since the second element does not recur independently (though it does in the synonymous *ætgædere*).

9.4 Compounds in English

All Germanic languages make compound nouns and adjectives freely, and English is no exception. In terms of the semantic relations between the parts of a compound there are three major types in English.[12]

In *endocentric* or *determinative* compounds the last element of the compound is its "head" and indicates a class of which the compound is a member. For instance, a *blackbird* (adjective + noun) is a kind of *bird* (noun) which is typically black; a *boathouse* (noun + noun) is a type of building or *house* (noun) to protect boats; someone who is *trigger-happy* (noun + adjective) is eager or *happy* (adjective) to pull the trigger; a person who is *half-blind* (adjective + adjective) is *blind* (adjective) by half, etc.

In *exocentric* compounds, sometimes called *bahuvrīhi* compounds (the technical term in Sanskrit), the final element is not the head; rather, the entire compound characterizes an unexpressed entity. For instance, a *bonehead* is not a kind of head; it means a person whose head apparently contains (nothing but) bone (thus no detectable brain). As Marchand 1969: 13–14 notes, compounds of this type must contain a zero-derivational morpheme which is their actual head. On those grounds he declines to consider them compounds, since strictly speaking they are derivatives of compounds by zero derivation. That is fair enough as far as it goes. What it does not take account of is the fact that (1) the underlying compound usually does not exist independently, and (2) only the compound—not its last overt element in isolation—can undergo the zero derivation. In other words, on the one hand there is no endocentric compound **bonehead* 'head of solid bone' or **tenderfoot* 'tender foot' from which the bahuvrīhis are derived, and on the other hand you cannot call someone a **head*, meaning 'person who has a head', or a **foot*, meaning 'person who has feet', by zero derivation; the compound and the zero morpheme go together. This is a good example of how distributional facts are often more important than bottom-up "piece-based" analysis

12. There may be others. See Marchand 1969: 11–30 for extensive discussion.

in linguistics. It is also a challenge for many theories of morphology, since it appears that an autonomous abstract structure must be posited to account for the facts.

A final major type are compounds in which one member is a verb which governs the other member in semantic terms (*Rektionskomposita* in German; Marchand 1969: 15–17). There are several ModE types. In the type *pickpocket* the verb is the first member and the compound is exocentric (much like French *gratte-ciel*); in the type *skyscraper* (which translates the French compound just adduced) the verb has been nominalized and the result appears in head position. An adjectival version of the latter construction is *heartbreaking*, using the participial suffix *-ing* rather than the agent noun suffix *-er*. As Marchand notes (ibid. pp. 15–17), the verbal compounds from which these nominal compounds might be supposed to be derived do not actually exist; i.e. there is no compound verb **skyscrape*, nor **heartbreak*. This is another instance of the distributional fact noted in the last paragraph: compounding and the derivational suffix are part of a single derivational package.

A full discussion of compounding in English is beyond the scope of this book; interested readers should begin with the comprehensive discussion of Marchand 1969: 11–127.[13] The rest of this section will make some observations about the history of different types of compounds in English.

Determinative and bahuvrīhi compounds were already numerous in OE; some can even be reconstructed for PGmc. (Carr 1939: 42–68, with extensive discussion), and it seems clear that compounds of these types were present in Proto-Indo-European, the earliest reconstructable ancestor of English. Since these formations are fully productive, Marchand is able to cite numerous examples of determinatives from every period of the language. Surviving OE examples are more numerous than might be expected; typical are *handbōc*, *reġnboga* 'rainbow', *sǣmann*, *hēahland* 'highland', *hwetestān* 'whetstone'. Surviving OE bahuvrīhis seem hard to find, but the type was very productive; typical are *mildheort* 'merciful' (lit. 'mild-hearted'), *ǣwiscmōd* 'ashamed' (lit. 'shame-minded'), *āneage* 'one-eyed', and *hēahstefn* 'with a high prow'. As the ModE translations show, there is a strong tendency to append the pseudoparticiple suffix *-ed* to compounds of this type. A few late OE examples can be found—for instance, beside *fēowerfēte* 'four-footed' (attested in the OE translation of Orosius) and *fēowerfōt* there is a single example of *fēowerfōted*—but there is typically a gap of several centuries between the attestation of such OE forms and the next appearance of their apparent descendants (see

13. For OE an exceptionally comprehensive and clear treatment is Kastovsky 2006: 228–34.

the *OED* s.vv. *three-footed*, *four-footed*, *one-eyed*, etc.), and it seems that pseudo-participle compounds became much more productive only in the fourteenth century (Marchand 1969: 266).

Compounds with internal government by a verb stem also existed in OE. The largest group ended in the agent nouns in *-a* and *-end*, which correspond functionally to ModE nouns in *-er* (see 9.1 above); typical are *heretoga* 'army-leader', *manslaga* 'murderer' (lit. 'man-slayer'), *mundbora* 'protector' (lit. 'protection-bearer'), and *æscberend* 'spear-bearer, warrior'. There was, of course, some overlap with compound names of professions such as *ārġēotere* 'bronze-founder' and *blōdlǣtere* 'bloodletter, physician'. Just as *-ere* eventually took over the function of making uncompound agent nouns, so also with compounds, though the compound formation does not seem to have been productive before the fourteenth century (Marchand 1969: 79). The story of OE internal-governing compound nouns in *-ing* and *-ung* is similar. Marchand (p. 75) cites *crismlīesing* 'untying the baptismal fillet' and *godspelbodung* 'preaching the gospel', and there are a number of others, but the ModE examples are all much later in origin; for instance, *homecoming*, *leavetaking*, and *childbearing* are late-fourteenth-century, and *housekeeping* (Marchand's type example) does not appear before the sixteenth century. The adjectival type *heartbreaking* is rare in OE; an example that survives in ModE is *weġfarende* 'wayfaring', but most examples are modern (Marchand 1969: 91). In short, though compounds with internal government by a verb stem were not foreign to OE, most modern examples are relatively recent innovations.

The ModE type of compound exemplified by *pickpocket* and *cutthroat* does not occur in OE; examples do not appear until the fourteenth century, and it is reasonable to suppose that they were coined in imitation of French examples (Marchand 1969: 380–2),[14] both because the type is normal in French and because the fourteenth century is the period in which the influence of French upon literary English becomes pervasive. Compounding of this type remains productive in ModE; to cite an example not found in the handbooks (so far as I know), in one of Ed McBain's police procedural mysteries a young woman contemptuously describes her romantic rival as an *eighteen-year-old piss-pants*.

14. However, Marchand's acceptance of Darmesteter's assertion that these compounds must reflect imperative sentences (ibid. p. 381) reflects a naïve conviction that abstract structures must somehow have originated from supposedly more transparent superficial ones. Note also that (pace Marchand) compounds of this type are numerous and possibly productive in Ancient Greek; typical examples include Ἐχέ-στρατος /ekʰé-stratos/ 'He-holds-the-camp', ἐκε-χειρίᾱ /eke-kʰeːría:/ 'truce' (lit. 'hold-hand'), Τερψι-χόρη /terpsi-kʰórɛː/ 'She-delights-in-dance', τερπι-κέραυνος /terpi-kéraunos/ 'delighting in the thunderbolt' (an epithet of Zeus).

Not all ModE compounds are spelled as single words. Many sequences spelled with internal white spaces are better analyzed as single compound words; for instance, some such sequences ending in a noun have the main stress not on the noun, as might be expected, but on the last preceding stressed syllable—a pattern typical of compounds.[15] Halliday 2004 observes that this type of compound is typical of scientific writing; he adduces the example *glass crack growth rate* 'rate of growth of cracks in glass' (ibid. p. 34). But the type is neither very new nor restricted to scientific discourse; in *The Sand Pebbles*, an American movie of 1966, Steve McQueen's character calls a valve in the ship's boiler room the *main steam stop valve*, in which *main* is probably just the ordinary adjective but *steam stop valve* 'valve which stops the steam' is clearly a compound. In fact, compounds of this type are fully productive in ModE, and they are routinely used both to compress a discourse and to provide continuity without exact repetition (Halliday 2004: 34–5, Kastovsky 2006: 206–7). They are interesting for at least two further reasons. Their great productivity shows that ModE is not as different from German in its use of compounds as is sometimes suggested: the two languages simply spell them differently. The other reason is more important. So far as I can tell, ModE productive compounding is no different in principle from the fully productive compounding of Classical Sanskrit (see, e.g., Whitney 1896: 480–515). For instance, in both languages a multi-part compound can usually be analyzed as binary-branching; Halliday's example above is unproblematically

[[[*glass crack*] *growth*] *rate*],

as his more discursive presentation demonstrates. A detailed comparison of the ModE and Sanskrit systems, both in formal terms (e.g. the "word-internal syntax" framework of Williams 1981) and in terms of the thematic relationships between the parts of compounds, might be interesting.

The compounds just described, though not recognized as lexemes in spelling, are made up of contiguous pieces. But ModE also has verb-plus-particle constructions which constitute discontinuous lexemes. Typical examples are *get up* 'rise from sleep', *get by* 'manage to survive', *come to* 'recover consciousness', *stand out* 'be conspicuous', *make out* 'engage in erotic foreplay', etc. They are lexemes because their meanings are not fully predictable from their component parts, but they are not morphological words because the components can be moved independently by the syntax of the language; for instance, *get up* can also be used transitively,

15. See Marchand 1969: 20–30 for comprehensive discussion of this and related problems.

and one can tell someone to *go get the others up* 'go and make the others get out of bed'. Whether OE had such lexemes is doubtful; the adverbs *inn*, *ūt*, and *upp*, and occasionally others, behave very much like the ModE particles *in*, *out*, *up*, etc. that are their descendants, but the OE verb-plus-particle combinations seem to be semantically transparent; even *cuman tō* 'arrive' is easily understood as a verb with a prepositional phrase whose object has been suppressed, equivalent to *cuman hider / þider*. The *OED* lists these combinations separately under their head verbs, so that historical information about individual examples is not difficult to retrieve, though a comprehensive survey would require considerable time and effort. Thus far, it appears to me that idiomatic meanings are rare at best before the fourteenth century, many appearing much later; surprisingly, *come to* 'recover consciousness' does not seem to be attested before the early nineteenth century. Once again, there is a similar phenomenon in German—the "separable prefixes" of verbs which are univerbated with the verb or not, depending on the clause's syntax—and in this case the developments were clearly parallel, not reflecting a common inheritance.

9.5 Compounding or affixation?

In ModE virtually all nouns, adjectives, and verbs have a form with no affixes (not even inflectional markers); those are "free" forms which can occur independently, as opposed to "bound" forms which cannot. Most ModE compounds are recognizable as compounds because they are concatenations of free forms in single prosodic words.

However, there are occasional exceptions, typified by *cranberry* and *raspberry*. The second element of both words is still fully transparent, but the first elements are not; *rasp* is no longer used by itself to denote raspberries, and the connection of *cranberry* with *crane* is apparent only to an etymologist (see the *OED* s.vv.). It is worth asking why we still consider such words to be compounds, instead of identifying *cran-* and *rasp-* as prefixes. I suggest that they are still compounds because they fit into a larger system of compounds which includes, e.g., *blackberry* and *blueberry*, still fully analyzable. In other words, it is the distribution of forms in a system which is decisive.

But there is actually an entire system of ModE multimorphemic words to which these diagnostics cannot easily be applied. The examples adduced in Plag 2018: 72 illustrate the problem well:

a. *bio*chemistry	b. *photo*graph	c. geo*logy*
*bio*rhythm	*photo*ionize	bio*logy*
*bio*warfare	*photo*analysis	neuro*logy*

Plag (ibid. p. 72) calls the morphemes that compose these words "neo-classical elements" and remarks, "It is not obvious whether the italicized elements should be regarded as affixes or as bound roots" (ibid. p. 73); but he goes on to point out (ibid. p. 73) that if we decide that they are affixes we will be obliged to conclude that a word like *biology* is composed of a prefix and a suffix with no root—an implausible analysis, to say the least. Semantically, these neoclassical elements behave like roots, and in fact they are adapted from Latin and Greek major lexemes. Plag concludes:

> The only difference between the neoclassical forms and native compounds is that these non-native elements are obligatorily bound. This is also the reason why the neoclassical elements are often called **combining forms.** We can thus state that neoclassical formations are best treated as compounds, and not as cases of affixation. (Plag 2018: 73)

For further discussion of this class of compounds the reader should consult Plag 2018: 152–6. As we will see in Chapter 11, this is not the only morphological peculiarity that has resulted from the wholesale borrowing of French, Latin, and Greek words into ME and ModE.

9.6 The fate of compounds

A type of development characteristic of the history of compounds should be noted here. Regular sound change typically makes compounds opaque, just as it makes inflectional paradigms opaque, for the simple reason that it proceeds without regard to morphological structure, meaning, or anything other than the phonological system. Occasionally, other changes can create similar opacities. The following examples will illustrate.

The ModE monosyllable *lord* is obviously not a compound by any definition, but it clearly was a compound a millennium and a half ago. Its phonological development was roughly *lord* < ME *lǭwerd* < *lhāverd* < OE *hlāford* < *hlāfweard*, lit. 'bread-guardian'; the normal OE form was already *hlāford*, and it always means 'lord' in OE texts, yet it must still have been analyzable, since the etymological spelling *hlāfweard* occurs once in the late OE *Paris Psalter*.

A slightly less opaque example is also well over a millennium old. Greek εὐαγγέλιον /euangélion/ 'good news; gospel' must have been loan-translated into OE as *gōdspell* in the seventh century, either soon after the missionaries sent by Pope Gregory the Great arrived in Kent in 597 or (less likely) during the period when Theodore (a native speaker of Greek, consecrated in 667) was Archbishop of Canterbury. But by early in the eighth century the first vowel of this word had been shortened before the following sequence of three consonants; we know that because it was mistranslated into OHG as *gotspel* 'news of God', with a short vowel (the correct translation would have been *guotspel*). In English this compound became increasingly opaque and was never "adjusted" to make it transparent again; a native speaker of ModE will be unaware that *gospel* originally meant literally "good news" unless (s)he has been told so explicitly.

Equally striking is the career of the OE compound *hāligdæġ* 'holy day'. The first vowel of this compound was shortened by the famous "trisyllabic shortening" sound change in the eleventh or (less likely) the latter part of the tenth century (Luick 1914–40: 328–9), but the resulting *Halliday* survives only as a family name. After OE *ā* was rounded to *ọ̄* (ibid. pp. 358–60), the compound was adjusted to fit its derivational base better, yielding *holidai* (short *o* being a lower mid vowel /ɔ/); the result survives in ModE as *holiday*. But that result has again become opaque, both in structure and in meaning; a modern Briton who "goes on holiday", or a modern American who "celebrates a holiday" (such as the Fourth of July), is typically unconcerned with holiness. The compound has therefore been recreated (at least in Catholic usage) as *holy day*, whose stress pattern (heavy stress on the first syllable) shows that it is, in fact, a compound, even though it is conventionally spelled with a space between its elements (see 9.4).

There are other similar examples, in ModE and in other languages (see, e.g., the entries for *housewife* and *hussy* in the *OED* online), but they exhibit the same basic principles of development.

Exercise

Look up the native adjective suffixes *-en*, *-ish*, and *-y* in Marchand 1969. From the information given there, give a brief sketch of how the productivity of each has changed over the course of the history of English. If you find Marchand's discussion insufficient, feel free to adduce evidence from other sources, such as the *OED*.

10 French derivational patterns in English

The division of material between this chapter and the next requires some discussion. Not only is French a direct descendant of Latin, preserving a large proportion of the Latin lexicon through generation after generation of NLA; like all the Romance languages, it has also reborrowed numerous Latin words from the written record of its ancestor and from the spoken Latin that was the medium of educated discourse throughout the Middle Ages and far down into the Renaissance. Many of those reborrowed Latin words were then passed on to English, with the result that any Latin loanword or affix in English can have arrived by one of (at least) two routes: it might have been borrowed directly from written Latin (most likely in the Renaissance) or it might have come through French (at almost any period). In addition, ordinary French words and affixes—whether or not they were inherited from Latin by direct descent—have been borrowed into English. We thus have three groups of loanwords and borrowed affixes from this nexus of sources: Latin direct, Latin-through-French, and (ordinary) French items (cf. the discussion of Durkin 2014: 236–40). The question is how to divide them up.

I have decided to treat all the identifiably Latin affixes, including the Latin-through-French, in the following chapter, reserving this chapter for borrowed material that is clearly French.[1] I do this for two reasons. On the one hand, it is often quite difficult to determine whether a Latin word or affix in English was borrowed directly from Latin or through the medium of a closely corresponding Latinate form in French. On the other hand, the distinction between native French material and reborrowings from Latin is generally easy to make, because the former has been affected by the dozens of complex but regular sound changes that French underwent, while reborrowings have usually escaped various characteristic French changes. Here is an example. There are numerous French

---

1. Some complex and indeterminate cases will be discussed in this chapter.

words ending in -ation, reflecting Latin -ătiōnem,[2] but not one of them was inherited from Latin by the usual route, i.e. being acquired by native learners in NLA generation after generation; they were all reborrowed from Latin in the Middle Ages. We know that because the French reflex of -ătiōnem by regular sound change is -aison; typical examples are oraison 'prayer' < ōrātiōnem, raison 'reason' < ratiōnem 'reckoning', saison 'season' < satiōnem 'sowing'. Some of the reborrowed examples appear relatively early, e.g. early twelfth-century les naciuns 'the gentiles' (modern les nations 'the nations'), but by then French had already undergone so many regular sound changes that to anyone familiar with the phonological development of the language the exceptionality of the reborrowed items is immediately obvious.

10.1 The process: borrowing and reanalysis

As I remarked in the preceding chapter, languages do not normally borrow pieces of words from one another, yet prefixes and suffixes of French and Latin origin have become productive in English. The process by which they did so was the same as that outlined for OE -ere in 9.2: affixed words and their derivational bases were both borrowed, the affixed word was recognized as such by native learners, and the affix was then "cut loose" for use with other derivational bases, eventually becoming productive. In the case of French loans in English this process can be observed operating in the historical record.

A case in point is -able (Marchand 1969: 229–30, Ringe and Eska 2013: 71–2). The Old French (OF) suffix had a wider range of functions than its ModE descendant, as is clear from an examination of examples borrowed into ME in the thirteenth century: merciable 'merciful', per-durable 'eternal', delitable 'delightful', defensable 'defensive', etc.; and as Marchand notes, it was generally the case that the derivational bases of these adjectives were borrowed too, though, of course, not always at the same time. The stage was thus set for the resegmentation of -able as a suffix for productive use in English, a development that will be sketched in more detail in the appropriate place below.

---

2. I cite Latin nominals in the accusative singular, since that is the etymological ancestor of most modern French singular forms. This is a simplification, since Old French still had a two-case system. Interested students should consult one of the standard historical grammars of Old French.

10.2 French prefixes in English

It is convenient to begin with a consideration of French prefixes, since the interchange between Latin and purely French forms is most tangled in just this area of derivational morphology. Latin had many lexemes, mostly verbs, with prefixes, most of which resembled prepositions (just like OE—see 9.3). OF inherited a fair number of such lexemes, and some were borrowed by English. However, many of the inherited prefixes did not become productive in OF or in English. Even a set of verbs such as OF *conçoivre* 'to conceive', *deçoivre* 'to deceive', *perçoivre* 'to perceive', *reçoivre* 'to receive' (modern French *concevoir, décevoir, percevoir, recevoir*) must have been only partly analyzable in OF; since it was not easy to extract meaningful prefixes from such sets, they did not give rise to productive patterns of word formation.[3]

Some of the OF prefixes which were borrowed into English were spelled like their Latin ancestors (e.g. *con-, pro-, re-*), so that one must examine the history of each loanword to discover which group it belongs to. Other OF prefixes were later adjusted in English so as to resemble their Latin sources more closely. For instance, both *interchange* and *intermeddle* were borrowed from French late in the fourteenth century (Marchand 1969: 171), and their earliest recorded ME forms are *entrechaungen* and *entremeddlen* (see the *OED* s.vv.). Spellings with French *entre-* continue to occur until late in the sixteenth century, but already before the end of the fifteenth the modern Latinate spelling *inter-* has begun to appear. OF *en-* has survived somewhat better, apparently because it can be assigned definite functions, especially 'put into/onto' (*endanger, emblazon, ensnare*, etc.) and 'make (into)' (*enslave, enable, enrich*, etc.; see Marchand 1969: 162–3), though spellings with *in-* also occur (ibid. pp. 163–4), and in some cases both have survived and been specialized in different uses (e.g. *ensure* vs. *insure*, the latter now mostly referring to financial insurance, the former never used in that sense, at least in the USA).

The prefixes beginning with *d-* present an especially complex and confused picture. Both Latin *dē-* 'down, off, away' and *dī-* 'apart' (the alternant of *dis-* which appeared before voiced consonants) developed by regular sound change into OF *de-*, whence modern French /də-/; typical examples are (modern French) *demander* 'to ask' < Lat. *dēmandāre* 'to entrust, to commend', *demeurer* 'to remain' < *dēmorārī* 'to linger, to delay', *devenir* 'to become' < *dēvenīre* 'to reach, to arrive at', *demi* 'half' < *dīmidium*. However, Lat. *dis-* 'apart', which occurred only before

---

3. Of course, this set has remained partly analyzable in ModE; see 11.3 for discussion of some interesting consequences.

voiceless stops, became OF *des-*; thus we find OF *destroitz* 'strait, narrow passage of water' < Lat. *districtus* 'pulled apart', *deschargier* 'to unload' < late Lat. *discarricāre*, *desplaire* 'to displease' < *displacere ← Lat. *displicēre*, etc. Since the function of *des-* overlapped with that of *de-* and since *des-* was a more distinctive marker of that function, it spread at the expense of *de-* in OF. For instance, we find not only OF *delivrer* 'to set free, to deliver' < late Lat. *dēlīberāre*, but also *deslivrer*, which cannot have a direct Latin source since *-sl-* does not occur in Latin.[4] The process of replacement was probably encouraged by a few inherited examples of *dē-* before verbs beginning with sC-clusters, e.g. OF *despoillier* 'to despoil' < *dēspoliāre*, *destruire* 'to destroy' < *dēstruere* 'to demolish'. Then in the sixteenth century *s* before consonants was dropped in French, with the result that *des-* became *dé-*; thus the modern French descendants of the last six OF words cited are *détroit, décharger, déplaire, délivrer, dépouiller,* and *détruire*. Since *dé-* superficially resembles Latin *dē-*, it was used to render the latter in reborrowings from Latin and in the coining of new Latinate words in French. An unhappy result is that English *de-* is etymologically multiply ambiguous; one must investigate the history of each example in detail in order to determine how it reached its current form.

A few clearly French prefixes have become productive in English; the most important examples are perhaps the following. Latin *contrā* 'against, opposite', which came to be used as a prefix only in late Latin (and then only rarely), survived in OF as *contre-* and became productive; typical OF examples are *contredit* 'objection, opposition' and *contreplege* 'reciprocating pledge, surety'. Early examples borrowed into English include *counterfeit* and *countermand*, but it was not until the sixteenth century that *counter-* became productive (Marchand 1969: 151–2). The same pattern—some early loans but only later productivity—appears in the cases of *mal-* 'bad' and *non-* 'not, un-'. Of early loans with *mal-* only *malapert* apparently survives; the common words *maladministration, malformed, malpractice,* etc. do not predate the seventeenth century, and many are later coinages (Marchand 1969: 174–5). The Latin words with the prefix *nōn-* cited in Marchand 1969: 179 are all late and specialized legal terms; as he notes (ibid. p. 179), the distribution of OF legal terms prefixed with *non-* was rather different, and it is the OF usage that is relevant to English. Of the ME loans, at least *non-payment, non-residence,* and *non-appearance* are still in use, but most modern examples, including all those that are not

---

4. Some examples of this replacement probably antedate the separate history of French; for instance, OF *desdeignier* 'to disdain' is perfectly cognate with Old Provençal *desdenhar*, apparently reflecting *disdignāre*, replacing Classical Latin *dēdignārī* 'to reject as unworthy'.

legal terms, are later coinages, and it is only in the nineteenth century that *non-* "takes off" as a general negator of adjectives (ibid. pp. 179–80). Finally, mention might be made of *sur-*, the OF descendant of Latin *super*. It has never been very productive in English, but in addition to the fourteenth-century examples *surname* and *surcoat*, the common noun *surcharge* appears in the sixteenth century and *surtax* late in the nineteenth, suggesting at least marginal productivity for this prefix.[5]

10.3 French suffixes in English

It is in this area of derivation that French influence on English morphology is most extensive and obvious. Not only have some twenty French suffixes achieved at least modest productivity in English, but in some cases related Latin suffixes have routinely been replaced by their French descendants in English derivational morphology. Some of the more important and interesting French suffixes in English are the following.

OF *-able* is the first example that comes to mind. As noted in 10.1, it appears in a steadily increasing number of French loanwords in English from the thirteenth century on. By the end of the ME period a large number of adjectives in *-able* and verbs from which they could be derived had been borrowed; Marchand's list (p. 229) includes *acceptable, agreeable, blamable, changeable, commendable, comparable, damnable, deceivable, desirable, determinable*, all in place by the middle of the fifteenth century, plus further examples which were, or could have been, derivable from nouns. Sometimes the members of a pair were apparently borrowed in the same generation, more or less; for instance, both *damn* and *damnable* first appear early in the thirteenth century. Sometimes there was clearly a wide temporal gap between the borrowings; for instance, *blame* appears in the twelfth-century *Trinity Homilies*, while *blamable* is not attested before Trevisa's *Polychronicon* late in the fourteenth century (and remains uncommon subsequently). But, of course, to a native speaker of English in, say, 1450 that made no difference; for such a person there were numerous adjectives in *-able* derived from verbs and meaning 'able to be Xed', where X was the verb from which the adjective was derived (as well as others with more idiosyncratic meanings, such as *comfortable* and *profitable*). It was easy to form new examples on the same semantic pattern, and, in fact, at least one had been derived from an English verb some generations before: *believable* first appears in the late-fourteenth-century Wycliffite bible. Now we begin to find *available* in 1451 ('able

---

5. Whether the fifteenth-century verb *surcharge* 'to charge (someone) too much' and noun *surcharge* 'second course (of a meal)' are relevant seems doubtful.

to be availed of'), *understandable* around 1475,[6] *eatable* in 1483, etc. (Marchand 1969: 230). Negative compounds with *un-* are especially numerous and often attested early (ibid. p. 230); for instance, *unknowable* appears first in Chaucer and *unspeakable* in the works of Richard Rolle. It seems clear that by 1500 *-able* was firmly entrenched in English as a fully native suffix. Later loans from Latin, though often spelled *-ible*, have been assimilated to the pre-existing pattern.

A suffix with an interestingly complex history is *-ity*, which represents OF *-ité*. As Marchand notes (p. 312), the French suffix occurred in that shape only in Latinate words; the purely native French suffix was *-té*, e.g. in *cité* 'city' < Lat. *cīvitātem* 'citizenship; citizens (collectively)', *sûreté* 'safety, security' < *sēcūritātem*, etc. But the only concession to Latin in the Latinate suffix was the unstressed linking vowel *-i-*, which had been lost or reduced to schwa centuries before in the genuine French words; the native syllable coda *-é* < *-ed* < Lat. *-āt-* was retained. English has treated this suffix in a comparable fashion. French words containing the native form of the suffix were borrowed into ME (including, e.g., *city*, which first appears early in the thirteenth century, *surety* about a century later, and *safety* late in the fourteenth century), but so were Latinate French forms. In fact, the earliest attested loanword with this suffix is Latinate *carited* 'charity', which occurs in *Peterborough* in the entry for 1137 in its most archaic Norman French form (also *kariteð* in *Vices and Virtues*, *kariteþ* in the *Orrmulum*, both rendering the early OF word-final fricative accurately). Most of the Latinate examples, however, seem to be fourteenth-century and later; of Marchand's list (p. 312) the earliest attested (*diversity, impassibility, singularity*) are all from the works of Richard Rolle in the first half of that century. The commonest early example, *necessity* (not listed by Marchand), appears simultaneously in the works of Wycliffe, Gower, and Chaucer late in the fourteenth century.

In the fifteenth century some of the older French loanwords in *-(e)té* began to adopt the Latinate suffix (Marchand 1969: 313); that is most obvious in the cases of *falsté* (Robert Manning, early fourteenth century) → *falsité* and *curiousté* (Wycliffe, Chaucer) → *curiousité*, but *chasteté* (*Ancrene Wisse*) and *skarceté* (fourteenth century) also underwent at least a change in spelling, whether or not there was any actual change in pronunciation. To that extent the native French suffix in English was assimilated to its Latinate cousin. However, the largest-scale assimilation proceeded in the opposite direction: scores of words borrowed directly from Latin replaced the suffix *-itās ~ -itāt-* with *-ity*. Obvious examples include *implacability, impeccability* (Marchand 1969: 313), *parity* and *disparity*,

6. This also appears in the Wycliffite bible, but there it means 'understanding'.

opportunity (already in Trevisa), etc. Of course, it is usually not possible to insist with absolute certainty that French had nothing to do with the borrowing, because often the same Latin words were being borrowed into French, with comparable results. But the most striking large-scale fact is that the purely Latin form of the suffix never appears in English at all. German provides a telling contrast. *University* was a medieval Latin word borrowed into all the western European literary languages with its suffix assimilated to native forms (Italian *università*, French *université*, Spanish *universidad*, etc.), and from the pattern of foundation of universities it is clear that the English got both the institution and the word from France and the Germans from Italy (cf. e.g. Koch 2008: 51, 60). But while the English word conforms to the Anglo-French pattern, German *Universität* has a form of the suffix obviously adjusted to agree better with Latin, and that is the only form of the suffix current in German (cf. Kluge and Seebold 1995 s.v. *-tät*).

At least two French suffixes, *-al* and *-ment*, have become important for the derivation of nouns from verbs in English. The history of the former is surprising and partly obscure. Though it ultimately reflects Latin neuter plural *-ālia*, its French reflex *-aille* is not very productive; the career of *-al* in English was launched by a handful of examples, many of them prominent in or even confined to legal language at first (Marchand 1969: 236–7). A list of Marchand's early examples with relevant information will perhaps be more informative than a discussion:

	date attested	loan from French?	legal term (at first)?
espousal	1325	yes	yes
rental	Langland	yes	yes
supposal	Wycliffe	yes	partly
arrival	Gower	yes	no
rehearsal	Chaucer	no	no
reprisal	1419	yes	yes
acquittal	1430	no	yes
refusal	1474	no	yes
reversal	1489	yes	yes
trial	1526	yes	partly

It can be seen that the early examples are, on the average, comparatively late; that loans from the Norman French legal language used in medieval England were prominent for a long time, but that native English coinages begin to appear in the late fourteenth century; and that even among the English innovations legal terms continue to account for a majority of the examples. It was in the sixteenth and seventeenth centuries that derivation of nouns from verbs with *-al* really began to "take off", and many of the examples commonest today (*appraisal, arousal, betrayal, dismissal, transferral*) date from the nineteenth century (Marchand 1969: 236–7).

By contrast, the history of -*ment* is comparable to that of -*able*; Marchand seems to have had no difficulty finding early examples. For instance, both *judge* and *judgement* appear in the *Ancrene Wisse* early in the thirteenth century; *advance* and *preach* likewise appear in that work, while *advancement* is attested from about 1325 and *preachment* from about 1330. Other such pairs of which one member is attested from before 1300 are *commence* (1320) and *commencement* (1250), *admonish* (1325) and *admonishment* (1275); *entice, impair*, and *assign* are all attested from 1297, and their derivatives follow over the next century: *enticement* in 1303, *impairment* in 1340, *assignment* in 1393. "By 1300, -**ment** was obviously a derivative suffix though many of the 14th and 15th century coinages were short-lived" (Marchand 1969: 331). It has remained a productive deverbal suffix ever since, though it is striking that a large majority of the examples are made to verbs borrowed from French (op. cit. pp. 331–2).

The verb-forming suffix -*ify* and the adjective-forming suffix -*ive* exhibit productivity "curves" similar to that of deverbal -*al*: each is first attested in English in a handful of words borrowed from French in the fourteenth century, and it is only in the sixteenth century that they become productive. However, in these two cases there is a further complication of interest: they are often used to render Latin -*ificāre* and -*īvus* respectively in Latin-to-English loans and in Latinate coinages within English (Marchand 1969: 300–1, 315–18). For that reason it seems likely that the observable increase in their productivity should be attributed at least partly to the much greater borrowing of words directly from Latin in the sixteenth century and later.

Two French suffixes have become conflated in English with similarly shaped suffixes of other origins. Adjective-forming -*ous* was borrowed in French words throughout the ME period: *dangerous* appears already in the *Ancrene Wisse; courageous, grievous, lecherous*, and *venomous* are attested from the decades around 1300; *adventurous, amorous, glorious, riotous, treacherous*, and *virtuous* appear before 1350, etc. The suffix became productive in several patterns (Marchand 1969: 339–41). But by the fifteenth century it was also being used to render its Latin ancestor -*ōsus* in words borrowed directly from Latin, and from about the same time it begins to appear on Latin loanwords that had a different suffix or no suffix, rendering instead the grammatical ending -*us; superfluous*, borrowed from Latin *superfluus*, appears as early as 1432 (ibid. pp. 341–2). That usage led to further patterns of productivity (ibid. pp. 343–5). The history of -*ous* is too complex to be summarized here; students should read Marchand's account.

The Latin agent noun suffix *-tor ~ -sor* survived in OF as *-tour ~ -sour*; in addition, the Latin suffix *-ārius*, which had been borrowed into OE as *-ere* (see the preceding chapter), survived in OF as *-ier*. French nouns with those suffixes were, of course, borrowed into ME, and Latin *-tor ~ -sor* was subsequently borrowed as part of loans direct from Latin. Since *-er* and *-or* are pronounced identically in ModE, the spellings have become interchangeable to some extent; at least in US universities, academic *advisors* and *advisers* are both common (though the Google test seems to show that *adviser* has the upper hand, with 2.12 billion hits as opposed to 250 million for *advisor*). Naturally, it is not always easy to determine the etymology of a particular example without consulting the documentary record as summarized in the *OED*. In this case too the interested student should read the account of Marchand 1969: 273–81.

Perhaps the most apt summary of this chapter is that while English has borrowed numerous affixes from French, not all have become equally productive; for instance, *-able* has been hugely productive with bases of every origin, *-ment* is quite productive but remains largely restricted to French bases, *-al* shares that restriction but has not been so productive, and *-ard* and *-ure* remain unimportant enough that it did not seem worth discussing them in this chapter.

Exercise

Look up the suffixes *-age*, *-ee*, and *-ess* in Marchand 1969. From the information given there, give a brief sketch of how the productivity of each has changed over the course of the history of English. If you find Marchand's discussion insufficient, feel free to adduce evidence from other sources, such as the *OED*.

11 Latinate derivational patterns in English

As we saw in Chapter 10, French affixes have had very divergent careers in English. A few, like *-able*, have become fully productive; some, like *-ment*, are productive but mostly restricted to deriving words from French bases; many have had only a marginal impact on the derivational morphology of English. The same sort of divergence is observable among Latin affixes in English, with one major difference: to a surprising extent the Latinate system of derivation remains a closed subsystem of English derivational morphology, even though some parts of it have "got loose" in the lexicon and are quite productive. This chapter will sketch the main outlines of this pattern. Greek affixes have been included because they form part of the Latinate derivational system.

11.1 Fully productive Latinate affixes

A surprising number of Latinate affixes have become productive in twentieth- and twenty-first-century English. They all share two character-istics: they are easy to identify and delimit, and they are semantically useful.

A substantial majority of the productive Latinate affixes are prefixes. The champion, in terms of productivity, is almost certainly *re-* 'again'. It entered the language as part of French loanwords beginning early in the thirteenth century (Marchand 1969: 189), but as Marchand admits, many of the examples—I would say most—could not be analyzed, at least not fully. By the middle of the fifteenth century there were enough analyzable examples to segment *re-* off; some of the new, transparent examples are based on French words, but others are clearly based on Latin (ibid. p. 189). A large number of new examples followed in the sixteenth and seventeenth centuries, and by now the prefix is very productive; one can *reread* a book, *resend* an email, and even *re-vouch* for someone. Marchand 1969: 188–91 gives many examples with discussion.

Many Latinate prefixes seem to have become productive because they occur in useful pairs. Typical are *pro-* 'in favor of' (Latin and Greek) and *anti-* 'opposed to' (Greek), of which the latter has a much longer history in English. The earliest meaning of *anti-* in English seems to have been 'rival' or 'false'; aside from *antichrist* (ca. 1300), the examples date from the end of the sixteenth century and later, beginning with *antipope* (Marchand 1969: 142). In the seventeenth century the prefix acquires its modern productive meaning; *pro-* follows as its antonym in the nineteenth (ibid. pp. 142–4, 186). A similar pair is *pre-* 'before' and *post-* 'after', the former becoming clearly productive in the sixteenth century and then much more productive later, the latter following in the nineteenth (ibid. pp. 182–5). Yet another pair is *hyper-* 'excessively' and *hypo-* 'deficiently' (both Greek), but only the former has become notably productive; it became productive in the seventeenth century and acquired its modern function in the nineteenth, whereas *hypo-* emerged as a barely productive antonym in technical terms very recently (ibid. pp. 167–8).[1] The prefixes *sub-* 'under, lower; smaller, less' and *super-* 'over', though antonyms in Latin, seem to be less closely linked in English word-formation (ibid. pp. 193–7). The former became fully productive in the sixteenth and seventeenth centuries with examples like *subtreasurer* and *subcommittee* and has remained productive ever since; the productivity of *super-* dates chiefly from the nineteenth century, and few antonymic pairs seem to have become generally used outside of biological taxonomy, though at least *substructure* and *superstructure* can be cited.

Other useful and productive Latinate prefixes (in addition to *de-* and *inter-*, briefly discussed in the preceding chapter) include *ex-* 'former', *semi-* 'half', and *trans-* 'through'; their histories in English are outlined in Marchand 1969. Though *semi-* appears as early as Chaucer, these prefixes share a salient characteristic with those discussed above: most surviving examples were coined in EModE and later.

Among Latinate suffixes three examples borrowed from Greek enjoy unusual productivity in ModE. The champion, so to speak, is *-ize*, which forms verbs meaning 'do the activity characteristic of the derivational base'—a maximally general function that is obviously closely connected with the suffix's productivity. As so often with Latinate affixes, there are at least some medieval examples borrowed from or calqued on French, but in this case the number is fairly substantial; Marchand 1969: 318 cites (among less durable examples) *baptize, authorize, canonize, evangelize,* and *solemnize* from the late thirteenth and fourteenth centuries, followed by *catechize, harmonize, moralize, organize, scandalize, tyrranize,* etc. in the fifteenth. The ecclesiastical nature of most of these words is obvious.

---

1. In the commonest example, *hypodermic* '(penetrating) under the skin', the prefix has a quite different and older meaning.

Towards the end of the sixteenth century, however, *-ize* "takes off", with dozens of new examples coined before 1700, and in the nineteenth century there is a further burst of productivity in the context of scientific discourse (ibid. pp. 318–19). By this point there are few restrictions on the use of *-ize*, which appears in such obviously English innovations as *itemize* and *winterize*; Marchand (p. 320) attempts a semantic classification of the major types.

Less productive, but still important, are the noun-forming suffixes *-ism* and *-ist*, which in Ancient Greek were derivationally related to the source of *-ize*. Nouns ending in *-ism* often indicate ideologies or systems of thought and belief, and that was the earliest use of the suffix in English (productively from the sixteenth century onward). However, *-ism* has spread beyond that lexical "homeland"; obvious examples with rather different meanings are *absenteeism, alcoholism, egotism, fanaticism,* etc. The suffix *-ist* was originally linked to *-ism*—e.g. a *Calvinist* is someone who adheres to *Calvinism*—but this suffix too has acquired a life of its own as a kind of semantically loose agent suffix; the examples *tourist, bassoonist,* and *archaeologist* give a good impression of its range. Marchand 1969: 306–10 offers extensive discussion.

11.2 The Latinate derivational system in English

In addition to the Latinate affixes which can be added productively to a wide range of English derivational bases (including many not noted above, all discussed in Marchand 1969), there is an entire English derivational subsystem which is aptly characterized as "neo-Latin". Though it is neither fully regular nor fully productive, it is very extensive, as the following discussion will show. Much more information about the system can be found in Minkova and Stockwell 2009.

The suffix *-ation* straddles the two derivational subsystems (Marchand 1969: 259–61). Deverbal nouns can be formed with this suffix from verbs ending in the French suffix *-ify* (*identify : identification,* etc.) or the Greek suffix *-ize* (*organize : organization,* etc.) or—perhaps less often — French or Latinate verbs with no overt suffix (*adapt : adaptation, damn : damnation,* etc.). But there is also a large group of such nouns which are derivationally related to verbs in *-ate*, frequently also adjectives in *-ative*, and sometimes other formations as well. For instance, we have a verb *legislate*, an action / result noun *legislation*, an adjective *legislative*, an agent noun *legislator*, and a less regular, but not unparalleled, collective noun *legislature*.[2] So also *contemplate, contemplation,* and *contemplative*;

2. These are all seventeenth-century neo-Latin or (from a Classicist's point of view)

alternate, alternation, and *alternative; authenticate* and *authentication,* etc. As Marchand notes, the noun in *-ation* is typically the oldest member of the set in English, and the verbs, at least, are backformed to the nouns. The process of backformation is still going on. For instance, *orientation* was originally formed from suffixless *orient,* and the backformed alternative *orientate* is still stigmatized in the USA, though it seems to be completely unobjectionable in Britain. In much the same way, *administer* and *administration* are both attested in the fourteenth century; *administrate* was backformed in the sixteenth, and while it continues to be used it has never ousted *administer* (whereas the seventeenth-century adjective *administrative* is universal, since it is the only alternative in that function).

Other Latin loanwords in *-tion* and *-sion* occupy similar positions in families of derived words; but unlike *-ation* they are not added to non-Latinate verbs because they are less easily segmented off from their roots. Thus *division* is obviously related to *divide, divisor,* and *divisive; contrition* is related to *contrite, deletion* to *delete, construction* to *construct* and *constructive,* etc. The system is neither fully regular nor fully productive, but it does not contain only words actually borrowed from Latin; for instance, *divisive* and *construct* were formed within English, and *delete* may have been.[3]

As a result of the large-scale borrowing of Latin words from the sixteenth century onwards and the coinage of new Latinate words on the basis of existing models, English now has a two-tiered system of derivational morphology: in effect, one system for the Latinate vocabulary and the other for everything else. Of course, the two are not hermetically sealed off from one another (as the case of *-ation* demonstrates), but they are clearly distinct. Several things about that situation are of interest to a linguist.

In the first place, the fact that the Latinate vocabulary of English began to expand rapidly in the sixteenth century can only reflect the spread of the Renaissance to northern Europe around 1500, bringing with it a renewed interest in Classical Latin literature and style. The speakers of English who borrowed and coined the new words were necessarily educated, and the educated class was small and comparatively wealthy. Yet dozens of Latinate words, at least, have become current in vernacular

pseudo-Latin words. The ultimate source is a post-Classical phrase *lēgis lātiō* 'passing of a law', where *lātiō* is derived from *lātus,* the suppletive perfect participle of *ferre* 'to carry' (!).

3. The oldest citations in the *OED* are variously spelled and different in meaning from the modern word; they may or may not be the same word. *Delete* in the modern sense and *deletion* both first appear around 1600. The Latin verb is *dēlēre; dēlētus* is its perfect participle.

speech; obvious examples are *direction, executive, individual, institution, operation, production, structure, tradition,* etc., many borrowed from French at first but clearly Latin in form. As a group, these Latinate words must reflect the influence of educated speech on vernacular speech. How that process operated in detail can no longer be recovered, but one inference seems safe enough: working people must have learned these words in contexts where they came face to face with their social superiors, at first in the law courts and in church, then (much later) in political and medical contexts. Universal education and the internet have surely played a part as well, but from the perspective of linguistic history those are very recent phenomena.

   Secondly, a large majority of the Latinate vocabulary is clearly not learned in early childhood and therefore is not "native" in quite the same sense as, say, the inflectional morphology and such fully productive affixes as *-ness* and *-able.* The Latinate system probably cannot be learned as a system by small children, simply because they do not have enough of its pieces to put it together, and in discussions of the system linguists have not always paid enough attention to that. Yet the Latinate system is clearly native to native speakers of English in *some* sense; after all, a native speaker knows that there is no **administrature* (parallel to *legislature;* we use *administration* in a concrete sense instead). The implications of these facts remain to be explored, perhaps by psycholinguistic experimentation.

11.3 Some consequences of the split in English derivational morphology

As we have seen, French and Latin affixes which are historically related, or in some cases are merely similar, have tended to be conflated in English. Nevertheless, the fact that the English lexicon includes several etymological strata of words—at a minimum, Anglo-Saxon, French, and Latinate—has given rise to a few cases of competing affixes with the same or similar functions. By far the largest-scale example involves adjectives with negative prefixes.

   Native *un-* was already very productive in OE and has continued to be so; coinages such as *unadventurous* and *unconditional* show that it can be prefixed to adjectives of any etymological source. Though there are adjectives to which *un-* cannot be prefixed, the restriction seems to be semantic rather than formal; see Marchand 1969: 203 for discussion (though it is not clear to me that Marchand has said the last word on the matter). By contrast, negative *in-,* the Latin cognate of *un-,*[4] can be

---

4. The Proto-Indo-European prefix was syllabic *ṇ-; see Ringe 2017: 72, 100.

prefixed only to Latinate words, though within the Latinate system it has been very productive. Whether a particular Latinate adjective has a negative with *in-* or with *un-* is, to some extent, idiosyncratic, and the balance has shifted over time (Marchand 1969: 168–70)—except that a Latinate adjective beginning with (non-negative) *in-* or *inter-* must be negated with *un-* (e.g. *uninhabitable, unintelligible*; ibid. p. 169), evidently to avoid a superficial repetition of /ɪn-/. The distribution of *non-* (discussed briefly in 10.2 above) is somewhat different. Originally used only with nouns (ibid. p. 179), it can now be used freely with adjectives, but most examples strike me as nonce coinages, created only if there is not already a negative adjective with *un-* or *in-*, or if it cannot be called to mind at the moment. Paradoxically, that makes it the default negative prefix, even though most examples are rare. The least used negative prefix is *a(n)-*, the Greek cognate of *un-* and *in-*: all examples are Latinate and most are technical in nature, the only obvious nontechnical examples being *agnostic, amoral, apolitical,* and perhaps *asymmetrical* (with related noun *asymmetry*).

A very different consequence of the complex history of English derivation has implications for the theory of morphology. Consider the following sets of derived words (first adduced in a modern context by Aronoff 1976: 11–15, though note the references at Marchand 1969: 5; see also Don 2014: 15, 18, Carstairs-McCarthy 2018: 24–6):

1. *perceive*	*perception*	*perceptive*	*percept*	
receive	*reception*	*receptive*		*receptacle*
deceive	*deception*	*deceptive*		
conceive	*conception*		*concept*	
	contraception	*contraceptive*		
	inception	*inceptive*		
2. *reduce*	*reduction*			
deduce	*deduction*	*deductive*[5]		
induce	*induction*	*inductive*		
produce	*production*	*productive*	*product*	
3. *repel*	*repulsion*	*repulsive*	*repulse*	
propel	*propulsion*	*propulsive*		
compel	*compulsion*	*compulsive*		

5. But *deduct* belongs to a different set with a different meaning (and *deduction* is part of that set too, with a different meaning from the *deduction* adduced here). The *OED* entries show that the semantic ranges of the verbs *deduce* and *deduct* once overlapped, but they no longer do. The situation of *induce, induct,* and *induction* is similar, except that there has been less overlap in the meanings of the verbs historically (though there is still some in technical discussions of electricity).

The prefixes of these words are all recognizable units; so are the suffixes *-tion ~ -sion* and *-tive ~ -sive* (cf. e.g. *relation* and *relative, expression* and *expressive*), and though *-t* and *-tacle* are less immediately recognizable, they occupy the same position and can plausibly be segmented off. In each set the remaining "piece" of the words exhibits uniform behavior:

1. *-ceive* /-siːv/ word-finally, but *-cep-* /-sɛp-/ before a voiceless coronal obstruent;
2. *-duce* /-d(j)uːs/ word-finally, but *-duc-* /-dʌk-/ before a voiceless coronal obstruent;
3. *-pel* /-pɛl/ word-finally, but *-pul-* /-pʌl-/ before a voiceless coronal obstruent.

Each of these alternations is irregular and unique in ModE. That there might be two or more homonymous items exhibiting such an alternation is implausible at best; we seem to be in the presence of single contentful units, i.e. morphemes. The system is even marginally productive: upon learning the rare verb *abduce* an educated native speaker has no difficulty producing the derived noun *abduction*. But as Aronoff points out (1976: 11–15), there is no common denominator in the meanings of most of these compounds which would allow us to extract meanings for their roots. *Propel* and *repel* do make sense, but their semantic relation to *compel* is opaque; in discussions of logic the word-families of *deduce* and *induce* are at least opposites; but the other compounds are completely opaque semantically. Moreover, because that is true, even the prefixes usually cannot be assigned definite meanings in this context: though *re-* does mean 'back' in *repel*, it does not mean 'back' or 'again' (as in *resend*) in the other items in these sets; though *de-* might mean 'down' in *deduce*, it does not mean 'down' or 'reverse' (as in *dethrone*) in the other items, etc. The compounds have definable meanings, which reappear clearly in their derivatives, but the prefixes and the stem mostly do not. We are in the presence of morphemes without definable individual content.

Marchand 1969: 5–6 takes the position that since the roots and prefixes of these words do not have assignable meanings, they are not morphemes; his contention is that a morpheme must be meaningful. To me that seems hasty; after all, *cran-* has no obvious meaning in *cranberry* (see 9.5), yet it is clearly a morpheme. Moreover, identifiable pieces of complex words with no semantic function are not particularly rare crosslinguistically; obvious examples are the "conjugation" vowels of Latin present stems and the "peg" prefix of Navajo.[6] If the brief of morphology is to analyze

6. Navajo morphology is heavily prefixing, and a verb form can have many prefixes; the older ones (closer to the verb stem at the end of the form) and the younger ones are

the structure of words, we need to account for these pieces, whether they have meanings or not.

Our current brief, however, is to describe how this odd situation came about. The compound verbs ending in *-duce* and *-pel* and their derivatives in *-ion* are words actually borrowed from Latin, and in Classical Latin they were still relatively transparent semantically, both because they could still be used in more or less literal senses (*compellere* 'to drive together', *indūcere* 'to lead into', etc.) and because the simplex verbs were still in common use (especially *dūcere* 'to lead', though *pellere* was still common in the meaning 'drive away, put to flight'). But English borrowed only the compounds because the simplices were not needed; the literal meanings of the compounds do appear in earlier ModE, but they were evidently outcompeted by the ubiquitous English verb-plus-particle combinations, and some of the compounds also drifted semantically in various directions in English. In short, these examples are a result of the wholesale importation of Latinate derivational morphology into English.

The compound verbs in *-ceive* are a stranger case. In this case the verbs are all French, but their derivatives are Latinate. Most members of this set were actually borrowed into ME; most of the Latinate members seem to have been borrowed through French, reflecting the growth of Latinate vocabulary in French in the high Middle Ages. Thus this word-set resulted from a "perfect storm" of contingent events, i.e. historical accidents. By 1450 the only words of this set listed above that had not yet appeared in English were *concept, inception, deceptive, perceptive, inceptive, percept, contraception,* and *contraceptive*. *Concept* and *inception* were borrowed directly from Latin late in the fifteenth century. The other words are more interesting. *Deceptive, perceptive,* and *inceptive* first appear in the seventeenth century; though Latin and French antecedents can be cited, it is reasonable to suspect that these three words reflect the productivity of the Latinate system of derivation in English. *Percept* does not appear until the nineteenth century, and though the *OED* says *pro forma* that it reflects the Latin past participle *perceptum*, they also note that it was obviously coined on the model of *concept*. *Contraception* and *contraceptive* appear late in the nineteenth century, the former coined as a kind of opposite to *conception* (of a child), the latter by rule. These late examples clearly attest the system's productivity.

Two further remarks on this last set may be in order. I have not listed *interception* above for a specific reason: its verb is *intercept*. Both noun and

---

separated by a phonological boundary called the disjunct boundary. The peg prefix *yi-* is inserted if there is no other vowel in the prefix complex to the right of the disjunct boundary. See Kari 1976: 36–45, 104–14 for discussion and examples.

verb appear first in the sixteenth century; the verb happens to be attested earlier, but it was almost certainly backformed to the noun, which was borrowed directly from Latin. That history is the reason why the pair is not a typical part of this set.[7] The absence of a verb *contraceive might be laid to its uselessness: *conceiving* a child is an act, but what would "contraceiving" one be? On the other hand, the fact that its potential kin are very late formations might also be held to account for the absence of any such verb.

7. As biologists and colleagues at Cambridge are aware, there is also a rare verb *incept*, likewise dating from the sixteenth century; see the *OED* s.v. See also the entries for *precept* (borrowed directly from Latin early in the fourteenth century) and the (rare or old-fashioned) derivatives formed to it.

12 Some aspects of modern English derivational morphology

This chapter will offer a brief look at aspects of English derivational morphology which were not treated in the preceding chapters, some because they are recent developments, but at least one because its genesis spans the entire history of English from OE to the present.

12.1 Zero derivation

In 9.1 and 9.2 I noted briefly that ModE has a process of "zero derivation", in which a noun or adjective can be used as a verb, and some verbs can be used as nouns, without any overt affix. It is time to take a look at that process and its origins.

In the Germanic subgroup of IE, including English, the rightmost component of a derived word—regardless of whether the word is suffixed or compounded—is usually its "head", which exclusively interacts with the rest of the morphosyntax and, if the word is a compound, behaves like the corresponding uncompound word. There are numerous consequences of this rule of "right-headedness". In German both the gender and the plural of a derived noun are usually determined by its rightmost component. For instance, all nouns derived with the diminutive suffixes *-chen* and *-lein* are neuter and have plurals with no affix; all nouns derived with the abstract suffixes *-heit* and *-keit* are feminine and have plurals in *-en*; the numerous compounds of *Zug*, literally 'pull', are masculine and have plurals in *-züge*, just like the noncompound noun, etc. English compounds of irregular verbs normally exhibit the same irregularities as the noncompound verb. For instance, the past tense of *become* is *became*, that of *understand* is *understood*, that of *withstand* is *withstood*, etc.

In English zero derivation the consequences of right-headedness do not seem to apply. That could simply be a consequence of the fact that the inflection of nouns and verbs, for instance, is not the same. However, a few examples strongly suggest that a different solution is correct. We have seen that compounds of *stand* normally exhibit the (otherwise unique) inflectional irregularity of the simple verb, yet the past tense of the verb *grandstand* 'attempt (ostentatiously) to get favorable attention' is *grandstanded*. The reason is that this verb is not, in fact, a compound of *stand*; it is derived by zero affixation from the noun *grandstand* 'main area of seating at a sports event'. If we posit actual affixes that have no phonological content, they should be at the end of the word, according to the right-headed rule. The structure of the verb will then be [grand$_{ADJ}$+[[stand$_{VB}$]+0$_{NN}$]]+0$_{VB}$: a noun is derived from the verb *stand* by zero affixation, it is compounded with the adjective *grand* to produce another noun (by the right-headed rule), and the compound noun is then converted to a verb by a further zero affix (cf. Williams 1981, Spencer 1991: 183–7, Don 2014: 47–8). One of the zero affixes is the head of the noun *stand*; the other is the head of the verb *grandstand*; both should govern the inflection of the lexemes which they produce (according to the right-headed rule). Moreover, we might expect zero affixes, which are productive, to produce lexemes belonging to the fully productive inflectional classes—and they do: the plural of *stand* is *stands*, and the past tense of *grandstand* is *grandstanded*. This is a strong argument that the zero affixes of ModE are not linguists' fictions; they have observable consequences for the grammar. Admittedly, at least one exocentric compound offers a partial exception to the overall pattern. Whereas the plural of *sabertooth* 'extinct big cat with saber-like teeth' seems consistently to be *sabertooths*, the plural of *tenderfoot* 'person who has tender feet (through lack of experience hiking and backpacking)' is variably *tenderfoots* and *tenderfeet*. What to make of this exception is not entirely clear, though it does seem clear that it is an exception to the general rule.

When did zero derivation enter the grammar of English? One can make a case that it was already in place in OE, though the number of examples at that stage was much smaller. Most nouns derived from verbs in OE had additional prefixes, like *ġefeoht* 'fight', or suffixes, like the n-stem agentive suffix of *cuma* 'newcomer' and *dēma* 'judge' (see 9.1) or exhibited a root vowel which was different from that in the present stem of the verb, such as *sang* ← *singan* or *wōp* 'weeping' ← *wēpan* (or, of course, more than one of these differences, e.g. *bryċe* 'breach' ← *brecan* 'break'); no native learner could have abstracted a rule of zero derivation from such pairs. However, there were more than two dozen such nouns which were formed from strong verbs with no apparent alteration, except that they were inflected as nouns; examples include *drinc, fær*[1] 'way,

---

1. The alternation between *æ* and *a* is automatic in some morphological environments in OE, though not in all; analysis of this noun as zero-derived is at least arguable.

proceeding' (*faran* 'travel'), *ġiefu*[2] 'gift', *heald* 'custody' (*healdan* 'hold'), *help*, *hrēow* 'regret', *lāc* 'play', *rǣd* 'advice', *sacu* 'conflict', *sealt* 'salt', *slǣp* 'sleep', *spann* 'span' (*spannan* 'yoke, attach'), *stīġ*[3] 'path' (*stīgan* 'go (up)'), *sting*, etc. (cf. Biese 1941: 21).[4] In addition, there were prefixed nouns derived from prefixed verbs with a regular shift of accent, which triggered a slightly different form of the prefix; commonly occurring examples are *anġinn* 'beginning' (*onġinnan* 'begin') and *andġiet* 'understanding, meaning' (*onġietan* 'understand'). I know of no evidence that such formations were productive in OE, but it seems reasonable to recognize at least a minor rule zero-deriving nouns from strong verbs at that stage of the language (cf. Marchand 1969: 363, Kastovsky 2006: 211–2).

The derivation of verbs from nouns and adjectives was rather different. Weak verbs of class I always exhibited i-umlaut of the root, so there was a clear difference between the verb and its derivational base except in those (fairly few) cases in which the root vowel was not affected by i-umlaut or, conversely, had already been umlauted in the base (e.g. *ċierran* 'turn, change', *dǣlan* 'divide, part', *rīman* 'count, number', *stillan* 'quiet, make still'). But in weak verbs of class II there was no change in the shape of the base, and such verbs were very freely derived from nouns and adjectives of all kinds; typical examples, among hundreds, are *andswarian* 'answer',[5] *blissian* 'be happy', *ealdian* 'grow old', *endian* 'come to an end', etc. It is very unlikely that native learners parsed the distinctive inflectional endings of class II weak verbs as a derivational suffix, for the simple reason that there were also many class II weak verbs that were not synchronically derived (so Marchand 1969: 362, by implication; cf. also Kastovsky 2006: 211–12); typical examples include *āscian* 'ask', *clipian* 'call', *leornian* 'learn', *lōcian* 'look', etc. Thus the productive derivation of class II weak verbs, at least, was probably a zero derivation process in OE (pace Biese 1941: 19, who does not distinguish carefully enough between derivational processes and inflection).

The ME elimination of the distinctive weak class II present endings, except in the south (see 6.5), made the derivation of new verbs from

---

2. The *-u* of this and other examples is a nominative singular ending, not a derivational suffix.

3. Replacement of velar *g* by palatal *ġ* in the noun is automatic in that phonotactic position.

4. It is clear that the nouns in this list were derived from the verbs, simply because strong verbs were always basic lexemes, never derived.

5. This verb is clearly derived from the noun *andswaru*—not the other way round—because its prefix is stressed, and verb prefixes are not normally stressed. Our information about the stress patterns of OE words comes not only from internal analysis, but also from OE verse, in which only stressed syllables alliterate.

nouns and adjectives a zero-derivation process if it was not one already: one simply inflected the noun or adjective stem as a verb. There was a reasonably steady increase of such formations from the twelfth century through the middle of the sixteenth (Biese 1941: 31–43); fluctuations in the rate of innovations are likely to be more apparent than real, given the uneven attestation of ME. The history of the zero derivation of nouns from verbs is different and more interesting. Though such a process does not seem to have been productive in OE, there are a few innovative examples in the twelfth-century *Trinity Homilies* (Biese 1941: 51–2), in the *Orrmulum* (ibid. p. 54), in Laȝamon (ibid. pp. 56–7), in the thirteenth-century *Ancrene Wisse* (ibid. p. 60), etc. No single document offers many such innovations, but there are a few in each of the longer documents. Many of these new nouns do not survive, but at least *attire, dread, fall, grant, look,* and *start* are still current in ModE. *Attire* (in Laȝamon) and *grant* (in the *Ancrene Wisse*) are noteworthy as being the first examples derived from verbs borrowed from French. It seems indisputable that by the early thirteenth century the zero derivation of nouns from verbs had become productive at low frequency.

Late in the sixteenth century zero-derivation processes begin to gather steam, and the marked increase in new examples is maintained until the middle of the seventeenth century (Biese 1941: 40–5). In the eighteenth century there is a lull, but in the nineteenth there is a veritable explosion of new examples, and it is clear that we have reached the current situation, in which zero derivation both of verbs and of nouns is more or less fully productive.

12.2 Resegmentation

Marchand has little to say about resegmentation because it is only marginally systematic, but in ModE it has become a significant way of coining new words. The type that most resembles other derivational processes is the division of existing words to yield morphemes that can be used to derive new words (Marchand 1969: 211–14). The earliest examples respect the etymological integrity of existing morphemes, either because the innovators were maximally literate or because the morphemes of the model were obviously segmentable in any case. For instance, *landscape* (also *landskip*) appears in the years around 1600 as a half-translation of Dutch *landschap*.[6] The obvious corollary *seascape* appears about two cen-

---

6. The word was first used in English of paintings; its use in reference to real vistas appears to be slightly but measurably later. A clear example (as *lantskip*) is found in Milton's *L'Allegro*, tentatively dated by Shawcross to ca. 1631.

turies later, in 1799—obvious because *land* and *sea* are basic antonyms, leaving *-scape* to be interpreted as a morpheme meaning 'panoramic painting'. Only slightly less transparent is *cablegram*, coined in 1868 to mean a *telegram* (1852) sent by submarine cable; anyone with a smattering of Greek (or an awareness of Latinate derivational patterns in English) will recognize *tele-* as a combining element meaning 'far', replaceable by some other morpheme.

Backformation (Marchand 1969: 391–5) can be seen as a special case of this type of resegmentation, in which one of the morphemes is replaced by zero according to an appropriate derivational model; North American *donate* from *donation*, and British *orientate* from *orientation*, are obvious examples.

But in the twentieth century a different procedure became common: namely, the segmentation of longer words on purely prosodic lines to yield new combining morphemes. Perhaps the earliest example is *burger*. The phrase *Hamburger steak* (often capitalized, since the food item was named for the city of Hamburg) is attested from 1889, and *hamburger* from 1908; an American restaurant menu from ca. 1930 attests *cheeseburger*, and *burger*, *beefburger*, and *porkburger* are all recorded from 1939–40 (see the *OED* s.vv.). Since, as everyone (including Marchand) remarks, hamburgers obviously contain no ham, the resegmentation of *-burger* as a combinable morpheme and then as a freestanding word cannot be the result of semantic misinterpretation; it must have been prompted by the prosodic structure of *hámbùrger*, whose primary and secondary stresses make it sound like a compound word, even though it does not exhibit composite semantics. Other examples followed. Marchand (p. 213) instances a parallel phenomenon starting from *fránkfùrter* (1894); most of the innovative compounds that he cites are not even recorded in the *OED*, no doubt because the word has been out-competed by *hot dog*,[7] but *krautfurter* ('hot dog topped with sauerkraut') is well attested from 1949. A highly successful resegmentation of this type began with *àlcohólic*. The adjective is first attested in 1732 (applied to thermometers); it was applied to drinks in 1823, to poisoning or intoxication in 1830, and to persons addicted to alcohol in 1845; in the latter application it appears as a noun in 1852. Nearly a century later, in 1947, *wòrkahólic* appears by prosodic resegmentation, and the word has become part of the standard English lexicon. (*Chocoholic* (1961) and *shopaholic* (1977), by contrast, still strike me as somewhat jocular; but then addiction to chocolate or shopping is

---

7. The stress pattern *hót dòg* shows that this is also a compound (see 9.4); it has given rise to parallel innovations, of which *chíli dòg* is current in Philadelphia as I write this.

not a social problem.) Similar examples are *-orama* (starting from *panorama*) and *-athon* (starting from *marathon*, originally a place name).

Truncation of long and (therefore) morphologically complex words is perhaps even more common as a derivational strategy in ModE; Marchand calls it "clipping" and devotes a brief chapter to it (Marchand 1969: 441–50). The truncation of personal names to yield nicknames is attested in various languages (for instance, in Ancient Greek) and appears already in ME, often with deformations of various kinds; for instance, Sundén 1904: 154, 161 cites *Hick* (for *Richard*) and *Kit* (for *Christopher*) from 1273 (in the *Hundred Rolls*). Early ModE examples are common, e.g. *Hal* (for *Harry* for *Henry*) in Shakespeare, or *Kate, Madge, Nick*, and *Tony*, all cited by Sundén 1904 from a play *The Weeding of Covent Garden* produced in 1658. Otherwise, however, "Clipping of words is a modern phenomenon" (Marchand 1969: 448). A few examples from the sixteenth century can be cited; Marchand (p. 449) lists *coz* (for *cousin*), *gent*, and *chap*, and the *OED* cites *exam* from 1568. There is a steady trickle of new examples in the succeding centuries—e.g. *wig* (for *periwig*, 1675), *memo* (1705), and *pub* (1800)—but it is especially in the nineteenth that the practice becomes common. Of course, many nineteenth- and twentieth-century examples denote items that did not exist in previous generations; it is thus no surprise that we do not encounter *bike, gas* (North American, for *gasoline*), *lab, taxi, bus, phone* (for *telephone*), *plane* (for *airplane* / *aeroplane*), etc. in earlier documents. But *doc* and *math* (North American) or *maths* (British) could have been coined much earlier, and so far as we know they were not. Though there appears to be little system in English truncation, the examples usually obey a practical rule: when the truncation is first made, hearers must be able to recover the fuller word that the truncation stands for. Thus *doc, gas*, and *math(s)* represent the beginnings of the fuller words because otherwise the first generation of hearers would not have known what the speaker intended; *phone* and *plane* represent the ends of the longer words for the same reason. Even prefixes and suffixes have occasionally been "cut loose" as complete words; *isms* in the sense 'ideologies' is attested from 1680 and has been in use ever since, and since at least 1986 *dis* has been used colloquially to mean 'disrespect'.

12.3 Sound symbolism

The extent to which sound symbolism is part of derivational morphology is debatable, but there is no doubt that it plays a part in the coinage of new words. Sometimes the result is an unanalyzable morpheme; for instance, *dweeb* (1982, according to the *OED*) makes a direct appeal to the phonological sensibilities of native speakers of English without invoking any derivational pattern. Marchand 1969: 405–27 is an extended discussion of this type of sound symbolism, with hundreds of examples. Sometimes, however, derivational morphemes are used for effect. A simple example is *humongous* (1970), evidently meant to recall *huge* but signalling its status as an adjective with a Latinate suffix which also serves to make the word bombastic. More elaborate (and more sophisticated) is *discombobulate* and its variants (1825), with two supposedly antithetical prefixes and two suffixes, all Latinate, affixed to a root with no definable meaning. Many such examples, including the ones just adduced, were clearly coined as jokes, and it is not surprising that some are now impenetrable, like other jokes from the distant past; see e.g. *gazebo* in the *OED*.

What is most interesting about sound symbolism is that its extensive use in English is not new and not always unsystematic. Bloomfield 1933: 245 points out that onomatopoeic verbs in English often occur in extensive rhyming sets (cf. also Marchand, op. cit. pp. 419–26). A tabulation of ModE words in -*ash* by semantic area, with the *OED*'s dates and etymologies, yields an interesting pattern:

	first attested	*etymology*
violent motion:		
thrash	ca. 950	Northumbrian byform of OE *perscan*
mash	ca. 1200 (*Owl & N.*)	← noun, attested in late OE
(*quash*)[8]	ca. 1200 (*Owl & N.*)	OF *quaisser*; -*sh* first in 1589 (!)
dash	ca. 1290 (*S. Engl. Leg.*)	doubtful
lash	ca. 1330	none
pash	ca. 1370 (Langland)	none
slash	1382 (Wycl. bible)	OF *esclachier* 'to break'?
crash	late XIV (*Morte Art.*)	none
gnash	1496	mod. of *gna(i)st* (a. 1300, ← ON)
clash	before 1518	none
gash	1562	← noun (1528), dialect form of *garse* (ca. 1200)
(*squash*)	1565	OF *esquasser*?? (probably not, cf. the date)
bash	before 1642	doubtful
smash	1699	none
water:		
plash	1565	none
splash	1699	← the preceding

8. This and the other parenthesized items do not now rhyme with most other words in -*ash*, but it seems clear that at an earlier period they did.

bright light:

flash	1387 (Trevisa)	none; originally of water; of light ca. 1400

other words in *-ash*:

ash	ca. 700	OE *æsċ*, cf. ON *askr*, etc.
(*wash*)	ca. 900	OE *wæscan*, cf. OHG *waskan*, etc.
ash(es)	ca. 950	OE *æsċe*, cf. ON *aska*, Goth. *azgo*, etc.
rash (adj.)	late XIV (*Pearl*)	← Middle Low German *rasch*
lash (nn.)	ca. 1440?	cf. Swiss German *laschen* 'shoelace'?
trash	a. 1529 (Skelton)	none
cash	ca. 1595	Fr. *caisse* 'box; merchant's counter'
sash	1599	← Ar. *šāš* 'muslin'
hash	1650s	← Fr. *hacher* 'to chop up'
rash (nn.)	1696	← Fr. *rache* (obsolete)
stash	1790s	none
brash	1824	← *brash* 'brittle'? (1566, no etym.)

(*Squash* (nn., ← Narragansett *asquutasquash*) never rhymed with most words in *-ash* and is occasionally spelled *squosh* in eighteenth-century sources.) In the first category a few of the earliest examples have solid etymologies, but most of the rest do not, and it seems likely that the examples relating to water and light are late spinoffs from the much larger first set. The pervasive absence of clear etymologies is an indication that people simply made most of those words up, using the sound symbolism of the syllable coda. By contrast, most other words in *-ash* have solid etymologies.

Nor are these the earliest examples of systematic sound symbolism from the recoverable history and prehistory of English. Strong verbs in any Germanic language are basic lexemes, not derivable from other words, yet Seebold 1970 records many sets of rhyming strong verbs with similar meanings variously distributed across the languages of the family. Typically, one can be traced farther back in time than the others. For instance, the basic PGmc. verb meaning 'fall' is reconstructable as **dreusaną*[9] on the basis of Gothic *driusan*, OE *drēosan* (poetic only),

---

9. By contrast, **fallaną* is attested in all the languages *except* Gothic and appears to be a Northwest Germanic innovation; its supposed cognation with Lithuanian *púlti* 'to fall' (pres. 3sg. *púola*) is problematic because the ablaut relations make no sense, while any connection with Armenian *phowl* 'collapse' or Greek *sphállein* 'to trip (someone) up' would involve irregular sound correspondences. Seebold is properly skeptical.— There was an even older verb **fetaną* which, unlike **dreusaną*, has cognates outside Germanic (Sanskrit pres. 3sg. *pádyatē*, etc.), but it seems no longer to have been the basic verb meaning 'fall' in Germanic; see Seebold 1970 s.v. *FET-A- 1 'fallen' (?)* for the facts and discussion.

and Old Saxon *driosan* (also poetic), but there is also a rhyming synonym *hrēosan* in OE. Its creation must antedate the separate history of OE because, though such a verb is not certainly attested elsewhere, ON preserves several derivatives, but there is no reason to suppose that it goes back to PGmc.; apparently, it was made up to rhyme with (the immediate ancestor of) *drēosan*. Other such sets can be retrieved from the tables in Seebold 1970: 42–65.

A type of sound symbolism which does seem to have originated fairly late in the history of English is the reduplicated formation exemplified by *zigzag* and *wishy-washy* and the rhyming formation exemplified by *claptrap* and *hanky-panky*. Marchand 1969: 429–34 gives a brief historical survey (followed by extensive discussion). Unless I have overlooked something, his earliest example dates from 1362 (*handy-dandy*); there are also four examples from the fifteenth century, but most are much later.

12.4 The distribution of derivational types over text types

Finally, it seems appropriate to call the reader's attention to a fact which is seldom discussed in detail. English words of different etymological origins are not distributed evenly over different types of English text; as a result, some derivational processes are encountered far more often in some text types than in others. It seems best to structure the discussion around a series of illustrative examples.

To begin with, consider the beginning of Chapter IX, Book II, in J. R. R. Tolkien's fantasy novel *The Lord of the Rings*. That chapter, called "The Great River", contains even more description than usual because it narrates a long journey by boat in the wilderness. The first three paragraphs together (Tolkien 1993: 427) are purely narrative and are just over 350 words long. Ten word-tokens are non-English names and can be left out of consideration. Of the remaining words, only 4 are Latinate—*decision*, *desolate*, *event*, and *quiet*—and the last 2 fit so well into the native English lexicon that they participate in the native derivational system (cf. *eventful*, *quietness*). A further 31 word-tokens—less than 10 percent of the total—are of French origin: *branches*, *changed*, *company*, *content* (adj.), *corner*, *course*, *desire*, *eager*, *enemy* (2x), *failed*, *hasten*, *hours*, *insisted*, *isle*, *journey*, *pace*, *passed* (2x), *perils*, *pestilence*, *pressing*, *region*, *relieve*, *river* (2x), *sign*, *vast*, and *voyage*, as well as the first morpheme of *formless* and the second of *Tindrock*.[10] Most of these words are so thoroughly embedded in the English lexicon that no Anglo-Saxon equivalents survive, and those

---

10. The first morpheme of this name is apparently an archaic variant of native English *tine*.

that do (such as *foe*) are usually archaic or poetic. There are also 20 word-tokens of Norse origin: *bank* (2x), *drift, husbanding, roused, them* (2x), *their* (3x), and *they* (8x), as well as the first morpheme of *Mirkwood* and the second of *grey-skinned*. They fit seamlessly into the native lexicon; the only remarkable thing about them is that an actual majority are forms of the 3rd-person plural pronoun. The remaining words in the passage—well over 280 altogether, or nearly 85 percent—are native English words. Though there are passages in Tolkien's fiction in which the proportion of French words is even smaller, I think this one is typical.

Of course, Tolkien was a specialist in English historical linguistics and medieval English literature, but it is not immediately obvious that he paid so much attention to his use of the lexicon that he could deliberately omit to use words not already current in the fifteenth century; the passage might use a mostly medieval vocabulary because of its subject matter. For comparison, consider a passage of similar length (370 words) from the first chapter of Roger Zelazny's science fiction novel *Lord of Light*, beginning with *The high-frequency prayers* and ending with *their most prominent Attributes* (Zelazny 1976: 10–1). Five of the word-tokens are Sanskrit names. Of the remainder, perhaps 21, or more than 5 percent, can reasonably be called Latinate: *atmosphere, attributes* (2x), *current, custody, deities, directed, fertility, fluent, invoking, kilowatts, lotus* (2x), *monastery, notable, operated, orthodoxy, prominent, static, universal*, and the second element of *high-frequency*. There are also some 46 tokens of French loanwords and derivatives of the same, or more than 12 percent of the total: *across, affair, ages, artificers, bronze, celestial* (2x), *chariot, circles, city* (3x), *despite, doubted* (4x), *engine, entire, excuse, favor, founding, giant, gouts, machine, matter* (2x), *metal, mountains, movements, orange, passing, place, prayer(s)* (3x), *pray-machine* (3x), *sockets, real* (2x), *remembered, technique, tended*, and *terms*. Twelve tokens of Norse loanwords occur—*big, called* (2x), *die* (2x), *them, they, though* (4x), and *wake* (the noun)—and as usual they are indistinguishable from native words. Finally, there is a single Hindi loanword, *jungle*. The differences from Tolkien's usage are not extreme, but they are noticeable. Most obviously, Zelazny refers to the sort of technology that one might expect in science fiction, such as machines that exploit electromagnetic radiation. Other differences result from different choices of imagination: Tolkien invented a world without jungles or monasteries, and his presentation of religion in Middle Earth is subtle and understated; Zelazny's world is different and differently reported, even without the science fiction aspect. But though Tolkien also uses most of the French loanwords and some of the Latinate ones that occur in this passage, they seem less thick on the ground, and not only those that got a new lease on life during the industrial revolution, such as *engine* and *machine*. The difference in style becomes most obvious with the last sentence of Zelazny's passage, in which I italicize the Latinate words:

> Under his breath, he called upon the more *notable* of the *current fertility deities, invoking* them in terms of their most *prominent Attributes*. (Zelazny 1976: 10–11)

It is not only the joke about profanity that is uncharacteristic of Tolkien; the style is completely different too, and the lavish use of Latinate words is part of the difference. Compare two instances of irony from the Appendices to *The Lord of the Rings*:

> 'When the council was over, [King] Helm stood up and laid his great hand on Freca's shoulder, saying: "The king does not permit brawls in his house, but men are freer outside." . . .' (Tolkien 1994: 381)
> But they answered: 'Durin's heir you may be, but even with one eye you should see clearer.' (ibid. p. 392)

In these two quotations, *council, brawl,* and *heir* are French loanwords, but the only Latinate word is *permit*. It appears that Tolkien does avoid non-native words, consciously or unconsciously.[11]

Of course, novels about the contemporary world can be expected to refer to modern technology and institutions without restriction, though it seems likely that there will still be some stylistic differences involving the choice of lexemes with different etymologies. Since the author does not often read such novels, he will leave that investigation to others.

Some distributions of etymologically distinguishable classes of lexemes depend on the subject under discussion, occasionally in ways that are surprising if one does not know history in much detail. A case in point is Bruce Catton's three-volume history of the Army of the Potomac, the most highly visible of the northern armies in the American Civil War. Two paragraphs in Volume 1 (*Mr. Lincoln's Army*), Chapter 1 ("Picture-book war"), section 3 ("You must never be frightened"), beginning with the sentence *These two regiments belonged to Sykes's division* and ending with *they had shown any and all straw-feet how to fight*, total 360 words, of which 12 are names not composed entirely of ordinary English words.[12] Latinate words are especially hard to distinguish from French loans in this passage, but it seems reasonable to me to call 17 of the word-tokens Latinate: *act, add, column, division* (3x), *except, federal(s)* (2x), *participant, présent* (adj.), *regular(s)* (4x), *unemotional,* and the first half of the adjective *regular-army*. At just under 5 percent this is comparable to the proportion

---

11. Note that the only obvious alternative to *permit* is the French loanword *allow.*
12. This formulation deliberately excludes the Black Hat Brigade.

in the passage from Zelazny. Norse loans are typically few, inconspicuous, and dominated by the 3rd-person plural pronoun: *baggy, get, leggings, their, them* (8x), and *they* (11x); and there is a single Arabic loanword, *sash*. But the number of tokens of loans from French is very large, by my count 57, or more than 16 percent of the total: *advance, appears, battalions, battery, battle, blue, brief, brigade, brigaded, bushy, canvas, capture, cheers, command, commander-in-chief* (both parts), *composed, crusty, dressed, during, entire, family, fine, front, general* (2x),[13] *jacket, joined, line* (2x), *lined, major, merciless, order, pants, parade, part, percentage, placed, quite, regiment(s)* (2x), *remembered* (2x), *retired, rolled, skirmish, soldiers* (2x), *solidly, suffered, tasseled, taunted, volunteers*, and *war*, as well as the second half of *regular-army*. Though some of these words are of very general meaning (e.g. *blue, brief, family*, etc.), a substantial proportion of the French loanwords in this passage are specifically military, and in fact the military vocabulary of English is largely of French origin. To those familiar only with the French defeats and Pyrrhic victories of the last century and a half that might seem puzzling, but of course the words entered English long before, chiefly in the sixteenth and seventeenth centuries. It needs to be remembered that between 1494 (or perhaps 1566, when Süleyman the Magnificent died) and 1871 France was usually the strongest military power in Europe, and every European army modelled itself on the French army and adopted French military terminology.

It is possible to find text even more heavily dominated by Latinate vocabulary. Examine a passage near the beginning of Chapter 3 of this book beginning with *This chapter is a sketch* and ending with *auxiliary verbs meaning 'be' and 'become'*, ignoring the headings in the middle. The passage is just over 400 words long, but several words should be excluded from consideration: the name *Anglian*, the eleven citations of OE forms and parts of forms, and (for simplicity's sake) the three examples of *1sg.* and *3sg.*[14] Ignoring those items too, I find the following 104 tokens of Latinate words, more than 26 percent of the total: *active* (2x), *addition* (2x), *adjectives, auxiliary, circumstances, completely, complex, complicated* (2x), *complications, constructed, dialects, different* (2x), *discussing, discussion, disputed, distribution, exceptions, exhibit, feminine, finite* (3x), *focusses, fortunately, functions, general, generally, grammatical, imperative* (3x), *included, indicative* (5x), *infinitive, inflected, inflection, inflectional* (2x),

13. I count *general* as a French loan, even though it could be considered Latinate, because in its military meaning it was unarguably a French innovation. By contrast, *regular* is an abbreviation of *regular army*; the case of *column* seems unclear.
14. For convenience I count each instance of "OE" as a single word, though of course it is read as two ordinary English words.

intricate, lexical, minimum, morphological, necessary, neuter, nominative, nominative-accusative (2x, abbreviated), *nonfinite, operation, opposition, participle* (4x), *passive* (2x), *phonological* (2x), *phonology, plural* (4x, once abbreviated), *prehistoric* (2x), *present* (6x), *presentation, reflecting, similar, singular* (4x), *structure, students, subjunctive, subsequent* (2x), *syllables* (2x), *syncretism* (2x), *system* (5x), *systematic* (2x), *transitive*, and *uninflected*. An obvious reason for this large proportion is that the technical terminology of grammar is largely Latinate (though see further below), and that would be even truer in many other technical subjects. Some others of these words are in general use, even in colloquial speech. But the style of academic discourse also contributes to the use of Latinate words. One tends to *take a look at* a reference book in speech, but to *consult* it in print; events which take place *subsequently* in print are usually just *later* in speech; a theory which is *built* around an observation in an informal lecture is likely to have been *constructed* around it by the time the lecture is published, and so on. The 54 French loanwords in the passage amount to almost 14 percent of the total, a greater proportion than in the passage from Zelazny and almost as great as in that from Catton: *avoid, based, changes, chapter(s)* (2x), *class, default, detail, developments, distinguished* (3x), *example* (2x), *form(s)* (8x), *history, important, nouns* (3x), *part, past* (5x), *person* and *2nd-person* (both parts), *place, point, restored, retains* (2x), *rules* (2x), *several, sound, stressed, suffice, survived, tense(s)* (3x), and *verb(s)* (4x). Most of these words are in common use, but *noun, tense*, and *verb* are only technical terms of grammar. By contrast, Norse loans scarcely make a showing—there is only one token of *they*—and the Dutch loanword *sketch* is wholly isolated.

Of course, it might also be pointed out that even in the most relentlessly technical prose an actual majority of the words on the page are still native English words; it is not only the inflectional morphology of our language that is still obviously Anglo-Saxon. But that is just another aspect of the phenomenon that this section has highlighted: Latinate words have not penetrated very deep into the basic vocabulary of our language, and even a majority of French loanwords are not part of the word-hoard learned in the earliest years of acquisition. That is why English has (at least) a two-tiered derivational system.

Bibliography

Aarts, Bas. 2012. The subjunctive conundrum in English. *Folia Linguistica* 46: 1–20.

Allen, Cynthia L. 2008. *Genitives in early English*. Oxford: Oxford University Press.

d'Ardenne, Simonne R. Th. O. (ed.). 1961. *Þe liflade ant te passiun of Seinte Iuliene*. London: Early English Text Society.

Arngart, Olof (ed.). 1968. *The Middle English Genesis and Exodus*. Lund: Gleerup.

Aronoff, Mark. 1976. *Word formation in generative grammar*. Cambridge, MA: MIT Press.

Baker, Mark. 1988. *Incorporation: a theory of grammatical function change*. Chicago: University of Chicago Press.

Bately, Janet M. (ed.). 1980. *The Old English Orosius*. London: Early English Text Society.

Bately, Janet M. (ed.). 1986. *The Anglo-Saxon Chronicle, a collaborative edition*. Vol. 3. *Ms. A*. Cambridge: Brewer.

Bennett, J. A. W., and G. V. Smithers. 1968. *Early Middle English verse and prose*. 2nd edn. Oxford: Clarendon Press.

Berko, Jean. 1958. The child's learning of English morphology. *Word* 14(2–3): 150–77.

Biese, Y. M. 1941. *Origin and development of conversions in English*. Helsinki: Finnish Academy of Sciences.

Björkman, Erik. 1900–2. *Scandinavian loan-words in Middle English*. Halle: Niemeyer.

Blakely, L. 1949. The Lindisfarne s/ð problem. *Studia neophilologica* 22: 15–47.

Bloomfield, Leonard. 1933. *Language*. Chicago: University of Chicago Press.

Böhnke, Max. 1906. *Die Flexion des Verbums in Laȝamons Brut*. Berlin: Mayer & Müller.

Booij, Geert. 2007. *The grammar of words*. 2nd edn. Oxford: Oxford University Press.

Britton, Derek. 1991. On Middle English *she, sho*: a Scots solution to an English problem. *North-Western European Language Evolution* 17: 3–51.

Brunner, Karl. 1965. *Altenglische Grammatik.* 3rd edn. Tübingen: Niemeyer.

Buck, Carl Darling. 1949. *A dictionary of selected synonyms in the principal Indo-European languages.* Chicago: University of Chicago Press.

Campbell, Alistair. 1962. *Old English grammar.* Revised edn. Oxford: Clarendon Press.

Campbell, James, Eric John, and Patrick Wormald. 1982. *The Anglo-Saxons.* London: Penguin.

Carpenter, Henry Cave Ayles. 1910. *Die Deklination in der nordhumbrischen Evangelien-übersetzung der lindisfarner Handschrift. Bonner Studien zur englischen Philologie* II. Bonn: Hanstein.

Carr, Charles T. 1939. *Nominal compounds in Germanic.* London: Oxford University Press.

Carstairs, Andrew. 1987. *Allomorphy in inflection.* London: Croom Helm.

Carstairs-McCarthy, Andrew. 2018. *An introduction to English morphology.* 2nd edn. Edinburgh: Edinburgh University Press.

Clark, Cecily. 1957. Gender in the *Peterborough Chronicle. English Studies* 38: 109–15.

Clark, Cecily (ed.). 1970. *The Peterborough Chronicle 1070–1154.* 2nd edn. Oxford: Clarendon Press.

Clark, Cecily. 1992. The myth of "the Anglo-Norman scribe." Rissanen et al. 1992: 117–29.

Clemoes, Peter, and Kathleen Hughes. 1971. *England before the Conquest. Studies in primary sources presented to Dorothy Whitelock.* Cambridge: Cambridge University Press.

Collier, Wendy. 2000. The Tremulous Worcester Hand and Gregory's Pastoral Care. Swan and Treharne 2000: 195–208.

Comrie, Bernard. 1976. *Aspect.* Cambridge: Cambridge University Press.

Conde-Silvestre, Juan Camilo, and Javier Calle-Martín (eds). 2015. *Approaches to Middle English.* Bern: Peter Lang.

Corbett, Greville. 1991. *Gender.* Cambridge: Cambridge University Press.

Cosijn, Pieter Jacob. 1888. *Altwestsächsische Grammatik.* The Hague: Nijhoff.

Cowgill, Warren. 1960. Gothic *iddja* and Old English *ēode. Language* 36: 483–501.

Cowgill, Warren. 1965. The Old English present indicative ending -*e.* Safarewicz, Jan (ed.), *Symbolae linguisticae in honorem Georgii Kuryłowicz* (Wrocław: Polska Akademia Nauk) 44–50.

Dance, Richard. 2003. *Words derived from Old Norse in early Middle English: studies in the vocabulary of the south-west Midlands texts.* Tempe, AZ: Arizona Center for Medieval and Renaissance Studies.

Davies, Mark. 2008–. *The Corpus of Contemporary American English (COCA): 560 million words, 1990–present*; https://corpus.byu.edu/coca/ (last accessed February 10, 2021).

DeGraff, Michel. 2009. Language acquisition in creolization and, thus, language change: some Cartesian-uniformitarian boundary conditions. *Language and Linguistics Compass* 3/4: 888–971.

Dekeyser, Xavier. 1986. Romance loans in Middle English: a re-assessment. Kastovsky and Szwedek 1986: 253–65.

Dekeyser, Xavier. 1987. Relative markers in the *Peterborough Chronicle: 1070–1154*. *Folia Linguistica Historica* 7: 93–105.

Dobbie, Elliott Van Kirk. 1942. *The Anglo-Saxon minor poems*. New York: Columbia University Press.

Don, Jan. 2014. *Morphological theory and the morphology of English*. Edinburgh: Edinburgh University Press.

Durkin, Philip. 2014. *Borrowed words: a history of loanwords in English*. Oxford: Oxford University Press.

Ekwall, Eilert. 1936. The Scandinavian settlement. Darby, H. C. (ed.), *An historical geography of England before A. D. 1800* (Cambridge: Cambridge University Press) 133–64.

Eliasson, Norman E. 1967. The origin of irregular *-t* in weak preterits like *sent* and *felt*. Arndt, Walter W., Paul W. Brosman, Jr., Frederic E. Coenen, and Werner P. Friederich (eds), *Studies in historical linguistics in honor of George Sherman Lane* (Chapel Hill: University of North Carolina Press) 210–20.

Embick, David, and R. Rolf Noyer. 2007. Distributed Morphology and the syntax-morphology interface. Ramchand, Gillian, and Charles Reiss (eds), *The Oxford handbook of linguistic interfaces* (Oxford: Oxford University Press) 289–324.

Fernández Cuesta, Julia, and Sara M. Pons-Sanz (eds). 2016. *The Old English gloss to the Lindisfarne Gospels*. Berlin: de Gruyter.

Fernández Cuesta, Julia, and Nieves Rodríguez Ledesma. 2007. From Old Northumbrian to northern Middle English: bridging the divide. Mazzon 2007: 117–32.

Fletcher, Richard. 1997. *The barbarian conversion*. New York: Henry Holt.

Förster, Max. 1920. Der Inhalt der altenglischen Handschrift Vespasianus D. XIV. *Englische Studien* 54: 46–68.

Fortescue, Michael D. 1984. *West Greenlandic*. London: Croom Helm.

Freeman, Aaron. 2018. Patterns of retention of the instrumental case in Old English. *North-Western European Language Evolution* 71: 35–55.

Fruehwald, Josef. 2016. The early influence of phonology on a phonetic change. *Language* 92: 376–410.

Fulk, Robert D. 2012. *An introduction to Middle English*. Peterborough, Ontario: Broadview Press.

Fulk, Robert D. 2014. *An introductory grammar of Old English*. Tempe, AZ: Arizona Center for Medieval and Renaissance Studies.

Fulk, Robert D. 2018. *A comparative grammar of the early Germanic languages*. Amsterdam: Benjamins.

Funke, Otto. 1907. *Kasus-Syntax bei Orrm und Laȝamon*. Vienna: self-published.

García García, Luisa. 2012. Morphological causatives in Old English: the quest for a vanishing formation. *Transactions of the Philological Society* 110: 122–48.

Glahn, Nikolaus von. 1918. *Zur Geschichte des grammatischen Geschlechts im Mittelenglischen vor dem völligen Erlöschen des aus dem Altenglischen ererbten Zustandes.* Heidelberg: Winter.

Gneuss, Helmut. 1993. *Anglicae linguae interpretatio:* language contact, lexical borrowing and glossing in Anglo-Saxon England. *Proceedings of the British Academy* 82: 107–48.

Goddard, Ives. 1988. Stylistic dialects in Fox linguistic change. Fisiak, Jacek (ed.), *Historical dialectology* (Berlin: Mouton de Gruyter) 193–209.

Görlach, Manfred. 1986. Middle English – a creole? Kastovsky and Szwedek 1986: 329–44.

Görlach, Manfred. 1991. *Introduction to Early Modern English.* Cambridge: Cambridge University Press.

Greul, Walter. 1934. *Das Personalpronomen der 3. Person Pluralis im Frühmittelenglischen.* Leipzig: Mayer & Müller.

Halliday, M. A. K. 2004. *The language of science.* London: Continuum.

Healey, Antonette diPaolo, John Price Wilkin, and Xin Xiang. 2009. *Dictionary of Old English web corpus.* Revised edn. Dictionary of Old English Project, University of Toronto; www.doe.utoronto.ca/pages/pub/web-corpus.html (last accessed February 10, 2021).

Herring, Susan, Pieter van Reenen, and Lele Schøsler (eds). 2000. *Textual parameters in older languages.* Amsterdam: Benjamins.

Hickey, Raymond. 2015. Middle English voiced fricatives and the argument from borrowing. Conde-Silvestre and Calle-Martín 2015: 83–96.

Hoenigswald, Henry M. 1960. *Language change and linguistic reconstruction.* Chicago: University of Chicago Press.

Hogg, Richard M. (ed.). 1992. *The Cambridge history of the English language.* Vol. 1. *The beginnings to 1066.* Cambridge: Cambridge University Press.

Hogg, Richard M. 2011. *A grammar of Old English.* Vol. 1. *Phonology.* Oxford: Wiley-Blackwell.

Hogg, Richard M., and David Denison (eds). 2006. *A history of the English language.* Cambridge: Cambridge University Press.

Hogg, Richard M., and Robert D. Fulk. 2011. *A grammar of Old English.* Vol. 2. *Morphology.* Oxford: Wiley-Blackwell.

Holthausen, Ferdinand (ed.). 1888. *Vices and virtues.* Part I. *Text and translation.* London: Early English Text Society.

Irvine, Susan. 2000. The compilation and use of manuscripts containing Old English in the twelfth century. Swan and Treharne 2000: 41–61.

Irvine, Susan (ed.). 2004. *The Anglo-Saxon Chronicle, a collaborative edition.* Vol. 7. *Ms. E.* Cambridge: Brewer.

Jackendoff, Ray. 1975. Morphological and semantic regularities in the lexicon. *Language* 51: 639–71.

Jacobs, Neil. G. 2005. *Yiddish: a linguistic introduction.* Cambridge: Cambridge University Press.

Jember, Gregory K., and Fritz Kemmler. 1981. *A basic vocabulary of Old English prose / Grundwortschatz altenglische Prosa.* Tübingen: Niemeyer.

Jespersen, Otto. 1954. *A modern English grammar on historical principles. Part VI: Morphology.* London: Allen & Unwin.

Jones, Charles. 1988. *Grammatical gender in English: 950 to 1250.* London: Croom Helm.

Kari, James. 1976. *Navajo verb prefix phonology.* New York: Garland.

Kastovsky, Dieter. 1992. Semantics and vocabulary. Hogg 1992: 290–408.

Kastovsky, Dieter. 2006. Vocabulary. Hogg and Denison 2006: 199–270.

Kastovsky, Dieter, and Aleksander Szwedek (eds). 1986. *Linguistics across historical and geographical boundaries. In honor of Jacek Fisiak on the occasion of his fiftieth birthday.* Vol. 1. *Linguistic theory and historical linguistics.* Berlin: Mouton de Gruyter.

Kato, Tomomi. 1974. *A concordance to the works of Sir Thomas Malory.* Tokyo: University of Tokyo Press.

Katz, Joshua T. 1998. *Topics in Indo-European personal pronouns.* Ph.D. dissertation, Harvard University.

King, Ruth. 2000. *The lexical basis of grammatical borrowing.* Amsterdam: Benjamins.

Kiparsky, Paul. 1982. *Explanation in phonology.* Dordrecht: Foris.

Kipling, Rudyard. 1894. *The jungle book.* New York: Century.

Kitson, Peter R. 1995. The nature of Old English dialect distributions, mainly as exhibited in charter boundaries. Fisiak, Jacek (ed.), *Medieval dialectology* (Berlin: Mouton de Gruyter) 43–135.

Kleinschmidt, Samuel. 1851. *Grammatik der grönländischen Sprache.* Berlin: Reimer.

Kluge, Friedrich. 1995. *Etymologisches Wörterbuch der deutschen Sprache.* 23rd edn, revised by Elmar Seebold. Berlin: de Gruyter.

Koch, Hans-Albrecht. 2008. *Die Universität. Geschichte einer europäischen Institution.* Darmstadt: Wissenschaftliche Buchgesellschaft.

Kodner, Jordan. 2020. *Language acquisition in the past.* Ph.D. dissertation, University of Pennsylvania.

Krause, Wolfgang. 1948. *Abriß der altwestnordischen Grammatik.* Halle: Niemeyer.

Kroch, Anthony. 1989. Reflexes of grammar in patterns of language change. *Language Variation and Change* 1: 199–244.

Kroch, Anthony, Beatrice Santorini, and Lauren Delfs. 2004. *The Penn–Helsinki parsed corpus of Early Modern English.* Department of Linguistics, University of Pennsylvania.

Kroch, Anthony, and Ann Taylor. 2000. *The Penn–Helsinki parsed corpus of Middle English.* 2nd edn (*PPCME2*). Department of Linguistics, University of Pennsylvania.

Kroch, Anthony, Ann Taylor, and Don Ringe. 2000. The Middle English verb-second constraint: a case study in language contact and language change. Herring et al. 2000: 353–91.

Krygier, Marcin. 1994. *The disintegration of the English strong verb system.* Frankfurt: Peter Lang.

Labov, William. 1994. *Principles of linguistic change*. Vol. 1. *Internal factors*. Oxford: Blackwell.

Labov, William. 2001. *Principles of linguistic change*. Vol. 2. *Social factors*. Oxford: Blackwell.

Labov, William. 2010. *Principles of linguistic change*. Vol. 3. *Cognitive and cultural factors*. Oxford: Blackwell.

Labov, William. Forthcoming. The regularity of regular sound change. To appear in *Language*.

Labov, William, Malcah Yaeger, and Richard Steiner. 1972. *A quantitative study of sound change in progress*. Philadelphia: National Science Foundation.

Laing, Margaret. 1992. A linguistic atlas of Early Middle English: the value of texts surviving in more than one version. Rissanen et al. 1992: 566–81.

Laing, Margaret. 1993. *Catalogue of sources for a linguistic atlas of Early Medieval English*. Cambridge: D. S. Brewer.

Laing, Margaret. 2013–. *A linguistic atlas of early Middle English, 1150–1325*, Version 3.2, University of Edinburgh; http://www.lel.ed.ac.uk/ihd/laeme2/laeme2.html (last accessed February 10, 2021).

Laing, Margaret, and Roger Lass. 2014. On Middle English *she, sho*: a refurbished narrative. *Folia Linguistica Historica* 35: 201–40.

Lasnik, Howard, and Nicholas Sobin. 2000. The *who/whom* puzzle: on the preservation of an archaic feature. *Natural Language and Linguistic Theory* 18: 343–71.

Lass, Roger. 1992. Phonology and morphology. Blake, Norman Francis (ed.), *The Cambridge history of the English language. Volume 2, 1066–1476* (Cambridge: Cambridge University Press) 23–155.

Lass, Roger. 1999. Phonology and morphology. Lass, Roger (ed.), *The Cambridge history of the English language. Volume 3, 1476–1776* (Cambridge: Cambridge University Press) 56–186.

Lea, Elizabeth Mary. 1894. The language of the Northumbrian gloss to the gospel of St. Mark. Part II. Inflection. *Anglia* 16: 135–206.

Lehnert, Martin. 1953. *Sprachform und Sprachfunktion im „Orrmulum" (um 1200)*. Berlin: Deutscher Verlag der Wissenschaften.

Lindelöf, Uno. 1901. *Die südnorthumbrische Mundart des 10. Jahrhunderts. Bonner Beiträge zur Anglistik* X. Bonn: Hanstein.

Liuzza, Roy Michael. 1994. *The Old English version of the gospels*. Vol. 1: text and introduction. London: Early English Text Society.

Liuzza, Roy Michael. 2000. Scribal habit: the evidence of the Old English gospels. Swan and Treharne 2000: 143–65.

Lucas, Peter J. (ed.). 1983. *John Capgrave's Abbreuiacion of cronicles*. London: Early English Text Society.

Luick, Karl. 1914–40. *Historische Grammatik der englischen Sprache*. Stuttgart: Tauchnitz.

Machan, Tim William. 2000. Language and society in twelfth-century England. Taavitsainen et al. 2000: 43–65.

McIntosh, Angus, M. L. Samuels, and Margaret Laing. 1989. *Middle English dialectology.* Aberdeen: Aberdeen University Press.

Marchand, Hans. 1969. *The categories and types of present-day English word-formation.* 2nd edn. Munich: Beck.

Marckwardt, Albert. 1935. Origin and extension of the voiceless preterit and the past participle inflections of the English irregular weak verb conjugation. *Essays and studies in English and comparative literature by members of the English Department of the University of Michigan* (Ann Arbor: University of Michigan Press) 151–314.

Mazzon, Gabriella (ed.). 2007. *Studies in Middle English forms and meanings.* Frankfurt: Peter Lang.

Meech, Sanford Brown, and Hope Emily Allen (eds). 1940. *The book of Margery Kempe.* London: Early English Text Society.

Meid, Wolfgang. 1967. *Germanische Sprachwissenschaft.* III. *Wortbildungslehre.* Berlin: de Gruyter.

Millar, Robert McColl. 2000. *System collapse, system rebirth.* Frankfurt: Peter Lang.

Millar, Robert McColl. 2012. *English historical sociolinguistics.* Edinburgh: Edinburgh University Press.

Millar, Robert McColl. 2016a. *Contact.* Edinburgh: Edinburgh University Press.

Millar, Robert McColl. 2016b. At the forefront of linguistic change: the noun phrase morphology of the *Lindisfarne Gospels.* Fernández Cuesta and Pons-Sanz 2016: 153–67.

Millett, Bella (ed.). 1982. *Hali meiðhad.* London: Early English Text Society.

Millett, Bella. 1992. The origins of Ancrene Wisse: new answers, new questions. *Medium Ævum* 61: 206–28.

Millett, Bella (ed.). 2005. *Ancrene wisse.* London: Early English Text Society.

Minkova, Donka, and Robert Stockwell. 2009. *English words.* 2nd edn. Cambridge: Cambridge University Press.

Mitchell, Bruce. 1985. *Old English syntax.* Oxford: Clarendon Press.

Moore, Samuel. 1927. Loss of final *n* in inflectional syllables of Middle English. *Language* 3: 232–59.

Moore, Samuel, Sanford Brown Meech, and Harold Whitehall. 1935. Middle English dialect characteristics and dialect boundaries. *Essays and studies in English and comparative literature by members of the English Department of the University of Michigan* (Ann Arbor: University of Michigan Press) 1–60.

Morris, Richard (ed.). 1868. *Old English homilies and homiletic treatises of the twelfth and thirteenth centuries.* London: Early English Text Society.

Morris, Richard (ed.). 1872. *An Old English miscellany.* London: Early English Text Society.

Morris, Richard (ed.). 1873. *Old English homilies of the twelfth century from the unique Ms. B. 14. 52 in the library of Trinity College, Cambridge.* London: Early English Text Society.

Morse-Gagné, Elise E. 2003. *Viking pronouns in England: charting the course of THEY, THEIR, and THEM.* Dissertation, University of Pennsylvania.

Mossé, Fernand. 1952. *A handbook of Middle English.* Tr. by James A. Walker. Baltimore: Johns Hopkins University Press.

Muir, Kenneth (ed.). 1950. *Collected poems of Sir Thomas Wyatt.* Cambridge, MA: Harvard University Press.

Noreen, Adolf. 1923. *Altnordische Grammatik.* I. *Altisländische und Altnorwegische Grammatik.* 4th edn. Halle: Niemeyer.

Noyer, R. Rolf. 1997. *Features, positions, and affixes in autonomous morphological structure.* New York: Garland.

Okasha, Elisabeth. 1971. *Hand-list of Anglo-Saxon non-runic inscriptions.* Cambridge: Cambridge University Press.

Page, R. I. 1971. How long did the Scandinavian language survive in England? The epigraphical evidence. Clemoes and Hughes 1971: 165–81.

Page, R. I. 1973. *An introduction to English runes.* 2nd edn. Woodbridge: Boydell.

Paul, Hermann. 1960. *Prinzipien der Sprachgeschichte.* 6th edn (= 5th edn of 1920). Tübingen: Niemeyer.

Paul, Hermann, Hugo Moser, and Ingeborg Schröbler. 1969. *Mittelhochdeutsche Grammatik.* 20th edn. Halle: Niemeyer.

Philippsen, Max. 1911. *Die Deklination in den „Vices and Virtues".* Erlangen: Junge & Sohn.

Plag, Ingo. 2018. *Word-formation in English.* 2nd edn. Cambridge: Cambridge University Press.

Richards, Julian D. 2000. *Viking age England.* Revised edn. Stroud: Tempus.

Ringe, Don. 2017. *From Proto-Indo-European to Proto-Germanic.* 2nd edn. Oxford: Oxford University Press.

Ringe, Don. 2018. Indicative-subjunctive syncretism in West Germanic. Gunkel, Dieter, Stephanie W. Jamison, Angelo O. Mercado, and Kazuhiko Yoshida (eds), *Vina diem celebrent. Studies in linguistics and philology in honor of Brent Vine* (Ann Arbor: Beech Stave Press) 390–6.

Ringe, Don, and Joseph F. Eska. 2013. *Historical linguistics: toward a twenty-first century reintegration.* Cambridge: Cambridge University Press.

Ringe, Don, and Ann Taylor. 2014. *The development of Old English.* Oxford: Oxford University Press.

Ringe, Don, and Charles Yang. Forthcoming. The threshold of productivity and the "irregularization" of verbs in Early Modern English. To appear in the proceedings of ICEHL 20.

Rissanen, Matti, Ossi Ihalainen, Terttu Nevalainen, and Irma Taavitsainen (eds). 1992. *History of Englishes.* Berlin: Mouton de Gruyter.

Ross, Alan S. C. 1936. Sex and gender in the Lindisfarne Gospels. *Journal of English and Germanic Philology* 35: 321–30.

Ross, Alan S. C. 1937. *Studies in the accidence of the Lindisfarne Gospels.* Leeds: School of English Language, University of Leeds.

Samuels, M. L. 1989. The great Scandinavian belt. McIntosh et al. 1989: 106–15.

Seebold, Elmar. 1970. *Vergleichendes und etymologisches Wörterbuch der germanischen starken Verben.* The Hague: Mouton.

Shawcross, John T. (ed.). 1971. *The complete poetry of John Milton.* Revised edn. Garden City, NY: Anchor.

Shinkawa, Seiji. 2012. *Unhistorical gender assignment in Laʒamon's Brut.* Frankfurt: Peter Lang.

Siddiqi, Daniel. 2009. *Syntax within the word.* Amsterdam: Benjamins.

Smith, Jeremy. 1992. A linguistic atlas of Early Middle English: tradition and typology. Rissanen et al. 1992: 582–91.

Smith, Jeremy. 2000. Standard language in Early Middle English? Taavitsainen et al. 2000: 125–39.

Smithers, G. V. (ed.). 1987. *Havelok.* Oxford: Clarendon Press.

Spencer, Andrew. 1991. *Morphological theory.* Oxford: Blackwell.

Stanley, E. G. 1969. Laʒamon's antiquarian sentiments. *Medium Ævum* 38: 23–37.

Stiles, Patrick V. 1996. Old English uncet and inċit. *North-Western European Language Evolution* 28/9: 557–68.

Sundén, Karl Fritiof. 1904. *Contributions to the study of elliptical words in Modern English.* Uppsala: Almqvist & Wiksell.

Swan, Mary, and Elaine M. Treharne (eds). 2000. *Rewriting Old English in the twelfth century.* Cambridge: Cambridge University Press.

Taavitsainen, Irma, Terttu Nevalainen, Päivi Pahta, and Matti Rissanen (eds). 2000. *Placing Middle English in context.* Berlin: Mouton de Gruyter.

Tatlock, John S. P., and Arthur G. Kennedy. 1963. *A concordance to the complete works of Geoffrey Chaucer and to the Romaunt of the Rose.* Gloucester, MA: Peter Smith. Reprinted from the edn of 1927 (Washington, DC: The Carnegie Institution).

Taylor, Ann. 1994. Variation in past tense formation in the history of English. *Penn Working Papers in Linguistics* 1: 143–58.

Thomason, Sarah Grey, and Terrence Kaufman. 1988. *Language contact, creolization, and genetic linguistics.* Berkeley: University of California Press.

Thüns, Bernhard. 1909. *Das Verbum bei Orm.* Weida im Thüringen: Thomas & Hubert.

Tolkien, John Ronald Reuel. 1993. *The lord of the rings.* Part one. *The fellowship of the ring.* New York: Ballantine.

Tolkien, John Ronald Reuel. 1994. *The lord of the rings.* Part three. *The return of the king.* New York: Ballantine.

Tolkien, John Ronald Reuel, and Eric Valentine Gordon (eds). 1967. *Sir Gawain and the Grene Knight.* 2nd edn, revised by Norman Davis. Oxford: Clarendon Press.

Townend, Matthew. 2002. *Language and history in Viking age England.* Turnhout: Brepols.

Treharne, Elaine M. (ed.). 2010. *Old and Middle English c. 890–c. 1450: an anthology.* 3rd edn. Oxford: Wiley-Blackwell.

Trudgill, Peter. 1986. *Dialects in contact.* Oxford: Blackwell.

Trudgill, Peter. 2000. *Sociolinguistics: an introduction to language and society.* 4th edn. London: Penguin.

Underhill, Robert. 1976. *Turkish grammar.* Cambridge, MA: MIT Press.

Vezzosi, Letizia. 2007. *Himself:* an overview of its uses in Middle English. Mazzon 2007: 239–56.

Vinaver, Eugène (ed.). 1971. *Malory: works.* 2nd edn. London: Oxford University Press.

Walkden, George. 2014. *Syntactic reconstruction and Proto-Germanic.* Oxford: Oxford University Press.

Warner, Anthony R. 1993. *English auxiliaries: structure and history.* Cambridge: Cambridge University Press.

Warner, Anthony R. 2017. English-Norse contact, simplification, and sociolinguistic typology. *Neuphilologische Mitteilungen* 118(2): 317–403.

Warner, Rubie D.-N. (ed.). 1917. *Early English homilies from the twelfth century ms. Vespasian D. XIV.* London: Early English Text Society.

Wełna, Jerzy. 1980. On gender change in linguistic borrowing (Old English). Fisiak, Jacek (ed.), *Historical morphology* (The Hague: Mouton) 399–420.

Wełna, Jerzy. 2009. The post-sonorant devoicing of [d] in the past/past participle forms of weak verbs (*sent, spend,* etc.). Krygier, Marcin, and Liliana Sikorska (eds), *Þe laurer of oure Englische tonge* (Frankfurt: Peter Lang) 21–33.

Whitney, William Dwight. 1896. *A Sanskrit grammar.* Leipzig: Breitkopf & Härtel.

Williams, Edwin. 1981. On the notions "lexically related" and "head of a word." *Linguistic Inquiry* 12: 245–74.

Wright, Joseph. 1905. *The English dialect grammar.* Oxford: Henry Frowde.

Yang, Charles. 2016. *The price of linguistic productivity: how children learn to break the rules of language.* Cambridge, MA: MIT Press.

Zelazny, Roger. 1976. *Lord of light.* New York: Avon.

Zwicky, Arnold M., and Geoffrey K. Pullum. 1983. Citicization vs. inflection: English N'T. *Language* 59: 502–13.

Index

Large sections of the book and concepts often encountered (such as *morpheme*) are not referenced here, nor are stages of English, nor Latin; basic grammatical concepts (such as *case* and *tense*) are for the most part noted only for section A. Names of scholars are given with first initials, and are listed only if cited more than once in widely separated passages; those cited once, or only in one small part of the book, are not listed in the index, since their citations should be easier to find starting from the subject matter of their work. Hans Marchand, who is cited constantly in section C, is also not indexed.

Persons whose speech or writing provides data are listed with first (or only) names.